Shane Claiborne is a living exper[...] mixed with grassroots activism; [...] with prison time for feeding the [...] aimed at cowards seeking coura[...]

—AIDEN [...]

FORMER MANAGING EDITOR, *ADBUSTERS*

Sometimes I think there is really only one Christian denomination in America: American Civil Religion—a consumerist, militarist, therapeutic, colonial, nationalist chaplaincy that baptizes and blesses whatever the richest and most powerful nation on the planet wants to do. But then I hear a voice like Shane's, and I know that at least a few follow another leader on a less-traveled road. Read this book and let it make you uncomfortable, as it did me. We need this kind of discomfort more than we know.

—BRIAN MCLAREN, AUTHOR,
A GENEROUS ORTHODOXY

Desperately urgent. Profoundly biblical. If even one in ten contemporary "Christians" dared to truly follow the one we claim to worship with half of Shane's unconditional surren-der to Christ, our evangelism would acquire an awesome power and our actions would transform our broken world.

—RONALD J. SIDER, PRESIDENT,
EVANGELICALS FOR SOCIAL ACTION

Shane expresses the kind of authentic Christianity that most of us are trying to avoid because the cost is too great. He proposes a lifestyle that prophetically proclaims what it means to be a follower of Jesus in the twenty-first century.

—TONY CAMPOLO, AUTHOR,
REVOLUTION AND RENEWAL

Written with endearing humor and astonishing courage, *The Irresistible Revolution* describes a young man's embrace of uncompromising commitment to Jesus' teachings.

—KATHY KELLY, AUTHOR, CO-FOUNDER OF
VOICES IN THE WILDERNESS

If you know Shane, read this book to hear his irresistible voice on every page. If you don't know Shane (or even if you do), read this book to hear the irresistible voice of Jesus on every page.

—LEONARD SWEET, AUTHOR, *SUMMONED TO LEAD*

This book will challenge you to sell all you have and follow Jesus to the margins.

—ROB MOLL, EDITOR, *CHRISTIANITY TODAY*

Like the author, the book is rich and rare, fresh, memorable and challenging, even to seasoned resisters. It is a gift to all who long to midwife the kingdom of God here and now, who want to impact the future, who would be the Church for which we long.

—ELIZABETH MCALISTER, COFOUNDER,
JONAH HOUSE COMMUNITY

If you embark on this journey, you will not only meet a tall, skinny lad named Shane, but you will also meet his homeless friends in Philly, the dying that he cared for in Calcutta, and the children he played with in Baghdad as the bombs fell—all of which raise uncomfortable questions about what it means to follow Jesus. Read this book at your own peril. Shane will challenge you to join the ranks of "ordinary radicals."

—TOM SINE, FOUNDER, MUSTARD SEED ASSOCIATES

THE IRRESISTIBLE REVOLUTION

10TH ANNIVERSARY EDITION

THE IRRESISTIBLE REVOLUTION

LIVING AS AN ORDINARY RADICAL

UPDATED AND EXPANDED

SHANE CLAIBORNE

ZONDERVAN

ZONDERVAN

The Irresistible Revolution
Copyright © 2006, 2016 by The Simple Way

Requests for information should be addressed to:
Zondervan, 3900 *Sparks Dr. SE, Grand Rapids, Michigan 49546*

This edition:
ISBN 978-0-310-34370-7 (softcover)
ISBN 978-0-310-34393-6 (ebook)

Library of Congress Cataloging-in-Publication Data

Claiborne, Shane, 1975–
    The irresistible revolution: living as an ordinary radical / Shane
Claiborne.—1st ed.
        p. cm.
    Includes bibliographical references.
    ISBN 978-0-310-26630-3
    1. Claiborne, Shane, 1975–2. Simple Way (Religious community:
Philadelphia, Pa.)—Biography. 3. Christian biography—United States. 4.
Christian life—United States. 5. Church and the world. I. Title.
BR1725.C472A3 2006
277'.3'083092   dc222005029961

The website addresses recommended throughout this book are offered as a
resource to you. These websites are not intended in any way to be or imply an
endorsement on the part of Zondervan, nor do we vouch for their content for
the life of this book.

Published in association with the literary agency of Alive Communications, Inc.,
7680 Goddard Street, Suite 200, Colorado Springs, CO 80920.

Cover design: James W. Hall IV
Cover Photo/Illustration: Shutterstock
Interior design: Denise Froehlich

First printing November 2015 / Printed in the United States of America

Love without courage and wisdom is sentimentality, as with the ordinary church member. Courage without love and wisdom is foolhardiness, as with the ordinary soldier. Wisdom without love and courage is cowardice, as with the ordinary intellectual. But the one who has love, courage, and wisdom moves the world.

—Ammon Hennacy
(Catholic activist,
1893–1970)

Dedicated to all the hypocrites, cowards, and fools . . . like me.

*May we find the Way, the Truth, and the Life in
a world of shortcuts, deception, and death.*

CONTENTS

FOREWORD

A MANIFESTO FOR A NEW GENERATION

Shane Claiborne is a good example of the old adage, "Be careful what you pray for." Evangelicals like to pray that Christian young people will learn to love Jesus and follow in his steps. Well, that's exactly what this young Christian activist is talking about in his remarkable new book, *The Irresistible Revolution*. But the places that following Jesus has led Shane are not exactly the comfortable suburban environs that many evangelical Christians inhabit today. And his journey of discipleship has taken him away from the cultural habits that many middle-class believers have become conformed to. Worst of all, his notions of fidelity to the gospel seem to directly counter the political loyalties that many conservatives on the religious right have made into an almost doctrinal litmus test of faith.

For several years now, Shane has been experimenting with the gospel in the streets of Philadelphia and Calcutta, in the intensity of Christian community, and even in the war zones of Iraq. In this book, he takes us on pilgrimage with him—sharing his passions while admitting his uncertainties, critiquing his society and his church while admitting his own human frailties and contradictions, revealing his hopes for changing the world while embracing the "smallness" of the efforts and initiatives he holds most dear.

As you read, you will soon discover that Shane's disaffection from America's cultural and patriotic Christianity came not from going "secular" or "liberal" but by plunging deeper into what the earliest Christians called "the Way"— the way of Jesus, the way of the kingdom, and the way of the cross. He is the first to admit that what he and his spiritual cohorts are doing seems quite radical, even crazy, and maybe insane. But he also has come to question the sanity of the consumer culture, the distorted priorities of the global economy, and the methodology of the warfare state, while, at the same time, rediscovering the biblical reversal of our social logic—that the foolishness of God has always seemed a little nuts to the world. They call their little community in Philadelphia "the Simple Way" and believe experiments like theirs hold the key to the future.

I am finding the reading of this book a delight, as I also find the author. I must admit that the young Shane reminds me a little of a young radical Christian about three decades ago when we were founding Sojourners magazine and community. We were also young evangelicals who found that neither our churches nor our society were measuring up to the way of Jesus—not even close. Our battle then was against a private piety that limited religion to only personal matters, then compromised faith in a tragic capitulation to the economic, political, and military powers that be.

We desperately wanted to see our faith "go public" and offer a prophetic vision with the power to change both our personal lives and political directions. I remember writing the draft of a new and very hopeful manifesto back in 1973 called the "Chicago Declaration of Evangelical Social Concern," which was signed by leaders from both an older and a younger generation of evangelicals and destined, we hoped, to really change things.

But then came the religious right with evangelical faith going public, but not in the ways we had hoped. Christian concerns were reduced to only a few "moral issues" (most having to do with sex and the dominance of Christian language in the public square), and pacts were soon made with the economic and political agenda of America's far right. After thirty years, America became convinced that God was a Republican, and the enduring image of Christianity became the televangelist preacher.

But now all that is changing, and the landscape of religion, society, and politics in America is being transformed. As I crisscross the country, I can feel a new momentum and movement. Many who have felt left out of the "faith and politics" conversation have now begun to make their voice heard. The monologue of the religious right is finally over, and a fresh dialogue has begun; it's a conversation about how to apply faith to social justice, and it is springing up across the land. A new convergence, across the theological spectrum, is coming together over issues like overcoming poverty, both in the forgotten places of our own country that Hurricane Katrina has revealed, and in the destitution and disease of the global economy that is awakening the world. Christians are naming the environment as "God's creation" and insisting on its care. Church leaders and evangelical seminary professors are challenging the theology of war and the religion of empire now emanating from the highest places of political power.

But perhaps the greatest sign of hope is the emergence of a new generation of Christians eager and ready to take their faith into the world. The Christianity of private piety, affluent conformity, and only "God bless America" has compromised the witness of the church while putting a new generation of Christians to sleep. Defining faith by the things you won't do or question does not create a compelling style of life. And a new generation of young people is hungry for an agenda worthy of its commitment, its energy, and its gifts.

Shane Claiborne's *Irresistible Revolution* is the best evidence so far that a new generation of believers is waking up and catching on fire with the gospel again. You can feel the author's fire throughout, and he claims that he is not alone. And I can testify that he is right—he is not alone. Shane is one of the best representatives of an emerging Christianity that could change the face of American religion and politics. The vision presented here can't easily be put into categories of liberal and conservative, left and right, but rather has the capacity to challenge the categories themselves. I've met the author's kindred spirits across the country and have worked with an extraordinary group of them at Sojourners and Call to Renewal. This book is a manifesto for a new generation of Christians who want to live their faith in this world, and not just the next. Read it and your hopes will rise. God is again doing something new.

—JIM WALLIS, AUTHOR OF *GOD'S POLITICS*, EDITOR OF *SOJOURNERS*, AND CONVENER OF CALL TO RENEWAL

INTRODUCTION

While the voices of blockbuster movies and pop culture cry out for a life outside the matrix of numb efficiency, Christianity often has offered little to the world, other than the hope that things will be better in heaven. The Scriptures say that the entire creation groans for liberation, and the echoes of that groaning can be heard in everything from hip hop to Hollywood. There is a pervasive sense that things are not right in the world, and the gentle suggestion that maybe they don't have to stay this way. The headlines tell stories of war and terror, sex scandals, corporate greed, prison corruption, the AIDS pandemic, police brutality, and the desperate poverty of our one billion hungry neighbors. Global initiatives like Live 8 and the ONE Campaign have gathered eclectic groups of celebrities and pop stars under slogans like "Make poverty history." But most Christian artists and preachers have remained strangely distant from human suffering, offering the world eternal assurance over prophetic imagination. Perhaps it should not surprise us that Jesus says that if the Christians remain silent, then the rocks will cry out . . . or the rock stars, I guess.

Meanwhile, many of us find ourselves estranged from the narrow issues that define conservatives and from the shallow spirituality that marks liberals. We are thirsty for social justice and peace but have a hard time finding a faith community that is consistently pro-life or that recognizes that there are "moral issues" other than homosexuality and abortion, moral issues like war and poverty. So some folks just end up trying to save individual souls from their sins, and others end up trying to save the world from "the system." But rarely do we see that the sickness of our world has infected each of us, and that the healing of our world not only begins within us but does not end with us. I recently received a letter from a young man that read, "I am alone, surrounded by unbelieving activists and inactive believers. Where are the true Christians?" A "silent majority" is developing as a growing number of folks are deliberately distancing themselves from the noise and arrogance that have come to mark both evangelical Christianity and secular activism.

In college, one of my professors said, "Don't let the world steal your soul. Being a Christian is about choosing Jesus and deciding to do something incredibly daring with your life." I decided to take him up on that challenge. At first I went on missions trips to "take the good news" to poor people. Then I discovered that they were the ones who brought the good news to me. Since then I have tried to shout that news to anyone who will listen, whether in evangelical megachurches or in the United Nations. The adventure has taken me from the streets of Calcutta to the war zones of Iraq. Following the footsteps of Jesus, I have found myself led to the halls of power and the slums of the destitute, amid tax collectors and peasants, and dragged into courtrooms and jail cells.

When one of my anarchist friends, a punk-rock kid deliberately far removed from anything reeking of

Christendom, heard that I was speaking at a congregation on Sunday morning, he called me up and said, "I didn't know you were a preacher." I laughed and explained to him my love for Jesus, my discontent with the church, and my hope for another world. He then said to me, "How about that, you're a preacher . . . I'd go to a church that would let you preach!"

I thought to myself, Wouldn't we all go to a church that believes in ordinary fools and ragamuffins and whose gospel is actually good news? I've grown to admire the humor of a God who uses foolish things to shame the wisdom of this world, and weaklings to remind the strong that they may not be as mighty as they think they are (1 Cor. 1:27). And in an era of smart bombs, maybe the world needs more fools. There have always been "fools" in the imperial courts, but it's an interesting age when folks trust the court jesters more than the court itself.

I have a confession I'm sure many of you will find refreshing and familiar: I don't really fit into the old liberal-conservative boxes, so it's a good thing we are moving on to something new. My activist friends call me conservative, and my religious friends call me liberal. I like how old G. K. Chesterton postured himself: If I'm too liberal for the conservatives and too conservative for the liberals, I might be right where God wants me to be. Defy categories. What I often get branded is "radical." I've never really minded that, for as my urban-farming friends remind me, the word *radical* itself means "root." It's from the Latin word *radix*, which, just like a rad-ish, has to do with getting to the root of things. But radical is not something reserved for saints and martyrs, which is why I like to complement it with *ordinary*. Ordinary does not mean normal, and I lament the dreadful seduction which has resulted in Christians becoming so normal. Thankfully, there is a movement of ordinary radicals sweeping the land, and ordinary people are choosing to live in radical new ways. So this is a book for ordinary radicals, not for saints who think they have a monopoly on radical and not for normal people who are satisfied with the way things are.

So I am a radical in the truest sense of the word: an ordinary radical who wants to get at the root of what it means to love, and to get at the root of what has made such a mess of our world. And many of my heroes were "radicals," trying to get back to the roots of Christianity. In the past, being labeled radical was nice because it made me feel sassy, and I never had to worry about folks taking me too seriously. It was a word you used to write someone off, usually folks who exaggerated the truth that the world was neglecting. But something strange has happened. Either I'm no longer radical, or there are a lot of ordinary radicals out there. People are actually paying attention. The question is no longer what to do if nobody listens but what happens when people actually take us seriously.[1]

What do we do when the foolishness of the cross actually makes more sense than the wisdom of the sword? What if a fragile world is more attracted to God's vision of

---

1. Obviously, not much is done differently. Whether the whole world is watching or no one at all, whether the message gets us an award or gets us killed, we just keep living and speaking the truth with love. As author and Holocaust suvivor Elie Weisel has taught me, sometimes we speak out to try to change the world, and other times we speak to try to keep the world from changing us. But after speaking so long to a world I thought would never really listen, it is a beautifully bewildering thing to feel so many of us dreaming something better for the world together. And what are we to do when radical becomes marketable and they start selling WWJB (Who Would Jesus Bomb?) bracelets, "Jesus was homeless" buttons, or bumper stickers that say, "Jesus was a human shield"? What if they ask us to write a book? Hmm.

interdependence and sacrificial sharing than to the mirage of independence and materialism? What do we do when we are the ones who have gone sane in a crazy world?

Everyone from *SPIN* magazine to *Christianity Today* has called us here at the Simple Way,[2] looking for another face of evangelical Christianity. I'm not sure if it's because people have grown discontented or have just lost interest, but the controversial evangelical voices of conflict politics and sexy media have grown stale and no longer reflect an emerging and evolving church in the United States (if they ever did). People are no longer convinced that the "Moral Majority" is either moral or the majority.[3]

When my dear friend and coconspirator Jim Wallis wrote his book *God's Politics*, many of us were astonished when it jumped onto the *New York Times* bestseller list. Religion and politics, the taboo dinner topics, are now two of the most popular things to talk about. And whether I was among wealthy expatriates in the Bahamas, the poor lepers of Calcutta, or the puzzled Christians in Iraq, I found that the solemn recognition that our world is very fragile is universal. And yet attentive ears can hear the ancient whisper reminding us that another world is possible.

There is a beautiful moment in the Bible when the prophet Elijah feels God's presence. The Scriptures say that a great and powerful wind tore the mountains apart, but God was not in the wind. After the wind, there was an earthquake, but God was not in the earthquake. After the earthquake came a fire, but the Lord was not in the

---

2. The Simple Way is the faith community in Philadelphia of which I am one of the partners and founders.

3. If you don't know what the Moral Majority is, consider yourself blessed and keep reading. Don't worry, you can check the history books.

fire. And after the fire came a gentle whisper. It was the whisper of God. Today we can hear the whisper where we least expect it: in a baby refugee and in a homeless rabbi, in crack addicts and displaced children, in a groaning creation. In the words that Indian activist and author Arundhati Roy proclaimed at the World Social Forum in Brazil, "Another world is not only possible, she is on her way. On a quiet day, I can hear her breathing." The whisper cries out for God to save the church from us Christians and breathe new life into the aging Body.

Sometimes folks (usually of an older persuasion) ask me if I am an evangelical Christian. As with any label—anarchist, activist, radical, Christian—I want to make sure we have a proper understanding before I answer. I always find it important to note that the Greek word *euangelion*, from which we derive our words *evangelical* and *evangelism*, is an ancient word that predates Jesus. It is a word Jesus takes from the imperial lexicon and turns on its head. For instance, in 6 BC there was a saying inscribed around the Roman Empire: "Augustus has been sent to us as Savior . . . the birthday of the god Augustus has been for the whole world the beginning of the gospel [*euangelion*]." The early evangelists announced another gospel, proclaimed an allegiance to another emperor, and conspired to build another kingdom. If by evangelical we mean one who spreads the good news that there is another kingdom or superpower, an economy and a peace other than that of the nations, a savior other than Caesar, then yes, I am an evangelical.

No doubt, there is much noise in evangelical Christianity. There are many false prophets (and false profits) out there, and all kinds of embarrassing things being done in the name of God. Religious extremists of all faiths have perverted the best of our traditions. But there is another movement stirring, a little revolution of sorts. Many of us are refusing to allow distorted images of our faith to define us. There are those of us who, rather than simply reject pop evangelicalism, want to spread another kind of Christianity, a faith that has as much to say about this world as it does about the next. New prophets are rising up who try to change the future, not just predict it. There is a movement bubbling up that goes beyond cynicism and celebrates a new way of living, a generation that stops complaining about the church it sees and becomes the church it dreams of. And this little revolution is irresistible. It is a contagious revolution that dances, laughs, and loves.

During the war in Afghanistan, folks in my community here at the Simple Way organized an all-night vigil and sleep-out at Love Park in Philadelphia to remember the refugees and the cost of war. Shortly afterward, we went out to grab a pizza at a fabulous hole-in-the-wall pizza joint where the grease makes the paper plates transparent. We had become close friends with the owner, who is from Afghanistan. He told us with tears in his eyes that he had seen us on the news and was deeply grateful. His family had become refugees, and he did not know what would happen to them. He said that what we were doing was beautiful but then added, "But we are only little people. We are like roaches, and they can crush us with their big feet." I said to him, "But there are many of us, and enough roaches can run an owner out of the house!" We all laughed. We are a modest revolution of roaches that can run money-changers out of temples or politicians out of office. And we can invite them to join us in creating another world.

But we live in a world that has lost its appreciation for small things. We live in a world that wants things bigger and bigger. We want to supersize our fries, sodas, and church buildings. But amid all the supersizing, many of us feel God doing something new, something small and subtle. This thing Jesus called the kingdom of God is emerging across the globe in the most unexpected places, a gentle whisper amid the chaos. Little people with big dreams are reimagining the world. Little movements of communities of ordinary radicals are committed to doing small things with great love.

Now, don't get me wrong. Even though people around the country thirst for something new, the elephant and the donkey are the largest and the most stubborn of animals. And though the masses cry out for a safer, more sustainable world, the bear and the bull of Wall Street are aggressive and are ready to tear apart anything that stands in their way. The truth is that much stands in the way of God's will for our world, beasts like what Dr. Martin Luther King Jr. called the giant triplets of evil: racism, militarism, and materialism. And the voices of resistance are little voices, but the voices of these ordinary radicals are beginning to harmonize in the most beautiful ways. The biblical prophets talked about the beasts of the empire and the market. Jewish uprisings toppled the beastly golden eagle of imperial Rome that was placed in front of God's temple. And the whispers of little prophets once again rise from the land.

Some of you reading this I know well. Some of you I don't know at all, which makes things a little awkward when trying to figure out how much (or how little) to share. I can't tone things down or throw in a joke when I see you getting feisty with me, or show you pictures when you get bored. I can't hear you giggle or see you cry. And I can't tell when you've had enough, and I can't entertain questions at the end of a section. So we're working with some serious limitations.

INTRODUCTION

This book is not really an autobiography in the formal sense, like *Malcolm X*. You have to be pretty famous or spectacular or dead to have an autobiography. I'll leave it to folks like Bill Clinton to write those. I'd feel a little pretentious writing a book called *My Life*, and I can't imagine anyone actually buying it, except my mom (who actually might buy enough to put it on the bestseller lists, but that's not the point). But I do write autobiographically, knowing that few things have more transformative power than people and stories. People are fascinated by real life and ordinary people, whether it's *The Osbournes* (or the *Kardashians*) or *American Idol*. So that's why I write autobiographically, not because I am somebody so spectacular that everyone needs to hear what I have to say, but just the opposite: I think my experiences have come to exemplify and caricature the struggles and ironies close to many of our hearts.

The strange thing is people also have a celebrity fetish. But there are enough celebrities and superstars. A pastor friend of mine said, "Our problem is that we no longer have martyrs. We only have celebrities." Most of the time, when I see Christian superstars like the late Jerry Falwell or the Reverend Al Sharpton, I feel like I'm watching professional wrestling. There's a lot of shouting and sweating, but the people seem too superhuman, and I'm not convinced all the moves are real. And as with any sports event, there are tons of spectators, desperately in need of exercise, who sit back and watch a handful of people who could really use a little break, and maybe a nice massage. All that's to say, I don't want to be another superstar Christian whom a lot of people yell at or ask to sign their T-shirts. Maybe that sounds a little dramatic, but I can't tell you how many starry-eyed young people come up to ask me for an autograph or to tell me I'm "awesome." If I am awesome, we have a problem. Either folks are being set up for disappointment, or they have not yet caught a glimpse of God. Only God is awesome. Besides, if people get too excited, I'll start to wonder whether I have really spoken the truth, for Jesus said, "Woe to you when everyone speaks well of you, for that is how their ancestors treated the false prophets" (Luke 6:26). So don't think too highly of me, and maybe some of you could write me angry letters (so I'll know I said something right).

So this is a book of stories. The things that transform us, especially us "postmoderns," are people and experiences. Political ideologies and religious doctrines just aren't very compelling, even if they're true. And stories disarm us. They make us laugh and cry. It's hard to disagree with a story, much less split a church or kill people over one. One of the best compliments I've ever gotten is, "You don't argue people into new ideas. You 'story' them in." Stories have power. They change the way we think. And certainly no one hurts others with the passion of those who do it in the name of God, and it's usually over ideologies and doctrines, not stories. Besides, people seem to loosen up after a good story.[4] I think that's why Jesus told so many stories—stories about ordinary first-century Mediterranean life, stories of widows and orphans, debts and wages, workers and landlords, courts and banquets.

Nonetheless, I know this is a risky venture. Dualism has infected the church, a dualism in which folks separate the spiritual from the political or social, as if the political and social issues were of no spiritual significance, and as if

---

4. Granted, there are those times Jesus tells a story and folks pick up stones and are ready to kill him, but we'll try to stick to the stories that disarm . . . or at least that keep folks laughing so they don't even think about getting their stones ready.

God had no better vision to offer this world. These stories, whether from the streets of Philly or the hospitals of Iraq, are political, social, and spiritual. The issues we will stir up can be volatile and gut-wrenching. But I think there are enough of us so discontented with the old answers and traditional camps—whether believers or activists, capitalists or socialists, Republicans or Democrats, pacifists or just-warriors—that the risk is worth it. The time has come for a new kind of conversation, a new kind of Christianity, a new kind of revolution.

AUTHOR'S NOTE

The decision to write a book was not an easy one for me when I first decided to write this book ten years ago. I will spare you the years of wrestling with the tension between living authentically small and evangelically large, and I can't catch you up on every aspect of this decision, like who took my glamour shot or why I chose Zondervan as publisher, nor might you even care. But before we get started, there are a few things I can do to keep it real.

There are enough people preaching to the choir, talking to people who look and think just like them. The point is not to give you all of the answers but to stir up some of the questions. Some of us haven't even asked the right questions, or found a church that would let us. I trust that as we ask questions together, the Spirit will guide us along the Way.

My goal is, and always has been, to speak the truth in love. There are a lot of people speaking the truth with no love, and there are a lot of people talking about love without much truth. And let's not get stuck in guilt. When I first sent this book to publishers a decade ago, a couple of them told me that people don't like reading books about hard issues involving social justice, because these books make them feel guilty. I hope that you will find, as thousands of other folks have, that I don't like guilt very much. It can't be what moves us to change the world, or ourselves. Most good things begin with a little guilt, but they never end there. A friend of mine says, "Guilt can be a good indicator, but it is a terrible motivator." Jesus came not to give us guilt but to give us life. We never fully arrive at the perfect lives or the perfect world we hope for, which is why grace is so magnificent. But we still must strive to see our hypocrisies and contradictions become less and less each day. We are all bound up in the filthy system, and if you find yourself particularly bound, take courage, as you will then have more grace as you liberate others.

We live in a consumer culture with enough stuff gathering dust on shelves. And there are enough white men writing books. Most good things have been said far too many times and just need to be lived. Ironically, over the past decade, the previous sentence has proved to be one of the truest and most quoted from the book. Alas, we will once again print the message as a ten-year edition. Thanks for reading it, and I do hope that revolution will become a way of life, not just a cliche. So as author and farmer Wendell Berry says in his preface to *Sex, Economy, Freedom, and Community*, "If you have bought this book, dear reader, I thank you. If you have borrowed it, I honor your frugality. If you have stolen it, may it add to your confusion."

Publishing a book validates what you have to say, and that's something we should all be careful of. I despise it when people write me off as a young idealist until they hear I'm writing a book or went to seminary.[1] When people hear you wrote a book, they listen to what you have to say.

---

1. Or worse yet, when I show up to speak at a fancy banquet and they don't let me in until they realize that I'm the speaker, and then they escort me to the front row apologizing the whole way. (It has happened a few times!)

That's dangerous because there are some bad books out there (not by Zondervan, of course—wink). And there are tons of good people with something to say who will never write a book. (How about Jesus, for starters?)

This is not the story of the Simple Way. I could not tell our story on my own if I wanted to. Besides, we'd need our own book series, or better yet our own reality TV show. (Just kidding. Don't get any ideas.) We support each other's vocations, and the Simple Way has walked with me and supported me in this project. I am one voice among the chorus that creates the harmony of our movement. I have had an incredible group of people by my side as I make decisions about speaking and writing. They hold me accountable. (That's a fancy way of saying they make sure I don't sell my soul to "the Man" or look at porn on the internet.) They ask me hard questions and check my motives. I am thankful for Michael, Brooke, Michelle, Amber, Richard, Chris, Joshua, Aaron, Scott, Darin, Jonathan, Will, Tony, Jamie, Bart, Jim, Tom, Ched, Ron, Betsy, and Margaret. And I am thankful for my wife, Katie Jo. I didn't have her when I wrote this book ten years ago, but I'm so glad we found each other. She also suggested that this anniversary edition could have a picture of her face on the front instead of mine, but that didn't fly with the design team.

If you are disappointed with this book and want your money back, let me know. (Actually, first try going back to the bookstore with the receipt, then give writing the publisher a shot. If you still have no luck, then try asking the Simple Way; maybe they'll feel sorry for you. If all else fails, tell me, and I'll send you a better book, which most likely will be used, and might be the Bible.)

It's also worth noting that in the years since I wrote this, my first, book, I have written a bunch more, but every one of them has been collaborative. This isn't an accident. Collaboration has been a deliberate act, and a richly rewarding one. I've loved writing with others folks I admire, and I can feel myself getting deeper and wiser as I do it. It has been an honor to conspire with legends such as John Perkins (*Follow Me to Freedom*) and Tony Campolo (*Red Letter Revolution*) and ice-cream man Ben Cohen of Ben and Jerry's (*Jesus, Bombs, and Ice Cream*). Some of these projects have involved dozens of diverse and immensely gifted people (*Common Prayer, Schools for Conversion*, and *Animate*). I'm not out to be a soloist but to build a movement. These days that means writing lots of forewords and endorsements and giving free and hopefully good advice to new writers. We have an entire community of speakers and writers now known as Red Letter Christians who are trying to harmonize, but not homogenize. We believe Jesus actually meant the stuff he said. We rejoice that Jesus has survived the embarrassing things we Christians have done in his name. And we want our Christianity to look like Jesus again.

Back to this book. Who knew you could make so much money writing a book? Thankfully, some of my friends and elders were forward-thinking (and optimistic) enough to arrange for the proceeds of this book to be given away. This also protected me from the entanglements of money, an obsession with sales, and the necessity to self-promote.[2]

Over the past ten years, we have sold more than 300,000 copies of this book. And we have been able to share nearly

---

2. I realize this runs the risk of tooting my own horn. But I think there is a greater risk in politely repressing questions of credibility. Many of us don't care how articulate someone is if they don't incarnate the message they preach, if we can't hear their words past the noise of their lives. So thanks for those of you who care where your money is going and who have the audacity to question my stewardship!

half a million dollars with "local revolutions" around the world. Every time you buy a book, you are helping to fuel the revolution. In this updated edition, I have added dozens of new groups to the list in appendix 1, and I keep discovering new ones every day. These are people who inspire me, and we add new names to the list all the time.

By the way, giving away the money from book sales is not a noble act of charity. It's the only thing that makes sense to me. Besides, this is not just my story, and I am not just exploiting the stories of others. This book has emerged from a movement of communities of faith and struggle, inspired by local revolutions and ordinary radicals, anchored in life among the poor and marginalized. So it is not only a responsibility but a joy and honor to share the profits with all of them.[3] May we continue to feed each other hope as we dance God's revolution together.

One more thing, a tenth anniversary edition thing: try to imagine reading something you wrote ten years ago. You might find you disagree with yourself. You might say things differently now. You might be gentler or more aggressive. Well, I've resisted the temptation to rewrite this book and decided just to give it a facelift, so this is version 2.0. We've tried to update outdated cultural references as best we could, though I'm not known for my hipness anyway. My interjections and additions appear in this different color font, and we've been careful to try to leave the content true to the original book. So it is a little vintage, and a little fresh.

---

3. In appendix 1 at the back of the book, you will find a list of ordinary radicals with whom I enthusiastically redistribute the money I receive from the publication of this book through the Simple Way's Jubilee Fund.

CHAPTER 1

WHEN CHRISTIANITY WAS STILL SAFE

It's what always happens to the saints and prophets who are dangerous: we bronze them, we drain them of their passion and life and trap them in stained-glass windows and icons, confining them safely in memories of the past. St. Francis becomes a birdbath, Malcolm X is put on a stamp, and Martin Luther King gets a holiday. And Jesus gets commercialized, whether it's the plastic night-lights or the golden crucifixes. (And now there is a bobbing-head "Buddy Jesus" for your car and the "Jesus is my homeboy" T-shirt.) It becomes hard to know who Jesus really is, much less to imagine that Jesus ever laughed, cried, or had poop that smelled.

I can remember when Christianity was still safe, comfortable, trendy. I grew up in the Bible Belt, in East Tennessee, where there's a church building on nearly every corner. I can't remember meeting anyone Jewish or Muslim, and I distinctly remember being dissuaded from dating a Catholic girl because she "prayed to Mary." I attended two or three different youth groups, whichever had the best entertainment and drew the largest crowd. Church was a place where there were cute girls, free junk food, and cheap snowboarding trips. I discovered a

Christianity that entertained me with quirky songs and velcro walls.[1]

In middle school, I had a sincere "conversion" experience. We took a trip to a large Christian festival with bands, speakers, and late-night pranks. One night a short, bald preacherman named Duffy Robbins gave an invitation to "accept Jesus," and nearly our whole youth group went forward (a new concept for most of us), crying and snotting, hugging people we didn't know. I was born again. The next year, we went to that same festival, and most of us went forward again (it was so good the first time) and got born again, again. In fact, we looked forward to it every year. I must have gotten born again six or eight times, and it was great every time. (I highly recommend it.)

But then you start to think there must be more to Christianity, more than just laying your life and sins at the foot of the cross. I came to realize that preachers were telling me to lay my life at the foot of the cross and weren't giving me anything to pick up. A lot of us were hearing "don't smoke, don't drink, don't sleep around" and naturally started asking, "Okay, well, that was pretty much my life, so what do I do now?" Where were the do's? And nobody seemed to have much to offer us. Handing out tracts at the mall just didn't seem like the fullness of Christian discipleship, not to mention it just wasn't as fun as making out at the movies.

I was just another believer. I believed all the right stuff—that Jesus is the Son of God, died and rose again. I

---

1. I'm hopeful that not everyone reading this grew up in the same bizarre world of youth-ministry entertainment, so for those unfamiliar with the velcro wall, it's a giant inflatable wall of velcro that you wear a special velcro suit for and bounce up and stick onto . . . all for Jesus.

had become a "believer," but I had no idea what it means to be a follower. People had taught me what Christians believe, but no one had told me how Christians live.

SPIRITUAL BULIMIA

So as we do in our culture, I thought perhaps I needed to buy more stuff, Christian stuff. Luckily, I found an entire Christian industrial complex ready to help with Christian music, bumper stickers, T-shirts, books, and even candy ("Testa-mints" . . . dead serious . . . mints with a Bible verse attached, candy with a Christian aftertaste). A friend of mine who owns a Christian bookstore told me I went easy on the Catholics here, who also know how to clutter and commercialize. He told me about a Catholic cologne—imported from Italy—so even if you don't feel holy, at least you can smell holy. They had lists of bands and the Christian alternatives to them, so I got rid of all my old CDs. (CDs were what we used to listen to music on back in the 1900s.) (And I must confess, I was a bit disappointed by the Christian counterfeit. I later heard legendary musician Rich Mullins grieving how bad a lot of Christian art is. He said, "You hear these Christian artists say, 'God gave me this song,' and then you listen to it and know why God gave it away." Who could compare to Guns N' Roses and Vanilla Ice?) And I bought books, devotionals, T-shirts. I developed a common illness that haunts Western Christianity. I call it spiritual bulimia. Bulimia, of course, is a tragic eating disorder, largely linked to identity and image, where folks consume large amounts of food but vomit it up before it has a chance to digest. I developed the spiritual form of it where I did my devotions, read all the new Christian books and saw the Christian movies, and then vomited information up to friends, small groups, and pastors. But it had never had the chance to digest. I had gorged myself on all the products of the Christian industrial complex but was spiritually starving to death. I was marked by an over-consumptive but malnourished spirituality, suffocated by Christianity but thirsty for God.

It was Mark Twain who said, "It's not the parts of the Bible I don't understand that scare me, but the parts I do understand." I don't know if you've read the Bible, and if you haven't, I think you may be in a better place than those of us who have read it so much that it has become stale. Maybe this is why Jesus says to the religious folks, "the tax collectors and the prostitutes are entering the kingdom of God ahead of you" (Matt. 21:31). For me, it became hard to read the Bible and walk away as if I had just watched a nice movie. Jesus never seemed to do anything normal. How about the fact that his first miracle was the old turning-water-into-wine thing to keep a party going? (Not a miracle that would go over well in some Christian circles.) And there's that time Jesus' friends leave him on the shore. If we had been in Jesus' shoes, some of us might have yelled for them to come back. Others might have jumped in the water and swum out to the boat. But Jesus just steps on the blessed water (Matt. 14:22–26). That's nuts. It scares his friends to death. Or take healing a blind person, for instance. I've seen people gather around and lay hands on the sick. Others anoint people with oil. But when Jesus wants to heal a blind guy, he picks up some dirt off the ground, *spits* in it, and then wipes it on the dude's eyes (John 9:6). That's weird. No one else did that. Can you imagine the other religious leaders? "Rabbi, could you hack me up a holy loogie?" Not a chance. No one else did stuff like that. Only Jesus would be crazy enough to suggest that if you want to become the greatest, you should become the least. Only Jesus would declare God's blessing on the poor rather than on the rich and would insist that it's not enough to love just your friends. I began to wonder if anybody still believed Jesus meant those things he said. I thought if we just stopped and asked, What if he really meant it? it could turn the world upside-down. It was a shame Christians had become so normal.

JESUS WRECKED MY LIFE

I know there are people out there who say, "My life was such a mess. I was drinking, partying, sleeping around . . . and then I met Jesus and my whole life came together." God bless those people. But me, I had it together. I used to be cool. And then I met Jesus and he wrecked my life. The more I read the gospel, the more it messed me up, turning everything I believed in, valued, and hoped for upside-down. I am still recovering from my conversion. I know it's hard to imagine, but in high school, I was elected prom king. I was in the in-crowd, popular, ready to make lots of money and buy lots of stuff, on the upward track to success. I had been planning to go to med school. Like a lot of folks, I wanted to find a job where I could do as little work as possible for as much money as possible. I figured anesthesiology would work, just put folks to sleep with a little happy gas and let others do the dirty work. Then I could buy lots of stuff I didn't need. Mmm . . . the American dream.[2]

---

2. Well, there was that brief stint when I wanted to join the circus. I went to circus school and became quite an accomplished unicycler, magician, juggler, stilt-walker, fire-breather, and fire-eater, although I never ended up joining the circus. Of course, now I know that working with the church is close enough, its own kind of circus, packed full of fools, freaks, and daredevils. Can you add a note to a footnote? Well, I'm about to. If you really dig the circus and want to see theology and circus meet, you'll love this ten-minute clip: *https://www.youtube.com/watch?v=KuNPABbYcG8*.

But as I pursued that dream of upward mobility preparing for college, things just didn't fit together. As I read Scriptures about how the last will be first, I started wondering why I was working so hard to be first. I heard a preacher put it like this: "If you find yourself climbing the ladder of success, be careful or else on your way up you might pass Jesus on his way down." And I couldn't help but hope that there was something more to life than pop Christianity. I had no idea what I should do. I thought about leaving everything to follow Jesus, like the apostles, and hitting the road with nothing but my sandals and a staff, but I wasn't sure where to pick up a staff.

There were plenty of folks talking about the gospel and writing books about it, but as far as I could tell, living out the gospel had yet to be tried in recent days. So youth group got a little old—the songs got boring, the games grew stale, and I found other places to meet fine women. I wasn't sure the church had much to offer. Of course, I didn't dare stop going to church, convinced that "going to church" is what good people do, and I didn't want to become like "those people" who don't "go to church." Heathens. Ha. So I sucked it up and went every week, often cynical, usually bored, but always smiling.

All the youth used to sit in the back row of the balcony, and we'd skip out on Sunday morning to walk down to the convenient mart for snacks before slipping back into the balcony. I recall thinking that if God was as boring as Sunday morning, I wasn't sure I wanted anything to do with him. And I remember joking with friends that if someone had a heart attack on Sunday morning, the paramedics would have to take the pulse of half the congregation before they would find the dead person. Yes, inappropriate, but funny, and I'm not sure it was far from the truth. A solemn deadness haunted the place. I remain convinced to this day that if we continue to lose young people in the church, it won't be because we made the gospel too hard but because we made it to easy. We will lose them not because the foosball table was broken or we didn't have the latest Xbox game in the youth room but because we didn't dare them to take Jesus seriously and connect the gospel to the world we live in. I learned in confirmation classes about the fiery beginnings of the Methodist Church and its signature symbol of the cross wrapped in the flame of the Spirit. Where had the fire gone? I learned about John Wesley, who said that if they didn't kick him out of town after he spoke, he wondered if he had really preached the gospel. I remember Wesley's old saying, "If I should die with more than ten pounds, may every man call me a liar and a thief," for he would have betrayed the gospel. Then I watched as one of the Methodist congregations I attended built a $120,000 stained-glass window. Wesley would not have been happy. Wesley's general philosophy on money was, "Get it out of your hands as quick as you can, lest it make its way into your heart." I stared at that window. I longed for Jesus to break out of it, to free himself, to come to rise from the dead . . . again.

JESUS FREAK

Then a couple of new kids transferred to our high school, and I heard a few rumors about them. They were from a "charismatic," nondenominational congregation that was much more "radical" than the United Methodists; they spoke in tongues and danced in the aisles. All right, I must admit, something in me was secretly fascinated. I wanted to see passion. But of course, I dared not admit my interest and joined my other friends making weird looks and cult jokes. So one day in the lunchroom, I was talking with some of my Methodist friends when we saw the two new students in the cafeteria, and I was commissioned (okay, dared) to go sit with them and ask them about the speaking in tongues, as all my friends looked on, snickering. Part of it was in jest, but there was another part of me that was intensely curious. Looking back, it's amazing they even gave me the time of day. But like good evangelicals, they invited me with open arms to worship with them, and I went. I quickly grew to admire their reckless, unguarded worship. And I met people who lived like they believed in heaven and hell, who cried and worshiped like they were actually encountering God. In this wild charismatic youth group, I also became a believer in miracles and the power of prayer. I saw people healed and lives transformed. The Holy Spirit became real to me. To this day I think most of the church needs a little more of the Pentecostal fire, and I long for those who believe in prayer to join forces with those who believe in action. I've seen both work miracles.

Before long, I ended up joining that congregation. I became a Jesus freak. I tried to convert everybody, from heathens to pastors. I organized the See You at the Pole meetings at our school, where hundreds of us met at the flagpole to pray, committed to bringing prayer back into the public schools. I was passionately pro-life and anti-gay,[3]

---

3. I must say I am still passionately pro-life, I just have a much more holistic sense of what it means to be for life, knowing that life does not just begin at conception and end at birth, and that if I am going to discourage abortion, I had better be ready to adopt some babies and care for some mothers. I like to say that I am pro-life from the "womb to the tomb"—from the cradle to the grave. In the 1990s, "pro-life" came to mostly mean "anti-abortion"—many of us acted like life begins at conception and ends at birth—but I see a new pro-life movement emerging that is not just anti-abortion but consistently *for life* and against death in all its

and I tore apart liberals. I helped organize the local Bush-Quayle campaign, running around slapping bumper stickers on cars whether the owners wanted them or not. Nobody could stop us Jesus freaks. I went to the malls to do goofy skits and hand out religious tracts to try to save innocent shoppers from the fires of hell. To this day, I have a certain respect for those religious fanatics who stand on street corners. At least they have a sense of urgency and passion and live as if what they are saying is true. The only problem with many of the street-corner preachers I've heard is that most of the things they say don't sound like the "good news." I like their zeal, but not always their message.

It was awesome being a Jesus freak, and I did it for almost a year, but the fiery newness of it died out, and when they actually let us pray in school, it sort of lost its glamour.[4] I saw the messiness of church politics and egotism. I was driven mostly by ideology and theology, which isn't very sustainable, even if they're true. I wondered if Jesus had anything to say about this world, and I began to question how much he cared whether I listened to Metallica. Sometimes when we evangelized, I felt like I was selling Jesus like a used-car salesman, like people's salvation depended on how well I articulated things. And that's a lot of pressure. I even heard a pastor explain that he used to work in the corporate world and now he was in a "different kind of business" with the "best product in the world." But I wasn't sure I was even selling them the real thing. Sometimes it felt like Jesus was

---

ugly forms—death penalty, war, poverty. Anything that destroys life erases part of God's image in the world. So let's imagine what it means to truly stand on the side of life and interrupt death.

4. We later referred to this feel-good, emotionally charged Christianity as "spiritual masturbation." It feels good but never really gives birth to anything.

a blue-light special at Kmart, or like I was in one of those infomercials in which people are way too happy to give you lots of cheap stuff you don't need. Really, all I had was a lot of Christian clutter, in my bedroom and in my soul.[5] I began to doubt whether the Bible stories looked like they did in Sunday school. I needed some relief for my overchurched soul. So I became quite disenchanted with the church, though I was still fascinated with Jesus.

I wanted to study and learn about Jesus. I wanted to see people who tried to live out the things that Jesus taught. My youth pastor pointed me to a little college up in Pennsylvania, Eastern College (later named Eastern University), where there were a number of wild Christians. One of them was the short, chubby dude, Duffy Robbins, who had spoken at the youth event where I got born again each year. And another was a wise, sassy, spitfire (and spitting) preacher named Tony Campolo, who chaired the sociology department. Both Duffy Robbins and Tony Campolo ended up becoming close friends and mentors, and still are to this day. At Eastern, I majored in both Youth Ministry with Duffy and Sociology with Tony. Duffy is much less chubby these days (he made me add this), is cutting-edge even though he's bald, and is still leading young people to Jesus all over the world. He's also very funny on Twitter. Tony and I are best buds; he's sort of a spiritual grandpa to me. We wrote a book together—*Red Letter Revolution*—and we lead a movement of "Red Letter Christians," which you'll hear more about later. Tony recently turned eighty and has been known to say, "You know you're old when your wife says, 'Let's go upstairs and have sex,' and you say, 'Pick one; I can't do both.' But he also says that we are all as old as

---

5. What a number of us grew to call "chicken poop for the soul."

our cynicism and as young as our dreams. I consider Tony a teenager because of his dreams, but I can run a lot faster than him. And I can walk up the stairs and have sex with my wife in the same night. When I mentioned the possibility of going there, my family freaked. No one went North.[6] My aunts warned me, "You are gonna git Yankified." My mom, who was already pleading with me to leave the fanatics and come back to the Methodists, told me, "If God wants you to go to school in Philadelphia, then God can pay for it." I guess God did. Before long, I was given a presidential scholarship and I headed to Philly. At one point, my mom said this made it sound like she didn't really support me, but she did. It was just hard to see her only son go to college eleven hours away. So let me be clear about something: I am the definition of a mama's boy. Yep, I said it. I couldn't ask for a better mom. She's been nothing but supportive over the years, even as I went to jail and to Iraq, although I didn't tell her I went to Kabul until I got home. We've traveled the world from the West Bank to New Zealand. Let there be no mistake: along with my wife, my mom is my closest friend, biggest fan, and constant inspiration. She has taught me what love is like—from the moment I was born.

JESUS IN DISGUISE

In college, I got involved in every club and student group, from the clown troupe to the gospel choir. But I just didn't

---

6. Some of you may think I'm exaggerating. But my high school was the Maryville Rebels, and Confederate flags branded everything we had. When I brought my yearbook with the flag on the cover up to college, a few folks gave me a gentle "that's not cool" acculturation talk. Thankfully, times change and Northerners know we wear shoes and have toilets down South, and my family knows that Yankees are not all stuffy liberals; though they will mess up your mind, it's not always a bad thing.

meet God in the halls of the Christian college like I had expected I would. One night, I was hanging with two buddies who told me they were going down to the city to hang out with their "homeless friends." I was a little startled. First, I couldn't believe that there were people living on the streets of Philly through the winter. (Keep in mind, I'm from Tennessee.) And second, I was puzzled that my college buddies, Chris and Scott, who sat around listening to death metal and talking like Beevis and Butthead, had become friends with them. Chris Lahr and Scott Matney—the guys who first took me to the streets—are still among my best buds. Chris and his family live about a mile up the street. Scott helped me renovate the abandoned house we live in. They have both been a huge part of the work here in Philly, twenty years later. Thankfully, they have better taste in music these days. Although Chris did make me go to a Napalm Death show for his birthday. It was strange seeing old men listen to death metal, and the lead singer had to wear a knee brace. So it goes. So they invited me, and I went . . . again and again. In fact, every chance we got, we would head for the city. At first I was scared to talk to anyone lest they hear my Southern accent and think me an easy target for a mugging. (I tried to fake a Philly accent, but that ended up sounding more British.) I was in for a lot of surprises, least of which was that not everyone who goes downtown after dark gets mugged. On one occasion, I left my credit card in my room at school in case we ran into trouble and I got my wallet stolen downtown. I returned the next day only to find that a colleague had stolen it from my dorm room (and charged hundreds of dollars on it) while I was in the "dangerous" city streets. The people in the alleys stole only my heart. Eventually, they became my friends. I met some of the most incredible people I'd ever met. We would stay up all night and hear each other's stories. It became harder and harder to come back to the comfort of our dorm rooms and leave our neighbors in their cardboard boxes (and to talk about "loving our neighbors as ourselves" in New Testament classes).

One night my friend Chris said to me, "I've been reading Mother Teresa." I knew we were in trouble then. He continued, "She says that we can't understand the poor until we begin to understand what poverty is like. So tonight we are going to sleep out on the street." My jaw dropped. I asked him not to mention this to my mom, and we headed out for the streets. Night after night, we would head down. The Bible came to life for us there. When we read the Bible on the streets of Philly, it was like watching one of those old-school 3-D movies with the red glasses. Before, we had never put the glasses on (so it just looked weird). But now the words jumped off the pages.

Back at college, I had asked one of my Bible teachers if he still believed in miracles, like when Jesus fed thousands of people with a couple of fishes and a handful of loaves. And I wondered if God was still into that stuff. I wanted miracles to be normal again. He told me that we have insulated ourselves from miracles. We no longer live with such reckless faith that we need them. There is rarely room for the transcendent in our lives. If we get sick, we go to a doctor. If we need food, we go to a store and buy it. We have eliminated the need for miracles. If we had enough faith to depend on God like the lilies and the sparrows do, we would see miracles. For is it not a miracle that the birds find enough worms each day? He was right. On the streets of Philly, we experienced miracles. We would wake up sometimes with a blanket on us or a meal beside us that wasn't there when we went to sleep. Other moments were so mystical I'm scared to try to crystallize them on paper lest you think I'm nuts . . . or even worse, that I'm a saint or a televangelist. (After all, this is only the first chapter.) It's enough to say I just wanted to be safe for God to trust with those little secrets that God seems to reserve for the weak and the destitute.

We read in the Scriptures that God says to take good care of strangers, for we could be entertaining angels without knowing it (Heb. 13:2). And I really think we saw angels and demons. One night we met a precious, fragile old woman who looked just like a granny about to pinch your cheek. As we walked by, she began whispering, "Jesus is dead. Jesus is dead," louder and louder until it became chillingly eerie. At a loss for words and taken a little off-guard, we just began quietly humming the tune of an old worship song. She put her hands on her ears and began shaking her head, her whole body squirming as if we were running our fingernails down a chalkboard. She rocked back and forth, shouting, "Get away from me! Get away from me!" And then she scurried down the street with her hands on her ears. I didn't even know if I believed in angels or demons, but I had the distinct sense that we were encountering them. They just looked so much different than they do in the horror movies and Hallmark cards.

At first, the supernatural was hard to recognize. I began to realize that the transcendent comes in many forms. Perhaps the devil is just as likely to wear a three-piece suit as to have horns and a pitchfork. And perhaps the angels look more like the bums in the alley than like feathered white babies.

I saw one woman in a crowd as she struggled to get a meal from one of the late-night food vans. When we asked her if the meals were really worth the fight, she said, "Oh yes, but I don't eat them myself. I get them for another homeless lady, an elderly woman around the corner who can't fight for a meal."

I saw a street kid get twenty bucks panhandling outside of a store and then immediately run inside to share it with all of his friends. We saw a homeless man lay a pack of cigarettes in the offering plate because it was all he had. I met a blind street musician who was viciously abused by some young guys who would mock her, curse her, and one night even sprayed Lysol in her eyes as a practical joke. As we held her that night, one of us said, "There are a lot of bad folks in the world, aren't there?" And she said, "Oh, but there are a lot of good ones too. And the bad ones make you, the good ones, seem even sweeter."

We met a little seven-year-old girl who was homeless, and we asked her what she wanted to do when she grew up. She paused pensively and then replied, "I want to own a grocery store." We asked her why, and she said, "So I can give out food to all the hungry people."

Mother Teresa used to say, "In the poor we meet Jesus in his most distressing disguises." Now I knew what she meant.

I found that I was just as likely to meet God in the sewers of the ghetto as in the halls of academia. I learned more about God from the tears of homeless mothers than any systematic theology ever taught me.

CHAPTER 2

RESURRECTING CHURCH

We were sitting in the college cafeteria eating dinner, complaining as usual about the food and going back for more (the woes of college students). Suddenly, a friend walked up to our table and threw down a newspaper, muttering, "You guys are not going to believe this." The top story was about a group of forty homeless families who were being evicted from an abandoned cathedral in North Philadelphia.

The families were with an organization called the Kensington Welfare Rights Union, made up mostly of homeless mothers and children who took care of one another. They had been living in a tent city a few blocks away from the cathedral, but conditions were worsening, with rats and flooding. As they looked around North Philly, they saw the wreckage of an industrial neighborhood—thousands of abandoned houses, vacant factories, and empty lots. St. Edward's cathedral had been closed down along with half a dozen other cathedrals in Philadelphia's poorest neighborhoods (and not without massive resistance from Catholics), and it had been left vacant for several years. Though the number of abandoned houses surpassed the number of homeless people, many of the people were stuck on an endless waiting list for subsidized housing. So, living in worsening conditions and with the government threatening to take custody of their kids, the families moved into St. Edward's as an act of survival and a refusal to remain invisible. Soon after, the Catholic archdiocese which owned the building announced that they had forty-eight hours to get out or face arrest. We could hardly believe our eyes.

We scarfed down the rest of our dinner with our heads spinning, wondering what we should do. This complicated the old "love your neighbor as yourself" thing, which had become so manageable. Now homelessness was not just adults on the downtown streets but women and children. It wasn't long before we were packed in a car heading into "the Badlands" in search of St. Edward's in a neighborhood we had always been told to stay clear of. Little did we know that God's got a thing for showing up in badlands like Kensington and Nazareth. Anytime I hear someone say nothing good can come from Kensington, I still like to say, "Careful. That's exactly what they said about Nazareth, and look who showed up there!"

JESUS WAS HOMELESS

After weaving through the streets of row houses in North Philadelphia, we came upon the monstrous cathedral. The building took up an entire block, with its school, convent, rectory, and sanctuary. The families had chosen to seek refuge in the historic sanctuary and had hung a banner out front that read, "How can we worship a homeless man on Sunday and ignore one on Monday?" It took us a minute to realize they were talking about our Savior as a homeless man. Timidly, we walked up to the large red doors and gave them a knock. We could hear the thumping echo through the marble cavern. Several folks clumsily opened the doors, and they embraced us without hesitation. Then they invited us in. And we would never be the same again.

They gave us a grand tour of the shantytown they had constructed inside, and introduced us to a few of the children, who promptly stole our caps and jumped on our backs. They poured out their hearts to us, their struggles and their dreams. They reminded us that we all need each other and assured us that if we all shared with one another, there would be enough for everyone. When we asked what we could do, they didn't seem as interested in our stuff as they were in us. They wanted us to join them in the cathedral and to bring our friends, and they alerted us to the urgency of the looming eviction.

With the laughter of the children ringing in our ears, and the weight of the families' struggle heavy on our hearts, we went back to our college, disturbed, aching, and aware of the ticking of the clock. There was no time to waste, so we wrestled, prayed, and started conspiring. We knew that people at our little Christian college were familiar with the verse where Christ says, "Whatever you did for one of the least of these brothers and sisters of mine, you did for me" (Matt. 25:40). So, early in the morning, we ran through campus hanging up flyers that read, "Jesus is getting kicked out of church in North Philly. Come hear about it. Kea Lounge, 10 p.m. tonight." And that night we gathered. Expecting no more than a dozen of our crazier friends to show up, we were shocked when over a hundred people packed out the little dorm lounge. We talked through the night, and a few of us announced our intention to join the struggle of the families and begin repairing a Church that was in ruins.

GOD, SAVE THE CHURCH

The next day, dozens of us poured into the cathedral, casting our lives next to the families', saying, "If they come for you, they'll have to take us too." And as you can imagine, the fact that dozens of students were risking arrest alongside the families made for quite a media spectacle. Folks from the city wondered who our parents were and thought through how horrible it looked to be arresting folks for seeking refuge in a vacant cathedral. The media jumped on the story and made it look like the church was kicking homeless people out (which wasn't a stretch, since the church *was* kicking homeless people out). The clock continued to tick away, and the momentum grew—city leaders, clergy, and advocates came out to support the families.

Near the end of the forty-eight hours, we rang the old bell in the tower of the cathedral to alert the people of the neighborhood, many of whom were already bringing donations and gathering outside. Around the forty-seventh hour, anticipating the arrival of city officials, we prepared a "Last Supper," with all the families and friends gathered around a table on the old marble altar to sing, to pray, and to break bread together, with lots of tears. The families asked for a show of hands of who would remain in the building, risking arrest, when the officials returned. As I raised my hand, a young girl named Destiny was sitting on my lap, and she asked why I was raising my hand. "Do you want to be able to stay here?" I asked. Destiny said, "Yes, this is my home." And I told her, "That's why I'm raising my hand." She hugged me and slowly lifted her hand into the air.

I will never forget when the officials came to evict the families. The families had just announced to the media that they had already talked with the owner of the building (the Almighty), and they declared, "God says this is his house and we are welcome to stay." Who's gonna argue with that? The representatives from the archdiocese pulled up to the curb, took two steps out of the car, saw the crowd, and crawled back into the car without uttering a word. So needless to say, the forty-eight hours came and passed.

Days and then weeks passed as we continued making daily trips to St. Edward's (since some of us decided it was best not to drop out of school). We knew that if the number of students ever diminished, the police and archdiocese officials would come back to evict the families, so we developed a plan. For the first time ever, we got a cell phone. And we got an air horn. When the officials came to evict the families, we would get the call and run into the middle of campus sounding the air horn, and a flood of students would stream into the gym parking lot, pile into a cavalcade of cars, and head down to St. Ed's, singing Tracy Chapman's "Talkin' Bout a Revolution" at the top of our lungs. It was a revolution. We stood on our lunchroom tables and preached, the words of the prophets dripping from our tongues. We took over chapel services and invited students to join the movement. The president gave her bed to the families in St. Ed's.

We became known as the YACHT Club (Youth Against Complacency and Homelessness Today). It was not a boating club, though we did have some boaters mistakenly call on occasion, and we didn't hesitate to ask them for money. The Spirit was tearing through our college campus like a wildfire, igniting us with passion.

The drama never diminished, with the archdiocese and city officials always scheming for new ways to quietly evict the families. Once, the archdiocese had gotten the fire marshal involved, a very politically suave tactic, since the fire department could come in and simply say, "We are doing this in the best interests of the families, since this building violates fire and safety standards, putting them at risk and endangering their kids." So we were frantically preparing for the arrival of the fire marshal. The night before the inspection, we were making whatever last-minute preparations we could when we heard a knock on the door. It was about midnight, so two of us walked to the door together, only to find two firefighters standing out front. Startled, thinking that they had come to prepare for the eviction in the middle of the night, we instinctively began talking in circles defensively. They gently interrupted us and said, "Wait, wait, you don't understand. We are here against orders. In fact, we could get in very big trouble for being here. But we know what is happening, and we know that it's not right. So we thought we'd come by and help you get ready for tomorrow because we know what they will be looking for." We humbly apologized.

After walking through the building pointing out things needing work, they drove us to the fire station and gave us boxes and boxes of smoke detectors. They helped us get exit signs and fire extinguishers, and then they left. The next day, the fire marshal showed up, walked through the place, and said, "I can't evict them. The building meets fire standards." We never saw the firefighter angels again. Maybe they were angels, though they didn't look like the pictures in Sunday school.

It felt like nothing could stop us, as if God really was on our side. I wasn't really sure how God felt about taking sides in difficult situations like this, but we had a real sense that even if we were being pursued by every department in the city, somehow the sea would split open and swallow them up (in the most loving way) in order to protect the families. I became a believer in miracles.

BECOMING CHURCH

Every week, dozens of us piled into Sunday services at St. Ed's, where we sang old hymns and freedom songs. It was a revival of sorts. Gospel choirs came, and we danced in the aisles. Catholic clergy led liturgies in very controversial services (since many Catholics take a vow of obedience to the church hierarchy, and we were testing the limits of that vow). Kids and homeless mothers preached the gospel. We shared communion—old apple cider and stale bagels or whatever we could find—and many of us were experiencing true communion for the first time in our lives.

The body of Christ was alive, no longer trapped in stained-glass windows or books of systematic theology. The body of Christ was literal, living, hungry, thirsty, bleeding. Church was no longer something we did for an hour on Sunday, and church was not a building with a steeple. As Don Everts says in his book *Jesus with Dirty Feet*, "Referring to the church as a building is like referring to people as two-by-fours." She came to life. The church became something we *are*—an organism, not an organization. Church became so fresh and vibrant, it was like we had brought something dead back to life. And perhaps we had. In fact, one of the old news headlines read, "Church Resurrected." There's some systematic theology for you.

And yet amid all the spiritual movement, we kept bumping into this other thing people still called church, and I wasn't sure what to make of it. It seemed so far from the Scriptures, so far from the poor, so far from Jesus. I felt like I was encountering angels, wrestling with demons, and touching Jesus' wounds, but the church seemed so far away.

One day we received a box of donations from one of the wealthy congregations near our college that will remain nameless.[1] Written in marker on the cardboard box were the words, "For the homeless." Excited, I opened it up, only

---

1. Let's just say it's two blocks north on Lancaster Avenue next to the 7-Eleven. (Just kidding. I'm not telling . . . nosey.)

to find the entire box filled with microwave popcorn. My first instinct was to laugh. We barely had electricity, much less a microwave, and popcorn wasn't on the top of the needs list. My second instinct was to cry because of how far the church had become removed from the poor. Later that same week, another group of folks brought donations by St. Ed's—the mafia. With the media jumping on the story, the mafia came by and gave bikes to each of the kids, turkeys to each family, and thousands of dollars to the organization. I thought to myself, I guess God can use the mafia, but I would like God to use the church.

Shortly afterward, I sat puzzled, grieving over the state of our church. "I think I've lost hope in the church," I confessed, brokenhearted, to a friend. I will never forget her response. "No, you haven't lost hope in the church. You may have lost hope in Christianity or Christendom or all the institutions, but you have not lost hope in the church. This *is* the church." At that moment, we decided to stop complaining about the church we saw, and we set our hearts on becoming the church we dreamed of.

We dreamed ancient visions of a church like the one in Acts, in which "there were no needy persons among them" because everyone shared their possessions, not claiming anything as their own but "sharing everything they had." We knew we could end poverty. The early church did, and the homeless families were doing it. We thirsted for the kingdom of God, and we knew that it could come "on earth as it is in heaven," as Jesus said. We were not interested in a Christianity that offered these families only mansions and streets of gold in heaven when all they wanted was a bed for their kids now. And many Christians had an extra one.

I remember hearing about an old comic strip back in the days of St. Ed's. Two guys are talking to each other, and one of them says he has a question for God. He wants to ask why God allows all of this poverty and war and suffering to exist in the world. And his friend says, "Well, why don't you ask?" The fellow shakes his head and says he is scared. When his friend asks why, he mutters, "I'm scared God will ask me the same question." Over and over, when I ask God why all of these injustices are allowed to exist in the world, I can feel the Spirit whisper to me, "You tell me why we allow this to happen. You are my body, my hands, my feet."

BORN AGAIN . . . AGAIN

It was in St. Ed's that I was born again . . . again. There is something mystical about finding God in the ruins of the church. At the time, I had no idea who St. Francis of Assisi was, but somehow the divine whisper that he and those young radicals heard in Italy in the thirteenth century was very familiar: "Repair my church which is in ruins." Now hundreds of years later, another bunch of young dreamers was leaving the Christianity that smothered them, to find God in the abandoned places, in the desert of the inner city. I felt so thirsty for God, so embarrassed by Christianity, and so ready for something more.

The adventure of St. Ed's ended with the families holding a press conference. Many of them had received housing, as people saw it on the news and donated homes, as city agencies were persuaded to provide housing, and as friends pulled together to make sure everyone was taken care of. The Kensington Welfare Rights Union announced that this had been a project of survival and had never been intended to be a permanent solution (with one bathroom and no heat!), and that they were thankful for the powerful movement of people standing with them in their struggle. Then they marched to the mayor's office to request that he try looking at the world through their eyes and walking in their shoes. And they took off their shoes and left them in a pile outside of his office with a standing invitation to see what life is like in the shoes of homeless families.

So that's how the story ended, but the legacy of St. Edward's cathedral is far from over. Books and films have been made about the story. The Kensington Welfare Rights Union is now part of an international movement of poor and homeless families fighting to end poverty, and it's rooted right here in our neighborhood.[2] Many of them are still our dearest friends and teachers, our theologians and elders.[3] The cathedral itself was left abandoned for years before it was auctioned off. Michael and Michelle Brix, founding partners of the YACHT Club and the Simple Way, were married there. Not too long ago, I met one of the nuns who had worked in the parish at St. Edward's and had been forced to leave when it was closed down. She confided in me that she had been devastated and mourned the tremendous mistake (I think she even dared to say sin) of the archdiocese's closure of the cathedrals in North Philly. And then she said, with tears in her eyes, that she only recently had been able to stand back and celebrate all that had been born amid the wreckage of that old cathedral. We do indeed have a God of resurrection, a God who can create beauty from the messes we make of our world.

It has been more than twenty years since the takeover of the cathedral. When the building was auctioned off, a little Pentecostal congregation bought it. The whole

---

2. The website for the Kensington Welfare Rights Union is *kwru.org*. The larger global movement of organized poor and homeless folks is the Poor People's Economic Human Rights Campaign (*www.economichumanrights.org*).

3. See *universityofthepoor.org*, which has an entire section on theology.

block—sanctuary, convent, rectory, school with forty class-rooms and gymnasium—all sold for about $100,000. But now it has extra special meaning—in 2011, Katie and I got married there (with permission!). Some of the families who used to live there in 1995 came to the wedding. We rang the old church bell again. And the exit signs we installed were still there.

Many of the families that lived in St. Ed's are still friends of mine. They continue to inspire me and challenge me. Cheri Honkala, the main organizer of the cathedral takeover, has continued to stir up all sorts of holy mischief. During the housing collapse, she announced a run for sheriff of Philadelphia, running as the "People's Sheriff," promising she would not evict people from their homes (which is one thing sheriffs do!). She even rode through Kensington on horseback during the campaign. In 2012, Cheri was the vice-presidential candidate for the Green Party. A few weeks ago, she called me needing blankets because she had homeless families building a tent city outside a government office.

The YACHT Club is still a vibrant group on Eastern University's campus, forging friendships with folks who live on the street and combatting complacency and injustice.

One of the lessons I learned during the whole St. Ed's debacle is this: for some strange reason, God doesn't want to change the world without us. There are times when we throw our hands up at God and say, "Do something!" and if we listen closely, we can hear God respond, "I *did* do something. I made you." Sometimes we are waiting on God, and God is waiting on us. When it comes to combatting injustice, this has proved to be true: God wants our help. Certainly God can work miracles without us. It's not that God needs us but that God wants us, and that is pretty spectacular. So next time you ask God to move a mountain, don't be surprised if God hands you a shovel. This is a divine conspiracy. We get to be a part of the action.

CHAPTER 3

IN SEARCH OF A CHRISTIAN

I remember when one of my colleagues said, "Shane, I am not a Christian anymore." I was puzzled, for we had gone to theology classes together, studied Scripture, prayed, and worshiped together. But I could see the intensity and sincerity in his eyes as he continued, "I gave up Christianity in order to follow Jesus." Somehow, I knew what he meant.

I wondered what it would look like if we decided to really follow Jesus. In fact, I wasn't exactly sure what a fully devoted Christian looked like, or if the world had even seen one in the last few centuries. From my desk at college, it looked like some time back we had stopped living Christianity and just started studying it. The hilarious words of nineteenth-century Danish philosopher Søren Kierkegaard resonated in my thirsty soul:

> The matter is quite simple. The Bible is very easy to understand. But we Christians are a bunch of scheming swindlers. We pretend to be unable to understand it because we know very well that the minute we understand, we are obliged to act accordingly. Take any words in the New Testament and forget everything except pledging yourself to act accordingly. My God, you will say, if I do that my whole life will be ruined. How would I ever get on in the world? Herein

lies the real place of Christian scholarship. Christian scholarship is the Church's prodigious invention to defend itself against the Bible, to ensure that we can continue to be good Christians without the Bible coming too close. Oh, priceless scholarship, what would we do without you? Dreadful it is to fall into the hands of the living God. Yes, it is even dreadful to be alone with the New Testament.[1]

I knew we were not going to win the masses to Christianity until we began to live it. So I went on a quest. I went looking for a Christian. I looked around hoping to find someone else who might be asking, What if Jesus meant the stuff he said? And I kept coming across dead people—the desert fathers and mothers of the fifth century, Francis and Clare of Assisi, Dietrich Bonhoeffer, Martin Luther King Jr., Oscar Romero (and it was hard to miss that these dead people might have lived a little longer had it not been for reading this little Book). And then there was Dorothy Day and Mother Teresa, sassy contemporary radicals. Rumor has it that the only time Dorothy Day and Mother Teresa met was in Philly. And rumor also has it that Mother Teresa attended our beloved parish at Sacred Heart in Camden when she was in town. Dorothy Day was an activist and a communist, a mother and a journalist, who converted to Christianity. As a Christian, she courageously spoke out against the roots of oppression, war, and poverty, and steered the Catholic Worker movement[2] through the 1900s, a renewal which has given birth to dozens of hospitality houses scattered around the world. Unfortunately

---

1. Søren Kierkegaard, *Provocations: Spiritual Writings of Kierkegaard*, ed. Charles E. Moore (Farmington, PA: Plough, 2002), 201.

2. *http://catholicworker.org*.

for my hunt, she died a few years back in 1980. Mother Teresa, on the other hand, was still alive. She seemed to be giving the gospel a pretty good shot and probably wouldn't be around too much longer. So my friend Brooke, with whom I had been dreaming since before St. Edward's, and I decided to write her a letter. "Dear Mother Teresa, we don't know if you give internships out there in Calcutta, but we would love to come check things out." We shared with her the story of St. Ed's and our newly born vision of church, as all our friends stood by hooting and hollering, "You are writing who?!" And then we waited. And waited.

MOMMA T

I am not the most patient person, so after a few weeks, I got a little fidgety. With summer approaching, I decided to just start calling nuns to see if any of them knew how to get ahold of Momma T. Some told me to write her again. Others wondered if it was a prank call. But finally I ended up talking to a precious nun in the Bronx. She told me, quite amused (I think she felt sorry for me), that she would let me talk to "Mother Superior" there in the Bronx. Feeling pretty good about talking to anyone with "superior" in their name, I got ready. Mother Superior picked up the line and we talked. She told me I needed to write a letter to Mother Teresa. I told her I had. She told me I needed to wait. I told her I had. Then she said she would give me a number for Calcutta, and I was not to give it out (darn telemarkers). So I got the digits for Mother Teresa.

I did some homework and found out that I needed to call at 2 a.m. and that the call would cost four dollars a minute. (So I resolved to talk fast, not easy for a Tennessee boy.) I was calling from our dorm lounge, on a pay phone. Pay phones were what we used to call people on in the

1900s. You put quarters in them. Crazy, huh? So this call took a lot of quarters. With my friend Brooke standing beside me, both of us praying someone would answer, we called at 2 a.m. from the pay phone in our college lounge. It began ringing. I was expecting to hear a formal greeting: "Missionaries of Charity, how can we help you?" Nope. I just heard an old raspy voice on the other end mutter, "Hullo." Thinking I had the wrong number in Calcutta with the tab rolling at four dollars a minute, I started railing: "Hi-I'm-calling-from-the-USA-trying-to-reach-Mother-Teresa-or-the-Missionaries-of-Charity—I'm-wanting-to-visit." On the other end, I heard the muffled voice say, "This is the Missionaries of Charity. This is Mother Teresa." My initial reaction was, "Yeah right, and I'm the pope." But I held back. I told her we had written and wanted to come work with her. She asked how long we wanted to stay, and I told her we would like to spend the summer, about two to three months. "That's a long time," she said, and I shot back, "Or two to three weeks, or two to three days . . ." Heck, two to three hours seemed nice. She said, "No, come for the summer. Come." Come? Where would we eat and sleep? So I asked her, "Mother Teresa, where would we eat and sleep?" She didn't worry a lot about that. She said, "God takes care of the lilies and the sparrows, and God will take care of you. Just come." Who am I to argue with that? I thanked her, and we hung up.

COME AND SEE

Whenever folks asked Mother Teresa about her work in Calcutta, how it was going, what life was like, she would say, "Come and see." Finally, we actually were. I was ready to see Christianity lived out. Brooke and I got a bunch of shots and headed to Calcutta together to live an incredible adventure working alongside Mother Teresa and the sisters among the "poorest of the poor." In the morning, we worked in an orphanage called Nabo Jibon, taking care of children with physical and mental handicaps, many of whom had been abandoned in the train stations. In the afternoons, I worked in Khalighat, the Home for the Destitute and Dying, the first home Mother Teresa had started.

Every week, we would take soap and bubbles and meet about a hundred street kids at a water hole. We'd set up a station to help bandage wounds, a station to sew clothes that were torn, and an area for washing off the kids and splashing each other. The brothers would cook a meal for everyone. Some of the kids just wanted to be touched with love, and some confessed that they cut themselves or scraped their knees just so they could be seen in the make-shift clinic, to be held and healed.

When we got there, I thought we were crazy, and then I saw that there were dozens of people from all over the world who had come there to join the work, ordinary radicals just trying to figure out how to love better. We quickly settled into a little hostel across the street from the Mother House, where Mother Teresa and the sisters lived. There were volunteers from all over the world, ranging in age from eighteen to eighty. Some had been there for years. They taught me to love, to risk, to dream. There were missional evangelicals, curious atheists, simple pilgrims, and wild revolutionaries.

One of my great inspirations was a man named Andy, who pretty much ran the home for the dying. (He had been there longer than most of the sisters.) Andy was raw and sassy and gentle. I remember him telling one of the young nuns, "Sister, can you visit Mr. Raju, the lovely man in bed number fourteen? He has s--- everywhere." The nuns didn't know how to respond; some would frown and some would giggle. I also remember Andy rolling his eyes with a smile and scolding me for pampering one person too long, because there were "so many who need to be loved."

One day, one of the patients I was very close to was on the verge of death. On my way home, I gave him a hug and stuck a protein cookie under his pillow. Busted. Andy saw what I had done, shook his head hopelessly with a big smile, and we left together to go to Mass. Eventually, Andy told me his story. (He didn't talk much about himself.) He used to be a wealthy businessman in Germany, and then he said he read the gospel and it "messed everything up." He read the part where Jesus commands the disciples to sell everything they have and give it to the poor (Luke 12:33), and he actually did it. I had met some fundamentalists before, but only "selective fundamentalists," not folks who took things like that literally. He sold everything he owned and moved to Calcutta, where for over ten years he had spent his life with the poorest of the poor. He told me that in a few years he might want to go back and visit his beloved mom for a bit, and then he would come back to be with the dying and destitute, his new family. I had gone in search of Christianity. And I had found it. I had finally met a Christian.

DYING TO FIND LIFE

I fell in love with the Home for the Destitute and Dying and spent most days there. I helped folks eat, massaged muscles, gave baths, and basically tried to spoil people who really deserved it. Each day, folks would die, and each day, we would go out onto the streets and bring in new people. The goal was not to keep people alive (we had very few supplies for doing that) but to allow people to die with dignity, with someone loving them, singing, laughing, so they were not alone. Sometimes folks with medical training would come by and be overwhelmed with frustration because we had so few medical supplies, and the sisters would hastily explain that our mission was not to prolong life but to help people die well. As Mother Teresa would say (telling the old story about throwing starfish back into the ocean even though they continue to line the beach in thousands), "We are called not to be successful but to be faithful." That sounds good, but it was the beginning of my years of struggling with the tension between efficiency and faithfulness. I remembered Gandhi's saying that what we are doing may seem insignificant, but it is most important that we do it. So we did.

While the temptation to do great things is always before us, in Khalighat I learned the discipline of doing small things with great deliberation. Mother Teresa used to say, "We can do no great things, just small things with great love. It is not how much you do, but how much love you put into doing it." Just as Andy would reprimand people for using too much soap when washing dishes (we mixed ashes with the soap to multiply it), I also heard many a volunteer scolded for not putting enough gravy on the rice, since the plate was being served to Jesus himself.

Khalighat is one of the places that showed me resurrection, that life is more powerful than death, that light can pierce darkness. Those dying people were some of the most vibrant people I had ever met. There is a morgue in the home for the dying. As you walk into it, a sign on the wall reads, "I'm on my way to heaven." And when you turn around to walk out, another sign says, "Thanks for helping me get there." I could truly say, "Where, O death, is your victory? Where, O death, is your sting?" (1 Cor. 15:55). Death was "swallowed up" (v. 54) by the laughter of the dying and the singing of the destitute. I knew what Jesus meant when he told Peter that the "gates of hell would not prevail" against the church, as I was finally seeing a church that was storming the gates of hell itself to save people from its horrors.

As I looked into the eyes of the dying, I felt like I was meeting God. It was as if I were entering the Holy of Holies of the temple—sacred, mystical. I felt like I should take off my shoes. I knew what Dorothy Day meant when she said, "The true atheist is the one who denies God's image in the 'least of these.'" The reality that God's Spirit dwells in each of us began to sink in. I had sung the old worship songs in youth group, like "Sanctuary" ("Lord, prepare me to be a sanctuary pure and holy"), but I don't think I ever realized that we really are the sanctuaries where the Spirit dwells. Our bodies are the temples of God, and that's not just a reason to eat less cholesterol. We are the body of Christ, not in some figurative sense, but we are the flesh and blood of Jesus alive in the world through the Holy Spirit—God's hands, feet, ears. When Paul writes, "I have been crucified with Christ and I no longer live, but Christ lives in me" (Gal. 2:20), he means it. Over and over, the dying and the lepers would whisper the mystical word *namaste* in my ear. We really don't have a word like it in English (or even much of a Western conception of it). They explained to me that *namaste* means "I honor the Holy One who lives in you." I knew I could see God in their eyes. Was it possible that I was becoming a Christian, that in my eyes they could catch a glimpse of the image of my Lover?

SOCIETY OF OUTCASTS

I began to understand what it meant when the curtain of the temple was torn open as Jesus died on the cross. Not only was God redeeming that which was profane but God was setting all that was sacred free. There's a whole stream of thought called "dirty theology," which explores the radical dynamic of Jesus' challenging what was deemed clean and unclean, holy and unholy, sacred and profane. From being born as a refugee, to dying on the cross, Jesus enters into the "dirty" world we live in. He does things like wash feet and heals people with unlikely things like dirt and spit. He calls the religious folks a "brood of vipers" and says the "tax collectors are entering the kingdom ahead of you." All of it is a challenge to see the world upside-down. Everything is redeemable, and God is found in unlikely places. It has been said that Jesus consistently challenges the chosen and includes the excluded. Now God dwelled not behind the veil in the temple but in the eyes of the dying and the poor, in the ordinary and the mundane, in things like bread and wine, or chai and samosas. And wherever two or three of us come together in community, God is there among us.

One of the most sacred places I went was a leper colony outside of Calcutta. I heard that one of the brothers was gone, and so I asked if I could have his bed (okay, his spot on the concrete floor). The brothers agreed, and I spent the last couple of weeks in India in the leper colony. Leprosy is still a dreadful illness among the "poorest of the poor." Very little is known about it. And there are no Magic Johnson–type celebrities to bring attention to the disease. There are no famous lepers. It is a disease of the outcasts, the untouchables. One of the lepers explained to me that oftentimes lepers don't even know the words *thank you* because they have never needed to say them. They had rarely experienced occasions when they used language of gratitude. But then there was this community of lepers, called Gandhiji Prem Nivas, which means "Gandhi's new life." I don't know how much you know about Gandhi, but he would have been proud. Gandhi had walked that very land a few years before envisioning a new society in the shell of the old, a movement of people who stepped out of the empire that was oppressing them and began creating a new way of life, marching to the sea to get their salt and spinning their own cloth. I saw Gandhi's dream alive.

Years back, folks had given the land along the railroad tracks (worthless for development) to Mother Teresa, and she began caring for lepers. Then the lepers began to care for one another. Now there are over 150 families, teaching one another "thank you." They grow their own vegetables, raise animals and fish. They make their own shoes. They sew their own clothes.[3] And they make saris for all the sisters, blankets for the orphanages, and bandages for a medical clinic there in the colony. The clinic is run by lepers who had been treated and now care for others. They even make their own prosthetic arms and legs out of wood for those who have undergone amputation.

I was the stranger at first (not many westerners there!), but a stranger who was quickly welcomed into their family. Each day, I made my rounds to visit new friends in the colony. I would sit and watch the shoemakers make shoes. They would custom fit each one, since every foot is uniquely affected by the disease. They made me a pair.

---

3. This is where I was first inspired to begin making my own clothes and shoes, which entails beautiful bonding moments with my mother, who teaches sewing and may have wished for a daughter, but I do what I can. Watch out, Liz, there's another Claiborne on the block. We still make clothes together each year. And over the years, we've made some pretty sweet stuff. I'll confess—I have a leopard sweatshirt (fake, of course). And a blanket we made that folds into a pillow. And we made a pair of circus pants that have velcro extensions to fit all of my different-length stilts. (The biggest is eleven feet tall!) Oh, and Mom made the tuxedo for my wedding. It was way beyond my skill set—each pocket had nine parts. I'm used to pockets with one part. I'll also confess a designer once offered to buy the pattern, until I told him the pattern was made out of newspaper.

I would head down the long corridor of spinning wheels, threaders, and looms as dozens of folks worked busily with huge smiles. I would stop and talk to my good friends Jon and Kisol, who worked together threading all the needles for the looms. Jon was an elder, an old man who had lived with leprosy for decades. He asked me about my family back in the US. When he heard that my dad had died when I was a kid, he told me I could call him Good Father. He adopted me. Kisol was a young guy, only eighteen years old. Both of his parents had died from the disease, and they had left him with his two young sisters to take care of. Jon and Kisol were hard to leave. They invited me to their homes. They fixed me tea and scrumptious Indian sweets. We would tell stories, jokes, pray together. We would sit around and laugh when John passed gas and blamed it on Kisol . . . you know, all the usual things you would imagine doing with lepers in Calcutta.

THE GREATER THINGS

Most days I would go to the clinic run by the lepers-become-doctors, and a line would form as people waited to be treated. The doctors would lay out a huge pile of cotton about four feet high, and my job was to roll cotton balls for them as they cared for one another. I would watch intently, fascinated by their love and compassion. One afternoon as things were winding down, one of the doctors had to leave early, but there were a few patients still waiting to be seen. He looked at me and emphatically said, "You know how this works; you have been watching. It's your turn." Startled, I just stared at him. I had been watching, and I did know what to do, but I wasn't sure I dared. I came forward and sat in the doctor's seat and began staring into the next patient's eyes, and the decision had already been made. I began carefully dressing the man's wound. He stared at me with such intensity that it felt like he was looking into my soul. Every once in a while he would slowly close his eyes.

When I was finished, he said to me that sacred word I had come to love: "Namaste." I smiled with tears in my eyes and whispered, "Jesus." He saw Jesus in me. And I saw Jesus in him. I remember thinking back to the stained-glass window my United Methodist church bought for over $100,000. I saw a clearer glimpse of Jesus in this leper's eyes than any stained-glass window could ever give me.

I knew that I had not just looked into the eyes of some pitiful leper in Calcutta but that I had gazed into the eyes of Jesus, and that he had not seen just some rich, do-gooder white kid from America but that he had seen the image of God in me. That is nuts. What would the world look like if we truly believed, as the apostle Paul figured out, that we no longer live, but only Jesus lives in us (Gal. 2:20)?

As I lived in the leper colony, the Bible came to life, changed from black and white to color, just like it did on the streets of Philly. I saw the gospel with new eyes. One of the texts that had always given me trouble was John 14:12: "Very truly I tell you, all who have faith in me will do the works I have been doing, and they will do even greater things than these, because I am going to the Father." You shall do even greater things? Here's the Son of the Almighty, God incarnate, telling us ragtag disciples that we will do the same things he has been doing. I don't know about you, but I haven't raised anyone from the dead lately. I haven't seen anyone turn water into wine (although I had a friend who tried). And I hadn't healed any lepers. Even though I touched them, they still went home lepers at the end of the day.

But I began to discover "the greater things." It was not just miracles. I started to see that the miracles were an expression not so much of Jesus' mighty power as of his love. In fact, the power of miraculous spectacle was the temptation he faced in the desert—to turn stones to bread or to fling himself from the temple. But what had lasting significance were not the miracles themselves but Jesus' love. Jesus raised his friend Lazarus from the dead, and a few years later, Lazarus died again. Jesus healed the sick, but they eventually caught some other disease. He fed the thousands, and the next day they were hungry again. But we remember his love. It wasn't that Jesus healed a leper but that he touched a leper, because no one touched lepers. And the incredible thing about that love is that it now lives inside of us. In the verses just after the one about the greater things, Jesus assures us that the Spirit now lives in us. Jesus says that he is going to the Father but will also remain inside of us, and we in him. We are the body of Christ, the hands and feet of Jesus to the world. Christ is living inside of you and me, walking the earth. We shall do even greater things because the love that lived in the radical Christ now lives within millions of ordinary radicals all over the planet.

For the record, I am a strong believer in miracles, and so many stories come to mind of miraculous providence. How about one quick one: A friend of mine was working down in Latin America in a health clinic they had set up. They had very few supplies, and one day they had run out of everything except a bottle of Pepto-Bismol. So when people showed up with all sorts of illnesses, all they could offer them was Pepto. But then, my friend says, "The crazy thing is people were getting healed." They were coming with all sorts of illnesses and injuries, and the missionaries would give them Pepto.[4] A

---

4. This is not a promo for Pepto-Bismol, nor would I suggest that this experience is replicable.

crowd of folks gathered from all over, and he said that some-how that little bottle never ran out. So I know miracles are real, story after story comes to mind. But beyond the miracles, what has lasting significance is love. We can do all sorts of miracles, but if we have not love, it is nothing. In the leper colony, I had the strange sensation that somehow God's Spirit was alive in me.

I have a friend who says one of the reasons we don't see many miracles in industrialized countries is that we don't really need miracles. When we get sick, we go to the hospital. When we get hungry, we go to the store. I have come to believe that when we live in a way that requires miracles, we will start to see them. One of my goals is to live in a way that invites and expects the miraculous. And most of the miracles I've seen have been in those all-too-few moments when I stepped out into a space of utter reliance on God. I want more of that.

Oh, one more story. I remember hearing about a clerk at the grocery store who had a customer in the checkout line pray for her and she was healed. She got so excited she grabbed the intercom phone and announced, "If anyone needs prayer or healing, come to lane 4!" We need more stories like that one. It does make you wonder what we do not see because we do not risk. Fear holds us hostage. We are not desperate enough to see miracles. I'm not ready to walk on water, but I'm also not ready to let the televange-lists and prosperity preachers hijack the supernatural stuff from the rest of us. Imagine what would happen if the prayer movement and social justice movement converged, and we had Christians who prayed like they depend on God and lived like God depended on them? Hallelujah. That would be a miracle, and I'm ready to see it.

The time had come to leave the leper colony and, very soon, Calcutta. First, I had to say bye to Jon and Kisol.

We hugged and cried. And I will never forget our last exchange. Jon had always liked my watch. It was digital, and he liked the beeps and all. As we said goodbye, I wrapped it on his arm. It went to the very last notch around his bony wrist. He looked at me and, shaking his head, said he had nothing to give. I said he had given me more than I could explain, and I said, "You adopted me." He smiled. Kisol had a necklace with two medals he wore around his neck every day, probably one of the only material possessions he treasured. They were the icon medals that Mother Teresa gives you when she prays with you to remember her blessing and continual prayers. Kisol had two of them, old and worn down, that he wore around his neck. Mother Teresa had given me a couple a few days before, and I wore them on dental floss around my neck. As I was leaving, Kisol took his medallions from around his neck and put them around my neck. And I gave him mine. We hugged and I left.

Gandhi would be proud of this little "experiment in truth" that bears his name. The lepers had shown me a glimpse of what God might have had in mind for the world. I remember praying in the leper colony each morning with the brothers, "Thy kingdom come, Thy will be done, on earth as it is in heaven." And perhaps for the first time, those were no longer empty words that I hoped would come true someday. They became words we are not only to expect to come true but also to enact. Such an idea was foreign to me in the materialism of my land, but it was so close to what I saw in the early church: a people on the margins giving birth to another way of living, a new community marked by interdependence and sacrificial love.

They had not chosen to live in "intentional community." Their survival demanded community. Community was their life. The gospel was their language. No wonder Jesus said, "Blessed are the poor, for theirs is the kingdom of God."

FIND YOUR CALCUTTA

After leaving the colony, I said the rest of my goodbyes and promised to write Andy. I went through the streets of Calcutta giving hugs, saying goodbyes, splashing in the monsoon puddles. A few of the beggars asked me if there was anything I could leave them. My bag was empty. I had given away all the bubbles, toys, candy, even my secret stash of Gatorade and emergency cash. I had nothing left to give but love. At last, I was at peace. Then the time came to leave Calcutta.

I had gone to Calcutta on a search for Christianity, hoping to find an old nun who believed that Jesus meant what he said. And I had found Christianity, but it didn't belong just to Mother Teresa. Eventually, we did meet Mother Teresa. In Calcutta, she was not "Mother Teresa the Saint," she was just "Mother," running around on the streets, hanging out with kids, caring for the sick, going to Mass each morning. Mother.[5] In fact, when we finally talked, I had very little to say. I just wanted a hug, and I got it. It was sort of like, "Yep, there she is, another ordinary radical in love with God and her neighbors."

After Mother Teresa died, I was in an interview with some reporter who asked me if Mother Teresa's spirit will live on. I said, "To be honest, Mother Teresa died a long time ago, when she gave her life to Jesus. The joy and compassion

---

5. My friend Brooke ended up going into the hospital at the same time as Mother Teresa, and the doctors said Mother Teresa just told them, "There are far too many people out there hungry, homeless, and alone for me to be in here lying around. Let me out." So they did.

and love that the world finds so magnetic are only Jesus, and that is eternal." I saw that eternal love all over Calcutta. I did indeed see Christ in Mother Teresa, but I also found Christ in the lepers, the children, the destitute, the workers. I even began to recognize that Christ lives in me.

Mother Teresa always said, "Calcuttas are everywhere if only we have eyes to see. Find your Calcutta." I was ready to come home. I knew that my Calcutta was the United States, for I knew that we could not end poverty until we took a careful look at wealth. I was to battle the beast from within the belly. I learned from the lepers that leprosy is a disease of numbness. The contagion numbs the skin, and the nerves can no longer feel as the body wastes away. In fact, the way it was detected was by rubbing a feather across the skin, and if the person could not feel it, they were diagnosed with the illness. To treat it, we would dig out or dissect the scarred tissue until the person could feel again. As I left Calcutta, it occurred to me that I was returning to a land of lepers, a land of people who had forgotten how to feel, to laugh, to cry, a land haunted by numbness. Could we learn to feel again?

I had the chance to return to Calcutta after Mother Teresa died, and the work was as vibrant as ever. The charisma of Mother Teresa and the Missionaries of Charity has been a great influence on our work in Philly. Even to this day, we have a saying above our door: "Today, let's do small things with great love . . . or not answer the door."

Since writing this book, I have helped dozens of folks make the pilgrimage to India. And like me, many of them returned only to realize that you don't have to go to Calcutta to find Calcutta. We only need to ask God to help us find our own Calcutta and give us the eyes to see the marginalized people next to us.

I'll never forget one businessman I met who, upon hearing about my trip to Calcutta said, "Wow, that's a terrible place that makes you come home and say, 'God bless America.'" I gently replied to him, "Actually, Calcutta is a beautiful place that makes you come home and say 'God bless Calcutta.'" He just sort of stared at me blankly.

CHAPTER 4

WHEN COMFORT BECOMES UNCOMFORTABLE

Just a few days after I returned from Calcutta, I headed to Willow Creek Community Church in the verdant Chicago suburbs, where I had arranged a one-year internship. The previous year, I had been doing a Bible study whose central premise was that rather than waiting around for God's special plan for your life, you should just go find where God is at work and join in. That made sense to me, so I did. (I didn't even finish the study.) Essentially, that's what led me to spend the summer in Calcutta and then to spend a year at Willow Creek.[1] God appeared to be powerfully at work in both places, but I had no idea how difficult the transition would be. Needless to say, when I walked into the atrium where they have a food court on the megachurch "campus," I knew I was a long way from the leper colony in India. The worlds of poverty and wealth collided, and I guess I felt a little dose of what the experts call culture shock. According to Mother Teresa, it is among the wealthy that we can find the most terrible poverty of all—loneliness. So perhaps I was still among the poorest of the poor, but these poor folks had some cash!

---

1. *http://willowcreek.org.*

CULTURE SHOCKED

I had heard the beautiful story of Willow Creek's beginnings as a bunch of young people who were pretty disillusioned with the church. They went door to door selling tomatoes and asking people how they felt about this peculiar thing called church. If folks they talked with were happily connected to a congregation, then they encouraged them to continue and moved on. If the folks they met were discouraged about or hostile toward church, then they would talk with them, explaining that they had something in common and were embarking on an adventure of trying to give birth to a new way of being church. Rooted in the vision of the early church and with the book of Acts on their lips, they started—small, sloppy, passionate. Now some thirty years later, they are one of the nation's largest congregations, with over twenty thousand folks coming onto the 150-acre campus each week. Now, forty years in, they are still rockin'—with eight regional campuses in Chicago and thousands of Willow Creek Association congregations around the globe.

Eastern College had agreed to let me do my final academic work at Wheaton College, which was just a half hour from the church, while I served my internship. So I took a light load of classes, anticipating diving headlong into work at Willow, where I worked in the early beginnings of their Axis services geared toward folks in their twenties, who were strikingly absent from most congregations. I also did some urban-plunge work busting folks out of the suburban bubble, and spent most of my days leading high school students in the little thousand-person student ministry. And every chance I got, I would head into downtown Chicago to hang out in inner city Lawndale, go to Uptown, or chill with the homeless guys who lived under Lower Wacker Drive.

I must say Wheaton wasn't the easiest place to be. There were beautiful breaths of fresh air and some folks who were radically seeking after God, and some great pranks (which I had better not mention in detail here, as they may still be looking for the culprits—ask me later). After ten years, I think I'm in the clear to mention one little prank at Wheaton. At Christmas, Wheaton has traditionally placed a huge lighted "JOY" sign atop one of the highest buildings on campus. One particular year, a large "POOP" sign was placed in front of the "JOY" sign, perhaps to remind folks of the original smell of the manger that first Christmas. However, the pranksters underestimated the size of the "JOY" sign and failed to make their cover-up large enough. So folks all over Wheaton saw a bright light that read, "POOPY." I may or may not know who did that. I also may or may not know the folks who put a tennis-ball shooter in the middle of the pipe organ so that folks were pelted by tennis balls during convocation. But even for this East Tennessee boy, it was very homogeneous, privileged, and white. So many people looked and thought the same way, it seemed like we were being robbed of the gift of diversity. I kept hearing Wheaton referred to as the "Harvard of Christian schools" and wasn't sure how God felt about that, since God seems to prefer to use foolish things to confound the wise. Not to mention they still had that pesky no-dancing rule at Wheaton back then. The times, they are a changin'. Wheaton no longer has that pesky no-dancing rule. You can now get your groove on at Wheaton.

My roommate at Wheaton, no doubt divinely appointed (with a little humor), was the head of the ROTC and happened to be one of the only nonwhite students at Wheaton. He explained to me that the only way he was able to attend Wheaton was with the ROTC scholarship, along with its mandatory US military service requirement, and he wasn't even from the US. We talked a lot about war and peace. He explained to me that he did not believe Christians should go to war. We had some good times together, including a debate we hosted (okay, rigged) for all of the ROTC cadets in which we "debated" just-war theory and surprisingly came out agreeing that when Jesus said, "Love your enemies," he meant not to kill them. I wish I could say that was the end of the ROTC at Wheaton. That's still in process. Although I must applaud Wheaton's decision to change its name from the Wheaton Crusaders to the Wheaton Thunder. As of 2016, Wheaton does still have an ROTC. Still working on that. It's helpful to know that Wheaton's founder and first president, Jonathan Blanchard, was a wild man— social reformer, abolitionist, a revolutionary of the best kind (also the namesake of one of Wheaton's main buildings, Blanchard Hall). No doubt Blanchard would continue shaking some things up today. In recent years, Wheaton has pioneered some stellar conversations on subjects like immigration and the death penalty through its Center for Applied Christian Ethics (CACE). Students also recently made national news for having a die-in and bringing attention to racial injustice in the US.

POOR LITTLE RICH MAN

The year I was at Wheaton, Rich Mullins was also there on a sabbatical of sorts. Rich Mullins was a popular Christian singer-songwriter who died a few years back in a car wreck. Before I met him, I probably wouldn't have cared very much, as I knew so little about him. The only song I knew by him was a worship song called "Awesome God," which I found a little old school, and I didn't care much for the part about God having "lightning in his fists," as it

sounded a little more like the Greek god Zeus than Yahweh.
My friend Joe used to sing his own cover of the song,
which I'd better not repeat here since it got him banned
from playing at college coffeehouses (and Zondervan won't
let me). Suffice it to say that it had something to do with
God kicking some serious butt. But then I heard that Rich
Mullins was a pretty crazy dude who hitchhiked a lot,
went barefoot all the time, and liked St. Francis of Assisi
(my newfound hero), so I became secretly intrigued. My
resident assistant at Wheaton told me Rich had come to the
school largely because he was writing a musical inspired by
the life of Francis, and that he was going to audition for a
part. Hmm . . . I was even more intrigued. Looking for any
opportunity to nurture the relationship with my RA (you
never know when that will come in handy, especially at
Wheaton), I asked if I could come along. So we went. Rich
and the Ragamuffins (his band) were there as folks audi-
tioned. I sat back, studied a bit, and watched. Some folks
were dismissed and others were called back to read again.
As fewer and fewer were left, my friend being one of them,
they found they needed an "extra" reader. At the time, I
had multicolored hair and I was wearing ripped jeans and a
Rage Against the Machine shirt sporting a black American
flag with the words "Evil Empire." I think they thought I
was cute, not really matching the Wheaton prototype. So I
was drafted to help read as the extra for the last auditions.

   After I had read a few lines, they had the nerve to
say to me, "We just need you to read plainly; lose the
accent." What? *Lose the accent?* (Again, born and raised in
Tennessee . . .) So I smarted off to them in good ole friendly
banter, and they soon discovered that my accent was not
an attempt at character development. Looking back, it's a
little weird to think how quickly we hit it off. They asked

me to go ahead and actually audition for the play. I told them I didn't have enough time for a play; they said neither did they. I told them I don't sing. They told me to try. So I agreed.

Rich had been playing an old hymn on the keyboard, and they would go down the line and each auditioner would sing the chorus in turn, so I hopped into the lineup. Hampered by my lack of rhythm and my tone-deafness, I had no idea when to come in, but I tried to fake it. Each attempt, I was several beats too late or too early, and I tried two or three times before giving up, with everyone hee-hawing. They all made fun of me, and it wasn't long until they invited me to join the show. They assured me there was one part that required no musical skill, and that the show was just as much about community as talent. So several months later, I ended up lip-syncing in the musical.

Meanwhile, I had a blast hanging out with Rich and the Kid Brothers of St. Frank, as they came to call themselves. Rich was one of those folks who assured me that the Gospels were not just for Mother Teresa and St. Francis, and that the Sermon on the Mount is as meaningful today as it was two thousand years ago.

I will never forget one of the chapel services where Rich spoke while I was at Wheaton. (Let me confess, I had stayed up all night playing Monopoly and slept through the whole thing, but I got the tape and listened to it later.) Rich stood up in chapel and said, "You guys are all into that born again thing, which is great. We do need to be born again, since Jesus said that to a guy named Nicodemus. But if you tell me I have to be born again to enter the kingdom of God, I can tell you that you have to sell everything you have and give it to the poor, because Jesus said that to one guy too . . . [And he paused in the awkward silence.] But

I guess that's why God invented highlighters, so we can highlight the parts we like and ignore the rest." Ha! If Rich hadn't died, he probably would've joined the list of notorious blacklisted chapel speakers. Since this book's original release, I've been able to reconnect with some of the band and some of Rich's closest friends and family. I joined them on a Ragamuffin Retreat to celebrate his life. (They may have more of those.) To this day, one of my favorite things to do on a chill day is listen to a recording I have of one of Rich's last concerts. It's something special. You can get it here: *http://kidbrothers.org/product/rich-mullins-live-dvd/*. Rich Mullins at his best.

COMFORT INTERRUPTED

So all this stuff with Rich at Wheaton was just like a bonus, and as I look back on it, the whole experience seemed to mysteriously fit into the whole journey out there in Chicagoland and Willow world.

The reason I had come to Chicago in the first place was Willow Creek, so nearly every day I was making the half-hour commute. That drive from Barrington to Wheaton became very familiar. I spent the time processing thoughts, recording many of my reflections on a handheld recorder as I drove. I had no idea how difficult it would be to live in the world of Wheaton and Willow just weeks after returning from the slums of Calcutta. I was working in one of the wealthiest congregations in the world and performing a play at the Harvard of Christian schools about the life of a little fool named Francis (which people would pay fifteen dollars to see). Define irony. I would be eating in Willow Creek's food court, still digesting my time with Calcutta's starving orphans. Sometimes I was incredibly frustrated and angry, wondering how these extremes could exist in the same world, let alone in the same church. Sometimes I just got cynical. That was the easiest thing to feel, as cynicism takes very little energy.

But it was hard to stay cynical, as I met more and more beautiful people. Many late nights, I would crash at the home of Sibyl and Dick Towner, both of whom were longtime members and leaders at Willow, and we quickly became good friends. Sibyl and Dick exuded a joy of childhood sweethearts that was so contagious people flooded into their home to feel the warmth of community. Dick and Sibyl came to our wedding and continue to inspire me, though they are no longer a part of Willow Creek (in the official sense, anyway . . . they moved). The first day I walked into their house, I saw one of Mother Teresa's books placed prominently in the center of the living room, and I knew everything would be okay. I quickly learned of Sibyl's love for Mother Teresa and ended up giving her a book that Mother Teresa had signed for me. Dick had been the financial director at Willow Creek for several years. He did their teaching on stewardship and money, and so we had many delightful hours of theological sparring and laughter. The more I met folks just like Dick and Sibyl at Willow, the more I saw how sincere they were. They cared for people and put stagnant nominal Christianity to shame. They took tremendous risks to invite people to experience love, grace, and community. They let homeless folks sleep inside the building on cold nights. They had an auto ministry to give cars to folks who needed them. Mechanics would volunteer their time, caring for single mothers who needed help with their cars. Front-row parking spaces were reserved for single moms. I saw the hospitality of the early Christians in a bizarre new context. It was still weird having a food court in the building, but then I discovered that they wanted people to be able to have dinner together as a family (granted, a big family) rather than to have to go to the mall or to franchises, and that the profits from the food court went to world hunger relief. They even made the courageous step to make sure all their coffee was fairly traded.[2] So I learned not to be so quick to judge. I truly felt that God was alive at Willow Creek, and it would have been very easy to write them off had I not.

But as I went back and forth to the Willow campus, there still seemed such a chasm between the good folks of the suburbs and the suffering masses in Calcutta or Lower Wacker. I ended up meeting with one of the founders of Willow, who shared with raw honesty how good they are at caring for the poor in their midst but how detached and insular that can become. He questioned whether it was enough to care for the poor that they happened to bump into in the suburbs. I could feel his heart, and I could still hear the echo of my teacher, Tony Campolo, back at Eastern College: "Jesus never says to the poor, 'Come find the church,' but he says to those of us in the church, 'Go into the world and find the poor, hungry, homeless, imprisoned,'

---

2. The United States consumes one-fifth of all the world's coffee, making it the largest consumer in the world. But few Americans realize that agricultural workers in the coffee industry often toil in what can be described as "sweatshops in the fields." Many small coffee farmers receive prices for their coffee that are less than the costs of production, forcing them into a cycle of poverty and debt.

Fair Trade is a viable solution to this crisis, assuring consumers that the coffee we drink was purchased under fair conditions. To become Fair Trade certified, an importer must meet stringent international criteria: paying a minimum price per pound of $1.26, providing much needed credit to farmers, and providing technical assistance such as help transitioning to organic farming. Fair Trade for coffee farmers means community development, health, education, and environmental stewardship. Check out *www.globalexchange.org and http://www.puravidacoffee.com*.

Jesus in his disguises." I couldn't help but wonder if we had highlighted only some of the verses in our Bibles, like Rich had said. I saw all the thousands of people who were becoming believers and it brought me great joy. And yet I could not help but wonder with Dorothy Day, "Have we even begun to be Christians?" I read Scriptures like Matthew 25:31–46, where Jesus tells us that ultimately we will be separated into two groups of people, sheep and goats, and the criteria will be how we cared for the poor, hungry, imprisoned, naked masses. I could not help but ask, When all is said and done and the thousands of Christians I was with are gathered before the throne, will we all be with the sheep?

I heard one of the teaching pastors at Willow Creek speak on the rich young ruler text that Rich had talked about in Wheaton's chapel. The teaching pastor said, "Now this doesn't mean you have to go sell your rollerblades and golf clubs," and he went on to "contextualize" the teaching to show that we just need to be careful not to make idols of our things. I wasn't so sure about that. Jesus doesn't tell the man to be a better steward, or to treat his workers fairly, or not to make money an idol. He tells this highly educated and devoutly religious young man that he lacks one thing: giving up everything he owns to give to the poor. Rich Mullins used to say that's because there are a lot of people coming to the Banquet, and God doesn't want all the luggage to deal with.

THE UNCOMFORTABLE CROSS

I decided to look a little closer at some of the rich young ruler text, which appears in Matthew, Mark, and Luke.[3]

---

3. Matt. 19:16–30; Mark 10:17–30; Luke 18:18–30.

After Jesus' teaching that you must enter the kingdom like a little kid, a wealthy man comes up and asks Jesus what he needs to do, and Jesus tells him he lacks one little thing. ("Lacks" is an interesting word to use, since the rich man thought he had everything.) And what might that one thing be? You can almost see him get excited. Then Jesus drops the big one: "Sell everything you have and give it to the poor!" The man's face sinks and he walks away with his riches.

I think it broke Jesus' heart to let the man walk away. The text says that Jesus looks at him and "loves him" as he walks away. But Jesus doesn't run after the man saying, "Hey, it's a journey, just give half," or, "Start with 10 percent." He simply lets the man choose his wealth.

In our culture of "seeker sensitivity" and radical inclusivity, the great temptation is to compromise the cost of discipleship in order to draw a larger crowd. With the most sincere hearts, we do not want to see anyone walk away from Jesus because of the discomfort of his cross, so we clip the claws on the Lion a little, we clean up a bit the bloody Passion we are called to follow. I think this is why the disciples react as they do. They protest in awe, "Who then can be saved?" ("Why must you make it so hard? We need some rich folks here, Jesus, we're trying to build a movement.") And yet Jesus lets him walk away.

Jesus doesn't exclude rich people; he just lets them know their rebirth will cost them everything they have. The story is not so much about whether rich folks are welcome as it is about the nature of the kingdom of God, which has an ethic and economy diametrically opposed to those of the world. Rather than accumulating stuff for oneself, followers of Jesus abandon everything, trusting in God alone for providence.

Willow Creek has helped coin the language of "seeker sensitivity," the idea that congregations need to carve out spaces for spiritual seekers to journey toward God, which is a good thing. And I am the first to say that we need more safe places, especially in the church, where folks can ask tough questions and seek truth together in humility and grace. I long for people to fall in love with God and each other, and so I'm a big fan of being radically inclusive, whether that means not turning off transsexuals or folks who drive SUVs. But I also became aware of how delicate that venture can prove to be. The temptation we face is to compromise the cost of discipleship, and in the process, the Christian identity can get lost. We don't want folks to walk away. We're driven by a sincere longing for others to know God's love and grace and to experience Christian community. And yet we can end up merely cheapening the very thing we want folks to experience. This is the "cheap grace"[4] that spiritual writer and fellow revolutionary Dietrich Bonhoeffer called "the most deadly enemy of the church." And he knew all too well the cost of discipleship; after all, it led to his execution in 1945 for his participation in the Protestant resistance against Hitler.

Funny that one of the first stories of the early church in Acts is the bizarre tale of a couple named Ananias and Sapphira, who withhold a portion of their possessions from the common offering and then lie about it. Peter confronts them in a way that seems quite rude (not very seeker sensitive), and then on top of it God strikes them dead (not very

---

4. The allure of cheap grace is not limited to seeker-sensitive mega-churches. It is attractive to many progressive Christian circles, in which cheap grace has many different faces, and hopefully this recognition will cause us to be a little more graceful with those we might accuse of cheapening it.

tolerant or inclusive). Perhaps we should be thankful that God isn't into that anymore, otherwise we'd have much smaller congregations. We would like to include people like the rich ruler and Ananias and Sapphira, but we would end up with the sort of Christianity that arose after Constantine, in which everyone can be a Christian but no one knows what a Christian is anymore.[5] Yet over and over in the Scriptures, Jesus warns people of the cost of discipleship, that it will cost them everything they have ever hoped for and believed in—their biological families, their possessions, even their very lives. He warns them to count the cost before putting their hand to the plow. And Jesus allows people to walk away.

It was very revealing when I asked someone why there were no crosses at Willow Creek, and he replied, "We try to be seeker sensitive, and the cross is not." On the other side of the coin . . . I remember hearing a story about Clarence Jordan, a pecan farmer and theologian down in Georgia. He was speaking to a wealthy congregation that had an enormous gold cross. He asked how much they had paid for it. They explained that it was a gift from a wealthy donor and told him how much it was. When he heard how much it cost, he said, "Wow! Ya'll got ripped off. Christians used to be able to get a cross for free!" Brilliant. To be fair, I know he was referring to the fact that many folks associate the pain of past church experiences with the traditional icons and

---

5. For many, the fourth-century reign of Constantine, the first Christian emperor, marks a significant point in church history. With the messy marriage of imperial power and the Christian cross, the Jesus movement shifted from persecuted to persecutor. Constantine flung open the door of the church to the rich and powerful, but it was at a great cost. Repentance, rebirth, and conversion were exchanged for cheap grace, and the very identity of what it meant to be a disciple of Jesus was lost. People joined the church in droves, but Christian disciples were hard to come by.

music, hymnals and pews, so Willow Creek got rid of those cultural barriers. And while they proclaim and live the message of the cross in many beautiful ways, there is still something profoundly unsettling about a church that has no crosses. True, the cross is not always seeker sensitive. It is not comfortable. But it is the cornerstone of our faith, and I fear that when we remove the cross, we remove the central symbol of the nonviolence and grace of our Lover. If we remove the cross, we are in danger of promoting a very cheap grace. Perhaps it *should* make us uncomfortable. After all, it wasn't so comfy to get nailed there.

BECOMING LOVERS

I once heard the saying, "God comforts the disturbed and disturbs the comfortable." In my suburban comfort, I increasingly felt disturbed by God. I became very uncomfortable in the comfortable suburbs. The beautiful thing was my discomfort arose not from a cynical judgmentalism but from a longing for something more. I did not want to settle for comfort. I did not want to settle for a life detached from the groaning of the slums or the beauty of playing in open fire hydrants and having block parties in the inner city. I wanted to see the community of Willow Creek shared with the lonely suffering masses that needed it so badly but would never make it to Barrington. The more I read the Bible, the more I felt my comfortable life interrupted.

So there I was my senior year in college, still feeling like I had no clue what I'd be doing after I graduated. After the musical with Rich, I knew I would not be performing on Broadway. (Lip-syncers are not in high demand.) And the more I read the Scriptures, the more uncertain I became about my plans for the future, or even of the wisdom of making plans in the first place, since God seems to be in the business of messing them up. It didn't help that I was majoring in sociology, the study of human inter-action. (How much more vague can you get, and what do you do with that degree?) And folks were asking me what I was going to do when I graduated from college. People always want to define you by what you do. I started saying, "I'm not too concerned with what I am going to do. I am more interested in who I am becoming. I want to be a lover of God and people."

I was convinced that what we do is not nearly as impor-tant as who we are. The question is not whether you will be a doctor or a lawyer but what kind of doctor or lawyer you will be. What would a twenty-year-old Jesus have said if they asked him, "What are you going to do when you grow up?" I don't know, maybe something like, "I'm going to turn the world upside-down. I'm going to hang out with prostitutes and tax collectors until people kill me." Or what would Peter have said? "Well, I was going to be a fisher-man, but then I met this dude, and he messed all that up."

I remembered Mother Teresa saying, "Do not worry about your career. Concern yourself with your vocation, and that is to be lovers of Jesus." So I started calling myself a "vocational lover." Whenever I would fill out forms (there are many of them your senior year of college) that had a blank for profession, I'd just write "Lover." My high school reunion handbook just listed me as a career lover. I'm okay with that.

MY LOVER

And right after asking, "What are you going to do?" the next question always seemed to be, "Have you met a lady?" I would smart off: "Yes, I have met lots of ladies. About every other person I meet is one." And they would stare blankly at me, disappointed. You've got to understand, I'm an only child and an only grandchild, on both sides—no first cousins—and I'm the only one to carry on the family line. So, much was at stake. There were great expectations, and I must admit that's a heavy burden for a young lad to shoulder. Folks wondered if I was gay or going to be a priest. Neither would have been good options in East Tennessee.

But it made sense to be single, and many of the people I had grown to admire had lived beautiful lives of singleness. And their lives would have been different had they been married (not bad, just different). Rich Mullins was one of those. One day over lunch, I asked Rich about why he was still single, and he looked at me funny. He said, "Open up the Bible." I assumed he was going to have me read the verses where Paul teaches that it is best to remain single and serve God (1 Corinthians 7). But we opened up to Matthew 19:10–12, just after Jesus' teaching on marriage and divorce, where the disciples say to Jesus, "If this is the situation between a husband and wife, it is better not to marry." And Jesus tells them that some are eunuchs,[6] and others have renounced marriage for the sake of the kingdom of heaven, and "the one who can accept this should accept it." I had never considered that before.

The church had not taught me that. I distinctly remember one of the children's services from my United Methodist church. The pastor brought all of the kids to the altar, held up a framed portrait of a perfect traditional family with

---

6. If you don't know what a eunuch is, see the diagram in the appendix. Just kidding, check the phone book and call up a pastor and ask her or him; it should make for an interesting conversation.

a mommy, a daddy, and two kids. He talked about how important family is, and he prayed with all the children that they would meet that special person God had for them. I left that children's sermon deeply convicted that I had better keep my eyes open. I thought that if I did not meet that special someone, then either I was not seeking God, or they weren't seeking God, or perhaps they had died an early death, in which case I'd just have to cope. It was as if every good Christian should marry, and yet the more I looked at good Christians throughout history, the less sure I was about that. The singles ministry had always been a place to get hitched. Finding a date may not be the top reason teenagers go to youth group, but it's gotta make the top five. And I'll be the first to admit I thought strategically when we joined hands for prayer.

Somehow I had missed the fact that singleness was a beautiful means of discipleship and that church history is filled with folks who followed God as singles—Jesus, for one; many of the disciples and martyrs, Francis and Clare of Assisi, the desert monastics, to name a few others. What would Mother Teresa's life have looked like if she had been married? Well, certainly different (again, not bad, just different).

At first it was a rational thing; I was attracted to the idea of God as lover. And then I began to experience God as lover, and quickly I became attracted to the Lover. I read Hosea and got the sense that life is a romance with the divine. I started meeting with a Catholic monk, who had taken a vow of poverty and celibacy. He told me, "We can live without sex, but we cannot live without love, and God is love."

I had come to see God as lover and provider and to desire a life of singleness and poverty—not very reassuring to my parents, who had sent me (their only child with no cousins) to college to get a top-notch education, meet a wifer-for-lifer, and become something important.

In May 2011, I got married to the lovely Katie Jo Brotherton in the old St. Ed's cathedral. I'll tell you more about that in the new section at the end.

THE AMERICAN JESUS

One of the last things I did in Chicago was write my senior thesis in sociology. Reading sociology while watching the church from a distance, I had become beguiled by pop Christianity and the market culture, so a thesis on "The American Jesus" seemed well on its way. I knew what Cornell West meant when he said, "We've taken the blood at the foot of the cross and turned it into Kool-Aid" and marketed it all over the world. Or as Rich Mullins sang, "They only want what they can own, but they can't own you." I found the classic sociologists articulating many of my thoughts on the commodification of God. Emile Durkheim, the classic forefather of sociology, wrote extensively about "totemism," the human tendency to form our conception of God in our own image. He said that oftentimes what human beings do, whether aboriginal tribes in the jungle or sophisticated clans (or not-so-sophisticated Klans) in industrial countries, is take the values and traditions that we most admire about ourselves and project them onto a totem. Eventually, we stand in awe of that totem and end up worshiping an incarnation of the things we love about ourselves. As George Bernard Shaw said, "God created us in his image, and we decided to return the favor." We create a Western conception of the Mediterranean peasant revolutionary who lived two thousand years ago, whom we can relate to and who cares about what we care about (eats at McDonald's and votes Republican). Or as the punk-rock band Bad Religion puts it, "We've got the American Jesus; he helped build the president's estate."

During one of the short-term mission trips I had gone on, a group of children were preparing a skit from the gospel story they had read. They came up to me and said, "Shane, we need you to play Jesus, because you are white and from America." Ouch! God forgive us, Buddy Jesus has become a white American resembling Mr. Rogers. What have we done? The bad news was that I had grown very weary of this Jesus. The good news was that there is another Jesus. I decided that one of the best ways to discover the historical Jesus is to deconstruct the American totem, to take him off the totem pole we have nailed him to.

So I did a little survey, probing Christians about their (mis)conceptions of Jesus. It was fun just to see how many people think Jesus loved homosexuals or ate kosher. But I learned a striking thing from the survey. I asked participants who claimed to be "strong followers of Jesus" whether Jesus spent time with the poor. Nearly 80 percent said yes. Later in the survey, I sneaked in another question. I asked this same group of strong followers whether they spent time with the poor, and less than 2 percent said they did. I learned a powerful lesson: We can admire and worship Jesus without doing what he did. We can applaud what he preached and stood for without caring about the same things. We can adore his cross without taking up ours. I had come to see that the great tragedy in the church is not that rich Christians do not care about the poor but that rich Christians do not know the poor.

When the worlds of poverty and wealth collide, the resulting powerful fusion can change the world. But that collision rarely happens. I could feel it happening inside of me. One of my punk-rock friends asked me why so many rich people like talking to me, and I said because I'm nice to them. He asked why I was nice to them. I said because I can see myself in them. That gives me a little patience and grace. I long for the Calcutta slums to meet the Chicago suburbs, for lepers to meet landowners and for each to see God's image in the other. It's no wonder that the footsteps of Jesus lead from the tax collectors to the lepers. I truly believe that when the poor meet the rich, riches will have no meaning. And when the rich meet the poor, we will see poverty come to an end.

CHAPTER 5

ANOTHER WAY OF DOING LIFE

If you ask most people what Christians believe, they can tell you, "Christians believe that Jesus is God's Son and that Jesus rose from the dead." But if you ask the average person how Christians live, they are struck silent. We have not shown the world another way of doing life. Christians pretty much live like everybody else; they just sprinkle a little Jesus in along the way. And doctrine is not very attractive, even if it's true. Few people are interested in a religion that has nothing to say to the world and offers them only life after death, when what people are really wondering is whether there is life before death.

As my teacher Tony Campolo used to ask, "Even if there were no heaven and there were no hell, would you still follow Jesus? Would you follow him for the life, joy, and fulfillment he gives you right now?" I am more and more convinced each day that I would. Don't get me wrong. I'm excited about the afterlife. We are going to party like there's no tomorrow (umm, and there won't be). And yet I am convinced that Jesus came not just to prepare us to die but to teach us how to live. Otherwise, much of Jesus' wisdom would prove quite unnecessary for the afterlife. After all, how hard could it be to love our enemies in heaven? And the kingdom that Jesus speaks so much about is not just something we hope for after we die but is something we are to incarnate now. I've had folks ask why I use this word *incarnate*. It's not a word everybody's familiar with, especially folks outside the church, but don't let that intimidate you. It's an important word that has everything to do with putting our beliefs into practice. One of my neighbors who speaks mostly Spanish broke it down. She said in Spanish *en carne* means "with meat." You order your burrito *con carne* and it comes with meat. Incarnation is about God with meat, in the flesh. In Jesus, the Word becomes flesh. God puts skin on and moves into the neighborhood to live among us. That's what incarnation means. Now we are to join the incarnation. We are to be the "body of Christ"—the hands and feet of Jesus. God is alive—in us now. We are to put flesh on God's love. That's how they will know we are Christians—not by our bumper stickers or T-shirts or tattoos but by our love. Jesus says the kingdom is "within us," "among us," "at hand," and we are to pray that it comes "on earth as it is in heaven." No wonder the early Christian church was known as the Way. It was a way of life that stood in glaring contrast to the world. What gave the early Christians integrity was the fact that they could denounce the empire and in the same breath say, "And we have another way of living. If you are tired of what the empire has to offer, we invite you into the Way." Even the pagan emperors could not ignore the little revolution of love. Emperor Julian confessed, "The godless Galileans feed our poor in addition to their own." And the Way had little cells multiplying all over that ole empire. Of course, everyone was forewarned that in this kingdom everything is backward and upside-down—the last are first and the first are last, the poor are blessed and the mighty are cast from their thrones. And yet people were attracted to it. They were ready for something different from what the empire had to offer.

Coming out of college, my friends and I were pretty unwilling to "conform to the pattern of this world," as the Scriptures say (Rom. 12:2). We knew all too well that there is a broad way that leads to death and that most people would take it, but we also knew that there is a narrow way that leads to life, and we wanted to find it (Matt. 7:13–14). In fact, people had begun to notice the ripples from our little student movement. I was asked to speak at Eastern's graduation ceremony, and to the chagrin of the dean, I told the story of how some friends and I were busted for rappelling out of the windows of one of the dorms. The dean had written us a warning that said, "Can you please enter and exit the buildings through the doors, like everybody else?" So my graduation message, "Crawl through the Window," went something like this: The doors of normalcy and conformity are dead. The time has come to give up on the doors and find a window to climb through. It's a little more dangerous and may get you into some trouble, but it is a heck of a lot more fun. And the people who have changed the world have always been the risk-takers who climb through windows while the rest of the world just walks in and out of doors. It got quite an ovation from everyone but the dean. We were ready for something new. A few years back, I was honored to receive an honorary doctorate from Eastern University, and I spoke at the convocation (which was a special day, by the way, joined by lots of family from Tennessee and my family in Philly). I spoke about "Holy Nonconformity," and for kicks I told the window story again, much to the dean's chagrin. (She is still there.) We have since reconciled and things are all good. (Alright, truth be told, she never was really that mad.) But then again, she doesn't know that we actually rapelled out of another three-story building using a bunk bed as an anchor. She never found out about that. Until now. Oops.

AN EXPERIMENT IN TRUTH

My friends and I had a hunch that there is more to life than what we had been told to pursue. We knew that the world cannot afford the American dream and that the good news is that there is another dream. We looked to the early church and to the Scriptures and to the poor to find it.

When Dorothy Day recalls the beginnings of the Catholic Worker movement, she says very unassumingly, "We were just there talking and it happened. We were just sitting there talking and people moved in. We were just sitting there talking and the lines began to form. . . ." The last line of her autobiography is, "It all happened while we sat there talking, and it is still going on." I know what she meant.[1] So about thirty of us from Eastern College continued dreaming together about another way of doing life. We stayed up night after night laughing and arguing, and eventually we came to a point where we knew we would never agree on exactly what causes homosexuality or whether Adam had a belly button (some things are best left unresolved), so we decided to go ahead and give our vision a shot. Besides, most of us were getting tired of talking and were ready to live. And I was living in a van (yes, down by the river), so we started looking for houses. As we did this little facelift on the original book, I decided to leave in the pop-culture references, even the ones that are a little dated. This reference to down by the river was a wink to the late Chris Farley (rest in peace, my brotha), who did a pretty spectacular skit as a motivational speaker who lived in a "van

---

1. This is from her autobiography, *The Long Loneliness.* Dorothy Day's writings have been a great inspiration to me, and especially in the early days of our community. One of my favorite compilations of her writings is Robert Ellsberg's book *Dorothy Day: Selected Writings* (Orbis, 1992).

down by the river." If you haven't seen it, I highly recommend it: *http://www.hulu.com/watch/4183*. It may change your life.

One of the first things we did was mail out letters to share stories and needs with the large cloud of supporters surrounding us. One of our first newsletters put it this way: "Once, there was a small group of kids who decided to go to a park in the middle of the city, and dance and play, laugh and twirl. As they played in the park, they thought that maybe another child would pass by and see them. Maybe that child would think it looked fun and even decide to join them. Then maybe another one would. Then maybe a businessman would hear them from his skyscraper. Maybe he would look out the window. Maybe he would see them playing and lay down his papers and come down. Maybe they could teach him to dance. Then maybe another businessman would walk by, a nostalgic man, and he would take off his tie and toss aside his briefcase and dance and play. Maybe the whole city would join the dance. Maybe even the world. Maybe . . . Regardless, they decided to enjoy the dance."

Poet Henry David Thoreau went to the woods because he wanted to live deliberately, to breathe deeply, and to suck out the marrow of life. We went to the ghetto. We narrowed our vision to this: love God, love people, and follow Jesus. And we began calling our little experiment the Simple Way. In January 1997, six of us moved into a little row house in Kensington, one of Pennsylvania's poorest neighborhoods, just minutes from old St. Edward's cathedral. It felt like we were reinventing the early church for the first time in two thousand years. (We were quite ignorant.) Thankfully, we had some humble elders who walked alongside us from the beginning. One of my favorite stories on that is of a visit from some Benedictine nuns. They approached one of my friends, Jonathan Wilson-Hartgrove, and told him how excited they were to hear about a new movement of folks living in community and praying together and all. Then they said humbly and unassumingly, "We want you to know that we are available if you want to talk with us. We may have some wisdom to offer you. We have been at it for a while . . . about sixteen hundred years." Thank God for wise nuns.

We had no idea what we were getting into. We had no big vision for programs or community development. We wanted only to be passionate lovers of God and people and to take the gospel way of life seriously.

Some of us dropped out of school; some finished. Some of us were pursuing careers; others left them. People sometimes ask us what we do all day on an "average day" at the Simple Way, and my answer has always been real short—either "Nothing spectacular" or "What is an average day?" It gets a little crazy since our lives are full of surprises and interruptions. Think about how many of the gospel stories happen because of interruptions and surprises. Jesus is "on his way" somewhere and someone pulls on his shirt, invites him to their house, runs out of wine at their wedding. With our obsession with time, routine, predictability, and schedules, we may miss out on things if we don't make space for interruptions. Many great things have been born here over the past twenty years because we allowed for interruptions—from St. Ed's to five minutes ago when I chose to answer the door. Constantly we have to remind ourselves that interruptions may not be just distractions; they may be divine appointments. I'll do my best to describe it to you.

We hang out with kids and help them with homework in our living room, and jump in open fire hydrants on hot summer days. We share food with folks who need it, and eat the beans and rice our neighbor Ms. Sunshine makes for us. Ms. Sunshine is still around, and she still lives up to her name. She's sort of a grandmother to us all. She no longer lives on the block, but we see her a few times a year. And we have new sunshines in our lives—so many aunts and uncles, sisters and brothers around here. My neighbors inspire me every day. Even as I was writing this, I had a little delivery of homemade soup and collard greens, and a kid who brought by a report card. Folks drop in all day to say hi, have a safe place to cry, or get some water or a blanket. So many folks have found their way of contributing to this redemptive work over the years. We have a group of folks called My Brother's Keeper who make all of our sleeping bags out of scrap material. And another group of folks who crochet plastic grocery bags into mats that can protect folks on the street from cold or rain. How cool is that? Sometimes we turn people away, or play Rock, Paper, Scissors to see who answers the door on tired days. We run a community store out of our house. We call it the Gathering, and neighbors can come in and fill a grocery bag with clothes for a dollar or find a couch, a bed, or a refrigerator. Sometimes people donate beautiful things for us to share with our neighbors; other times they donate their used toothbrushes. The specific stuff we do, like the thrift store, has changed over the years. Some of these things, like sharing food each week, we still do—and now it is led by neighbors who have been the recipients of food bags—helping others get food. Other stuff, like the thrift store, have changed. We supported a wonderful store called Circle Thrift around the corner where they do a much better job than we did with much more space than we had. So families here can still get anything they need, but we don't have to do everything ourselves. The only down side of not having it in our house is we no longer have a massive walk-in closet with a ready supply of wild vintage clothing and costumes for every occasion. Oh well.

We reclaim abandoned lots and make gardens amid the concrete wreckage around us. Not to brag, but our gardens won first place in the citywide garden competition. We believe in cooperation, not competition, but we'll take that one, ka-ching. We plant flowers inside old TV screens and computer monitors on our roof. We later discovered you can get cancer from growing food out of a television. So—note to self—be sure you grow only flowers out of TVs and computers. We see our friends waste away from drug addiction, and on a good day, someone is set free. We have seen so many people beat addiction over the years. One of our favorite places is New Jerusalem *(www.newjerusalemnow.org)*, a recovery community where we see the possibility of being set free and where we learn about our own addictions. We are all recovering from something. We see police scare people, and on a good day, we find an officer who will play wiffleball with his billy club. Definitely one of my favorite days was seeing a cop use his billy club for wiffle ball—exactly what billy clubs should be used for. We rehab abandoned houses. We now have a new nonprofit called Simple Homes that works entirely on housing: *http://www.fullercenter.org/philadelphiapennsylvania*. We are able to get houses as cheap as a dollar and fix them up, so families can own their own homes. It usually costs about $30,000 to do one, so let us know if you want to help. Our motto is "Building a better world, one house at a time." And we mourn the two people who died in this property (where I am now writing).[2] Fascinating—I wrote the first edition

---

2. I write one day a week from the inside of an abandoned house we have renovated. I can hear the kids outside finishing a mural on the side of the house that will read, "My people will beat their weapons into plows and study violence no more" (from the prophets Micah and Isaiah). The kids are breaking down toy weapons to make a mosaic plow for the mural.

in an abandoned house where someone had been killed. I wrote the new stuff for the ten-year edition in a different abandoned house where someone also had been killed. We deliberately move into the darkest corners to bring them back to life. The early Christians spoke about resurrection not just as a one-time event two thousand years ago but as something we are invited to participate in. So every time we bring dead space back to life or make ugly things beautiful, it is the work of Jesus. Resurrection happens every day. We try to make ugly things beautiful and to make murals. We now have murals on nearly every open wall "canvas" around here. One neighbor said the murals are like our stained-glass windows. We've got murals thirty feet square. We've got a remix of a piece from infamous graffiti artist Banksy on our house. We have another one we made from melted-down guns (which we invited kids to donate in exchange for juggling balls). Many of them were painted by the kids and dozens of neighbors and our eccentric "traveling artist for the Lord," Dimitre Kadiev, who hitchhikes out here every year. If you know you are going to encounter some ugly stuff, it's important to surround yourself with beauty. And it's fun. Instead of violence, we learn imagination and sharing. We share life with our neighbors and try to take care of each other. We hang out on the streets. We get fined for distributing food. We go to jail for sleeping under the stars. We win in court. We were arrested multiple times for breaking anti-homeless laws like sleeping in the parks and sharing food. Those same laws resurfaced recently and have been passed in more than fifty cities around the country. More on that later. We have friends in prison and on death row. From the beginning, I have given this book away to people living in prison and on death row. These folks, and courageous groups led by victims of violence who stand against execution, inspired me to write the new book *Executing Grace*. We stand in the way of state-sanctioned execution and of the prison industrial complex.

We have always called ourselves a tax-exempt 501c3 *anti*profit organization. Yep, we still consider ourselves an antiprofit organization. (Many nonprofits still make a lot of profit off work with people in poverty.) We wrestle to free ourselves from macrocharity and distant acts of charity that serve to legitimize apathetic lifestyles of good intentions but rob us of the gift of community. We visit rich people and have them visit us. We preach, prophesy, and dream together about how to awaken the church from her violent slumber. Sometimes we speak to change the world; other times we speak to keep the world from changing us. We are about ending poverty, not simply managing it. We give people fish. We teach them to fish. We tear down the walls that have been built up around the fish pond. And we figure out who polluted it. One of the more recent things we have been doing addresses what some have come to call the "food desert," meaning the more dense the urban population is, the less access there is to nutritious food. One person said, "It's easier to get a gun in our neighborhood than a salad." So we grow a lot of food, and our newest project is an urban aquaponics system, fish and plants growing together in an integrated way—fish underground and a greenhouse on top. Pretty sweet. Video here: *https://vimeo.com/42713166.*

We fight terrorism—the terrorism within each of us, the terrorism of corporate greed, of American consumerism, of war. We are not pacifist hippies but passionate lovers who abhor passivity and violence. We spend our lives actively resisting everything that destroys life, whether that be terrorism or the war on terrorism. We try to make the world safe, knowing that the world will never be safe as long as millions live in poverty so the few can live as they wish. We believe in another way of life—the kingdom of God—which stands in opposition to the principalities, powers, and rulers of this dark world (Eph. 6:12).[3]

So that's an average day. As I reread this average-day bit ten years later, it's amazing how much is different, and equally amazing how much has stayed the same. Even as I write this I can hear kids playing in the street and continual knocks at the door. And I look out the window to see new murals that weren't there ten years ago. Katie and I live across the street from the original house we all started in. We collectively own about a dozen properties on the same block, with community gardens and murals sprinkled everywhere. The form of community is different, but the spirit is very much the same. Now it feels like we have grown beyond the intentional community house and are growing an intentional community village.

Since those early days, we've made plenty of mistakes and have never learned the secret to not hurting each other. We have begun asking new questions and have challenged each other to risk more. Some of the faces have changed, and some of us are still here. Now some of us are married, and some have chosen singleness, and some have kids.[4] We recognize each of these choices as a gift. We have created

3. This whole average-day spiel was modified from various newletters and periodicals from our early days, not the least of which appeared in the provocative Canadian *Adbusters* magazine (*www.adbusters.org*).

4. Mike and Michelle Brix, founding partners here at the Simple Way, traveled around the country in an RV for a year visiting different communities to catch glimpses of different styles of living in community with families and kids. They kept a log of their travels, which is on our website (*www.thesimpleway.org*). Mike and Michelle now have two kids and live a few miles away. They are still among my closest friends.

some healthy structures and rhythms for our communal life, such as our Sabbath and our modified common pool of money, to which we each contribute $150 for living expenses each month. Just as you hear "many hands make light work," it's also true that many wallets make cheaper bills. We have managed to live off little by sharing a lot—cars, washers, tools, etc. The particulars are always changing, but the Spirit is the same. We hold our possessions with open hands and try to share needs as they arise. Nowdays, we have several different ways of sharing money for emergencies, medical bills, etc. More on that later. We have described the layers of our common life as an onion, at the core of which are the partners who covenant to love and cherish each other (the hardest and most beautiful thing we do), and each of us shares healthy responsibilities and expectations. We've hashed out our nonnegotiables and tried to understand those we do not agree with. We have created a statement of our faith so folks know we are not a cult. And so folks will know we are not just believers, we have created a statement of our practices, which range from simplicity and nonviolence to beauty and play.[5]

New folks have brought energy and imagination, and we've seen new visions born—from circuses and theater camps to superheroes[6] and a new monasticism. Did I mention I love the circus (minus any animal abuse, of course)? Ten-minute video I did on why the circus is important: *https://www.youtube.com/watch?v=KuNPABbYcG8*. Our programs

---

5. Our statements of faith and practice and details about our community structure can be found on our website (*www.thesimpleway.org*).

6. In the event that you have not heard of the USAntiheroes, they are a group of intergalactic superheroes committed to creating a better universe and can be found at *www.usantiheroes.com*—a project of the Worldwide Justice League.

revolve around the needs and gifts in our community and are always changing. They never define us, for we set out not to start programs but simply to be good neighbors. Neighbors have come and gone over the past decade. So sometimes we are feeding fifty folks out of our kitchen, helping a dozen kids with homework, fixing up abandoned houses, or planting urban gardens. In the summers, we run collaborative arts camps with the Yes! And . . . theater company,[7] mixing suburban and urban kids and carving out space for imagination and dreams. The kids create dance, music, art, characters, a set, and build a show together. We now have so many partner communities[8] and organizations

---

7. Yes! And . . . (www.yesandcamp.org) is a community of artist-educators who are (1) working to reawaken a sense of playfulness, wonder, and imagination through collaborative arts education, (2) equipping children to reclaim their power as invested, active contributors in society, and (3) training educators to transform communities by recognizing, celebrating, and nurturing the diversity, creative nature, and voice within every person.

8. One of our closest sister communities is Camdenhouse, across the river in New Jersey (www.camdenhouse.org). Two of the folks who started Camdenhouse are old friends of mine from the student ministry at Willow Creek, and others studied theology together in the rain forests in Belize. They do beautiful work reclaiming abandoned spaces and creating urban gardens on old waste sites. (Camden is an environmental disaster zone, with brown fields and toxic Superfund sites surrounding their inner-city neighborhood. Camden was rated the worst place to live in the US.) And they do a beautiful job teaching us all new ideas for sustainable living, as well as articulating the theology and philosophy underlying their work. In addition to a pottery studio and a bee hatchery, they have now built a giant urban greenhouse and natural-bread oven on what used to be forsaken spaces, what we call "practicing resurrection." They have different jobs, include married and single folks, and are closely connected with the Catholic parish of Sacred Heart (across the street from their house), and several folks teach in the school. Camdenhouse is still rockin'. Some of the founders have left, and new folks have come. And Sacred Heart continues to be one of the most magical places to worship. It's where Mother Teresa went when she came to town.

that it really feels like a movement much bigger than the Simple Way. And we are just one little cell within the Body, very full of life but only a small part of the whole. Cells are born and cells die, but the Body lives forever. Sometimes if feels like this little place has served as an incubator for dreams, helping them hatch and grow wings. At one point we had seventeen ministries under the Simple Way. And our goal has been not to have an empire or a franchise but to support a movement. We are honored to have been a little hatchery for other spectacular nonprofits and communities to be born or to develop, incredible work like Centurion's Guild (support network for veterans), New Sanctuary Movement (movement for immigrant justice and immigration reform), Timoteo (male-mentoring sports league), and so many others . . . one big, beautiful family.

SHOUTING THE GOSPEL WITH OUR LIVES

Remembering the invitation that Mother Teresa always gave to curious seekers, we have from the beginning invited people to "Come and see." And people have, hundreds. As an evangelical, the only way I know to invite people into Christian faith is to come and see. We've created some good "come and see" on-ramps for visiting. We have open houses here at the Simple Way. We also have Schools for Conversion (weekend gatherings) that happen all over the place: http://www.schoolforconversion.org/. And for folks on the younger side (18–30), Mission Year is the best place to start—a one-year community experience, sort of the closest thing we have to an internship: www.missionyear .org. After all, I'm not just trying to get someone to sign a doctrinal statement, but to come to know love, grace, and peace in the incarnation of Jesus, and now in the incarnation of the body, Christ's church. So if someone asked me to introduce them to Jesus, I would say, "Come and see. Let me show you Jesus with skin on." Sometimes we have evangelicals (usually from the suburbs) who pretentiously ask how we "evangelize people." I usually tell them that we bring folks like them here to learn the kingdom of God from the poor, and then send them out to tell the rich and powerful there is another way of life being born in the margins. For Jesus did not seek out the rich and powerful in order to trickle down his kingdom. Rather, he joined those at the bottom, the outcasts and undesirables, and everyone was attracted to his love for people on the margins. (We know that we all are poor and lonely anyway, don't we?) Then he invited everyone into a journey of downward mobility to become the least. As the old Franciscan slogan goes, "Preach the gospel always. And when necessary, use words." Or as our seventy-year-old revolutionary Catholic nun, Sister Margaret, puts it, "We are trying to shout the gospel with our lives." Many spiritual seekers have not been able to hear the words of Christians because the lives of Christians have been making so much horrible noise. It can be hard to hear the gentle whisper of the Spirit amid the noise of Christendom.

A VOICE FOR THE VOICELESS? NOT US

Not too long ago, those of us at the Simple Way were about to speak before a congregation. The person doing the introduction said, "These folks are a voice for the voiceless." And something inside me hurt. I gently corrected them. Everyone has a voice. I know many amazing people have used the old "voice for the voiceless" line (Oscar Romero, Mother Teresa, even the book of Proverbs). But it just felt strange. Perhaps we are too quick to assume folks cannot speak for themselves.

We are not a voice for the voiceless. The truth is that there is a lot of noise out there drowning out quiet voices, and many people have stopped listening to the cries of their neighbors. Lots of folks have put their hands over their ears to drown out the suffering. Institutions have distanced themselves from the disturbing cries. When Paul writes in Romans 8 that the entire creation is groaning for its liberation, he goes on to say that "we ourselves, who have the firstfruits of the Spirit, groan inwardly" (v. 23). This is the chorus of the generations of seemingly voiceless people that we have joined. And God has a special ear for their groaning, regardless of who else is listening. The best word I have come up with is *amplify*. Our job is to amplify the voices that are not being heard. I've especially seen this in the current racial injustice movement in America, arising from events like Michael Brown's death in Ferguson. When folks don't feel heard, they shout louder. And if we still don't listen, we make the world a very fragile place. Dr. King said, "Riot is the language of the unheard." What often happens is that oppressed people try to voice their pain and anger, and people cover their ears. Tears are met with tear gas. But listening is a holy act. And so is amplifying those who have been muted. When we amplify the voices of the oppressed, we make the world safer and better. So let's be people who amplify the voices of the unheard.

It is a beautiful thing when folks in poverty are no longer just a missions project but become genuine friends and family with whom we laugh, cry, dream, and struggle. One of the verses I have grown to love is the one where Jesus is preparing to leave the disciples and says, "I no longer call you servants. . . . Instead, I have called you friends" (John 15:15). Servanthood is a fine place to begin, but gradually we move toward mutual love, genuine relationships. Someday, perhaps we can even say those words that Ruth said to Naomi after years of partnership: "Where you go I will go, and where you stay I will stay. Your people will be my people and your God my God. Where you die I will die, and there I will be buried" (Ruth 1:16–17).

And that's when things get messy. When people begin moving beyond charity and toward justice and solidarity with the poor and oppressed, as Jesus did, they get in trouble. Once we are actually friends with folks in struggle, we start to ask why people are poor, which is never as popular as giving to charity. One of my friends has a shirt marked with the words of late Catholic bishop Dom Helder Camara: "When I fed the hungry, they called me a saint. When I asked why people are hungry, they called me a communist." Charity wins awards and applause, but joining the poor gets you killed. People do not get crucified for charity. People are crucified for living out a love that disrupts the social order, that calls forth a new world. People are not crucified for helping poor people. People are crucified for joining them.

ORDINARY RADICALS

Sometimes people call those of us in our community radical. As I said before, if by radical we mean "root," I think it is precisely the right word for what we are trying to do—get down to the roots of what it means to be Christian disciples. Most of the time, though, I think that if what we are doing seems radical, then that says more about the apathy of Western Christianity than about the true nature of our discipleship. And this is why "radical" has to be coupled with "ordinary." Our way of life was typical in the days of the early Jesus movement. We are like the Marys and

Marthas, and Peter's family—houses of hospitality, which was the standard call of the early Christians, who abandoned their personal possessions to a new family. This is to say nothing of the countless others who gave up everything and left their homes with no money or food or even sandals to follow Jesus. Christendom seems very unprepared for people who take the gospel that seriously.

One of the things that has fascinated me about the days of the early church is how those who abandoned homes and possessions to follow Jesus lived in such union with those who opened their homes to them and the poor. Gerd Theissen calls the two groups the "wandering charismatics" and the "local sympathizers."[9] The wanderers were traveling apostles and relied on the support of the sympathizers. Both shaped the early church. They did not look down on each other. The sympathizers did not write the wanderers off as radicals or freaks, and the wanderers did not judge the sympathizers as sellouts. They loved and supported one another. From our earliest days, we have seen the importance of that partnership as we have commissioned wanderers and nomads who travel like the apostles did, or like the later circuit riders of the church (who traveled on horseback, which is a little harder nowadays). These new pilgrims help to cross-pollinate our communities and lives. We have had folks travel the country by bike, by car, on foot, using biodiesel, and by RV, seeking to intersect our lives in the Christian underground. I finished this chapter traveling on a bus that has a converted diesel engine that runs on used vegetable oil. (We'd just hit up restaurants for their old oil, and busted out a little circus [*www*

---

9. Gerd Theissen, *Sociology of Early Palestinian Christianity* (Philadelphia: Fortress, 1978).

.runawaycircus.org] to earn our dinner).[10] Some folks, like our sister community, Psalters, live permanently nomadic lives.[11] Many of my Psalters friends continue to make incredible music and prophetic art, and many of them are in the Philadelphia area. We went on tour together when I released the book *Jesus for President* in 2008, hitting up thirty or so cities in a national tour traveling in a bus that ran on veggie oil. You can hear Psalters on the audio (and video) version of *Jesus for President* and in the film *Ordinary Radicals.* Psalters are also featured in *Jesus, Bombs, and Ice Cream.* Several of the former Psalters folks are now a part of a nomadic circus called Carnival de Resistance. And you can still find a lot of the Psalters classics online (and free, of course). Oh, and my Psalters friends played music for my wedding. Last month, with the full support of Sacred Heart parish in Camden, we just commissioned another brother to travel across the US by bike, spreading the news of what's happening in Camden and Philly and bringing back the stories of the people he meets. He went out with nothing but faith and his bike, dependent on God's providence and the church's hospitality. I will add this—the nomadic life is very difficult to sustain in a healthy way. It takes discipline to create healthy rhythms on the road and healthy relations in tight quarters. Just as I appreciate the nomadic life, I also

---

10. The veggie bus ran almost entirely on used oil we picked up at restaurants. Friends across the country are pioneering this movement, converting vehicles and even holding grease festivals to educate folks on renewable energy. Joshua Tickel's book is a good resource: *From the Fryer to the Fuel Tank: The Complete Guide to Using Vegetable Oil as an Alternative Fuel.* A growing number of people of faith and conscience are imagining new ways of living that will create a safer, more sustainable world. (It will be a long time before we have wars over used vegetable oil . . .) This is just one example.

11. *www.psalters.org.*

have come to appreciate stability. We often talk about a "theology of place"—the importance of loving our city and our neighborhood and making it home. It is important that the gospel happened in real places, in homes and villages— like Bethany, Capernaum, and Galilee. Sometimes we have to stay in a place for a while and tend the garden before we see a harvest of fruit. One of the ancient monastic vows is stability, and my pal Jonathan Wilson-Hartgrove has written a great book on that called *The Wisdom of Stability*. This is one of the challenges of youth—everyone wants to do everything . . . for six months, and then move on. But it takes time to grow trust in relationships. Wounds take time to heal. While it can be radical to live a nomadic life, it can also be radical to stay in one place more than five years.

DESPECTACULARIZING THINGS

Again, it's easy to see these things as spectacular, but I really believe that's only because we live in a world that has lost its imagination. These things were normal in the early church. It's just what conversion looked like. We must be careful not to allow ourselves to be written off as radicals when church history and the contemporary Christian landscape are filled with ordinary radicals. But today people crave the spectacular. People are drawn to lights and celebrities, to arenas and megachurches. In the desert, Jesus was tempted by the spectacular—to throw himself from the temple so that people might believe—to shock and awe people, if you will. Today the church is tempted by the spectacular, to do big, miraculous things so people might believe, but Jesus has called us to littleness and compares our revolution to the little mustard seed, to yeast making its way through dough, slowly infecting this dark world with love. Many of us who find ourselves living differently from the dominant culture end up needing to "despectacularize" things a little so that the simple way is made as accessible as possible to other ordinary radicals.

Sometimes people call folks here at the Simple Way saints. Usually they either want to applaud our lives and live vicariously through us, or they want to write us off as superhuman and create a safe distance. One of my favorite quotes, written on my wall here in bold black marker, is from Dorothy Day: "Don't call us saints; we don't want to be dismissed that easily."

The truth is that when people look at us like we are sacrificial servants, I have to laugh. We've just fallen in love with God and our neighbors, and that is transforming our lives. Besides, I think if most other folks knew Adrienne and the kids, a beautiful family that has been living with us after coming out of the shelter system, they'd do the same things we are doing. It just makes sense not to have families on the street or in abandoned houses, especially when we have a spare bedroom. Honestly, the way of life we have chosen often seems more natural than the alternative. The alternative—moving out and living in the suburbs—seems terribly sacrificial (or painfully empty). As I reread this bit on the suburbs, it sounded pretty harsh. I've visited some splendid suburban experiments in community and responsible living, and I see tons of suburban folks doing wonderful things with their lives. I know this can sound a bit like "I have suburban friends," but it's important to note that many studies show that people experience a deep loneliness in the suburbs, and many of the same problems of addiction and domestic violence. The difference from my neighborhood is that in the suburbs, there's more room to hide. I also find it important to name the fact that historically, much of suburban sprawl resulted from people moving out of neighborhoods where there was high crime, poverty, or people who "don't look like us." And that gravity is very different from the gravity of the gospel, which calls us into the pain rather than away from it. What must it be like not to have block parties or not to actually know the people around us? There are times when I have been very frustrated with wealthy folks for hoarding their stuff. But now I know enough rich folks to know the loneliness that is all too familiar to many of them. I read a study comparing the health of a society with its economics, and one of the things it revealed is that wealthy countries like ours have the highest rates of depression, suicide, and loneliness. We are the richest and most miserable people in the world. I feel sorry that so many of us have settled for a lonely world of independence and riches when we could all experience the fullness of life in community and interdependence. Why would I want a fancy car when I can ride a bike, or a TV when I can play outside with sidewalk chalk? Okay, sometimes I still want the hot tub on the roof, but the rest I can live without. And I mean *live* without. Patting Mother Teresa on the back, someone said to her, "I wouldn't do what you do for a million dollars." She said with a grin, "Me neither." I almost feel selfish sometimes, for the gift of community. The beautiful thing is that there is enough to go around.

Once we get past the rebellious or reactive countercultural paradigm and muster up the courage to try living in new ways, most of us find that community is very natural and makes a lot of sense, and that it is not as foreign to most of the world's population as it is to us. Community is what we are created for. We are made in the image of a God who is community, a plurality of oneness. When the first human was made, things were not good until there were two, helping one another. The biblical story is the story of community, from beginning to end. Jesus lived and modeled community with his little band of disciples. He always sent them out in pairs, and the early church is the story of a people who were together and were of one heart and mind, sharing all in common. The story ends with a vision of the new community in the book of Revelation, where the city of God is dressed beautifully for her lover, this community called the New Jerusalem, where heaven visits earth and people are fully reconciled to God and each other, the lion lays down with the lamb, mourning turns to dancing, and the garden takes over the concrete world!

But that doesn't mean community is easy. For everything in this world tries to pull us away from community, pushes us to choose ourselves over others, to choose independence over interdependence, to choose great things over small things, to choose going fast alone over going far together. The simple way is not the easy way. No one ever promised us that community or Christian discipleship would be easy. There's a commonly mistranslated verse where Jesus tells the disciples, "Come to me, all you who are weary and burdened, and I will give you rest. Take my yoke upon you and learn from me. . . . For my yoke is good and my burden is light." People take that to mean that if we come to Jesus, everything will be easy. (The word *good* is often mistranslated as "easy.") Ha, that's funny. My life was pretty easy before I met Jesus. In one sense, the load is lighter because we carry the burdens of the world together. But he is still telling us to pick up a yoke. Yoke had a lot of different meanings. It was the tool used for harnessing animals for farming. It was the word used for taking on a rabbi's teaching (as Jesus seems to use it here). Yoke was also the word used for the brutal weight of slavery and oppression that the prophets call us to break (Isaiah 58, among other passages). One of the things I think Jesus is doing is setting us free from the heavy yoke of an oppressive way of life. I know plenty of people, both rich and poor, who are suffocating from the weight of the American dream, who find themselves heavily burdened by the lifeless toil and consumption we put upon ourselves. This is the yoke we are being set free from. The new yoke is still not easy (it's a cross, for heaven's sake), but we carry it together, and it is good and leads us to rest, especially for the weariest traveler. I recently heard someone say that even Jesus didn't carry his cross alone. A friend named Simon helped him carry his cross. Who are we to try to bear our cross alone?

In fact, if our lives are easy, we must be doing something wrong. Momma T also used to say, "Following Jesus is simple, but not easy. Love until it hurts, and then love more." My friend Brooke, with whom I went to India and later started the Simple Way, used to have the words "Simple but not easy" painted on her wall. And at one point, when things were particularly difficult, I graffitied over them, changing it to "Simple and hard as crud." Dorothy Day of the Catholic worker movement understood this well. She said, "Love is a harsh and dreadful thing to ask of us, but it is the only answer."[12] This love is not sentimental but heart-wrenching, the most difficult and the most beautiful thing in the world.

A DIFFERENT KIND OF TAX COLLECTOR

We've been very careful at the Simple Way never to claim that we have the corner on the market for "radical

---

12. Robert Ellsberg, ed., *Dorothy Day: Selected Writings* (Maryknoll, NY: Orbis, 1992), 339.

Christianity." Nor have we even tried to spread a brand
or model. And the incredible thing is that the stories of
ordinary radicals are all over the place, stories of everyday
people doing small things with great love, with their lives,
gifts, and careers. I heard about a group of massage thera-
pists who spend their days washing and massaging the
tired feet of homeless folks. Some manicurists told me
they go to old folks homes and ask which old ladies have
no visitors or family, and then they sit with them, laugh,
tell stories, and do their nails. On some of our marches for
peace and justice, chiropractors join us in the evenings to
take care of people's tired bodies so that we will be ready
for another day of marching. Around the corner from us,
our close friends at the House of Grace Catholic Worker
run a free clinic where nurses, doctors, chiropractors, and
dentists care for folks who do not have health care. The
House of Grace clinic is still going strong. And now we have
another great clinic around the corner called Esperanza,
providing quality health care on a sliding scale based on
income. There's a whole movement of Christian health clinics
around the country, sort of a medical underground: *https://
www.cchf.org/*. Hallelujah for missional medicine! There are
lawyers who bail us out of jail, advocate for human rights,
and go with us before zoning boards that have no categories
for understanding how we live.[13] We had a plumber show
up and offer to live with us for a month and just fix all the

---

13. We have gone before courts and zoning boards for violating all sorts
of codes. We have been told we cannot invite people into our home to
eat, because the Simple Way does not have a food distribution license.
We have been told that we are breaking a "brothel code," which makes
it illegal for unrelated people to live together. Funny, one of my favorite
moments was when we went before zoning and the inspector's name
was Jesus (not an uncommon Latino name), and our Jewish lawyer said,
"Once again, Jesus is causing us all kinds of trouble." Lovely.

plumbing on abandoned houses and in neighbors' homes. We ended up needing more than a month! Thank God for missional plumbers! It makes you think we need to think of missions not just as a bunch of people who go to a foreign land but folks who ask how they can use their gifts right here at home. Perhaps we should begin commissioning school teachers, electricians, postal workers, and sanitation folks as missionaries—pray over them, anoint them with oil, and send 'em out! The examples are as numerous as the number of vocations. After writing this book, I met some robotics engineers who told me they were considering what it means to be kingdom-minded in their work. They heard about the landmines scattered all over Afghanistan and the little children who are paid to disarm them (and who often get injured doing this work). So this group of robotics engineers told me, with faces gleaming with excitement, that they were designing robots that can dismantle landmines. Then little kids won't get their hands blown off and families can walk across fields without fear. That's what I'm talkin' about. But the calling is the same: to love God and our neighbors with our whole lives, careers, and gifts.

In the early days of our community, it was as if we had a "radical disciple" mold, and everyone had to fit into it. But as we have matured (Matured? Maybe aged in wisdom . . .), we have seen the beauty of diverse vocations and the multidimensionality of Christian discipleship. One of the best things communities like ours do is carve out a space for people to discern and redefine their vocations. Vocation comes from the same root as *voice*, denoting the hearing of a divine call. Beyond knowing that God has a purpose for our lives, most of us (especially non-Catholics) spend little energy seeking our vocation, especially in light of how the needs and sufferings of our neighbors might inform how we use our gifts for divine purposes. There are plenty of people who are miserable in their jobs, for they have not listened to God's call. And I would add there are many Christians who are not fulfilled in their spiritual lives because they have no sense of their gifts or purpose, and they just run to the mission field to save souls rather than transform lives and communities using their gifts and those of the people they live among. Both lead to emptiness and burnout. Frederick Buechner said, "The place God calls you to is the place where your deep gladness and the world's deep hunger meet." I've come to see that this is the difference between a career that is just about paying the bills, and a vocation that is about seeking first the kingdom of God. A vocation is when we take our passion and connect it to the world's pain. Then we do what we are gifted at, and it alleviates the suffering of others. Everybody wins. Don't settle for a job; find your vocation.

The concept of multidimensional discipleship is essential as we consider how to retain a radical discipleship that is multiethnic, intergenerational, and includes singles and families. I always find it funny when folks ask if you can do community with a spouse and kids. Most communities I've seen have families and kids (minus the monastic orders with strict celibacy rules, of course). Several communities even celebrate that the kids outnumber the adults, more little people than big ones. I'm currently trying to help some married folks write the book *Revolution . . . with Kids*. Meanwhile, the Christian Community Development Association is a great resource for folks trying to live radically with a family (*www.ccda.org*). Otherwise we will just end up surrounded by people who look like us, think like us, and respond to the gospel in exactly the same way we do. And that would rob us of the gift of community and of what it means to be a body with many different parts. What an extraordinary thing it must have been to sit around a table with that eclectic mix of Zealot revolutionaries, Roman tax collectors, peasants, Samaritans, prostitutes, and fishermen, all conspiring to find a radical new way of life.

In the early church, whenever converts sought baptism, their entire careers were reimagined. Just as baptism was a symbol of people's dying to their old lives and rising to new ones, so there was the very real sense that the old ways of living were gone and something new was here. For some, like the tax collector Zacchaeus, whom Jesus calls down from the sycamore tree where he had climbed up to see Jesus from a safe distance, the face-to-face encounter meant that his career was radically redefined—socially, economically, politically. He does not sell everything, but he sells half of everything, and then pays people back four times what he owed them, enacting the ancient Levitical teaching of Jubilee where debts are forgiven and possessions are redistributed. (We need some Jubilee tax collectors!) Zacchaeus was still a tax collector (though he may have gone broke eventually), but now he was a different kind of tax collector. For others, the encounter with Jesus meant that they needed to leave their jobs, like another tax collector named Levi (Matthew). He meets Jesus and leaves it all behind, inviting his tax collector friends to join the movement.

Some may leave their jobs. Others will redefine them. We are all called to nonconformity. As Romans 12 says, "Do not conform to the pattern of this world." But living a creative life that doesn't conform to the status quo doesn't mean we'll all do the same thing. Nonconformity doesn't mean uniformity. When we truly encounter Jesus and the poor, we may still be a tax collector, but we will be a different kind of tax collector. We may still be a doctor, but we will be a different kind of doctor. I've found it helpful to think about who we are more than what we do. The real question is not what are you going to do when you grow up but who are you becoming. More important than whether you are going to be a doctor or a lawyer is *what kind* of doctor or lawyer you are going to be. Hippolytus (ca. AD 218) said it like this in the third century: "The professions and trades of those who are going to be accepted into the community must be examined. The nature and type of each must be established . . . brothel, sculptors of idols, charioteer, athlete, gladiator . . . give it up or be rejected. A military constable must be forbidden to kill, neither may he swear; if he is not willing to follow these instructions, he must be rejected. A proconsul or magistrate who wears the purple and governs by the sword shall give it up or be rejected. Anyone taking or already baptized who wants to become a soldier shall be sent away, for he has despised God."[14] Many of us feel an inner collision between the old life and the new one. One executive told me he sold his entire company and didn't even keep any of the money, because it had only made him miserable. Another executive told me he was trying to implement a sliding-scale wage (based on family size) that valued everyone equally, so the CEO was not making more money than the janitor or receptionist.[15] One friend in

---

14. Hippolytus, "Church Order in the Apostolic Tradition," in *The Early Christians in Their Own Words*, ed. Eberhard Arnold (Farmington, PA: Plough, 1997), 16.

15. The United Nations reported in 1992 that income disparities between the world's richest and poorest have doubled since 1960. Today, the wealthiest 20 percent of the world's population receives almost 83 percent of the world's income, while the poorest 20 percent receives less than 2 percent! In 1965, the average US worker made $7.52 per hour, while the person running the company made $330.38 per hour; today, the average worker makes $7.39 per hour, the average CEO $1,566.68 per hour—212

the military left because of his reborn identity and is now painting murals and preaching nonviolence with us here in Philly. Logan Mehl-Laituri went on to start Centurion's Guild, a support group for current and former service members (*http://centurionsguild.org/*). He and I traveled back to Iraq together—without weapons. And he has now written several books about peacemaking, including *Reborn on the Fourth of July* and *For God and Country (In That Order)*.

It's sort of like if you work for a porn shop and have a conversion experience. Most of us would probably agree it's a good idea to rethink your career track. But why wouldn't we do that for other born-again disciples? What if someone works for Lockheed Martin (the world's largest weapons contractor) or a notorious human rights abuser like Coca-Cola or Nestle or Disney or Gap?[16] We have had many people—professionals,

---

times more! (Ched Myers, "God Speed the Year of Jubilee!" *Sojourners*, May–June 1998). Even more recently, *Forbes* magazine showed that eighty-six people own the same amount of wealth as half the world (3.5 billion people). There are CEOs now making more than $5,000 an hour. The average worker has to work a month to make what the average CEO makes in an hour. On a happier note, here's a great interview with the CEO of Japan Airlines, who laughs at the thought of making more than his coworkers and thinks it totally normal to eat in the cafeteria with them: *http://www.redletterchristians.org/is-there-such-thing-as-a-good-ceo-video/*.

16. Coca-Cola has been accused of arming its factories in Columbia with paramilitary thugs. Nestle has been accused of mass-marketing an infant formula as a breast-milk substitute to third-world women. Disney has been accused of maintaining sweatshops in Haiti and Bangladesh, and Gap has been accused of having similar factories in Cambodia and China. These are a few of the companies who continually appear as human rights violators documented by corporate watch groups across the globe. Some, like Gap, have made significant improvements, but usually only after public outcry brought attention to their abuses and they lost lawsuits, like the Saipan case in 2004. A few of my favorite groups working for corporate accountability and who suggest healthy alternatives are: *Globalexchange.org, Sweatshopwatch.org, Corpwatch.org, Hrw.org* (Human Rights Watch), *Iccr.org* (Interfaith Center on Corporate

parents, economists, nurses, military officers—come through our community and begin asking fresh questions about their vocation, what the voice of the Spirit is calling them to do with their lives. As I wrote my death penalty book, *Executing Grace*, I interviewed several executioners and prison workers who felt this same collision and left their jobs. And in North Carolina, doctors have refused to take part in executions, which has meant a moratorium on the death penalty. And the medical community has backed them, insisting it is a violation of their oath "to do no harm." All of us are called to be faithful to Christ first, even if it could cost us our jobs.

Not everyone responds exactly the same way. Some will give up their houses and leave their fields. Others will offer their possessions to the community and form hospitality houses like Mary and Martha, and Peter's family. Others will hold back from the common pool and lie to God, and they will be struck dead like Ananias and Sapphira. (Just kidding, hopefully . . .) There are the Matthews who encounter Jesus and sell everything. But then there are also the Zacchaeuses who meet Jesus and redefine their careers. So not everyone responds in the same way, but we must respond. We must seek our vocation listening to the voice of God and the voices of our suffering neighbors. Both Zacchaeus and Matthew responded to the call of Jesus in radical ways that did not conform to the pattern of the world. And then there is Bryan Stevenson, who graduated from Eastern, where I went to college, then went to Harvard and graduated with honors. As an African-American from Harvard, he could have worked anywhere and named his

---

Responsibility). I heard there is now a phone app that helps you shop responsibly, and rates companies based on different indicators of justice, like wages, abuse, child labor, and environmental harm. If it doesn't exist, maybe you can invent it.

salary. But he went to Alabama to defend folks on death row and folks wrongfully convicted who couldn't afford a good lawyer. When *Time* magazine went to do a feature story on him, he was living in a little apartment with next to nothing to show for his success. They asked him, "Why would you be this kind of lawyer?" His response: "Why would I not be this kind of lawyer?" Brilliant. He now heads up Equal Justice Initiative (*www.eji.org*), doing some of the most liberating work in the country. Desmond Tutu recently called him "America's young Mandela." And here's Bryan's epic Ted Talk: *http://www.ted.com/speakers/bryan_stevenson*.

Here in Philly, I have a friend named Atom. He's a scientist who uses big words and usually needs a translator, and he started working on his PhD when he was twenty-one. Then he started hanging out with folks here at the Simple Way and reading the Bible. His initial reaction was to leave everything, be a bike messenger, and pray all night. (His mom recently introduced me as one of the people who messed up her son.) But the more he sought God and his gifts, the more he felt his own vocation emerging. As he studied science in the context of his global neighborhood, he saw that lack of access to clean water was the biggest killer of children in our world—over twenty thousand die each day from curable water-borne diseases. Economists predict that within the next decade, the leading cause of violence and war will be not oil but water. So Atom has dedicated much of his life to studying and working with indigenous communities to solve this solvable crisis, and all hubbed out of a simple life on our block in inner-city Philly.[17] I recently learned about another water project that adds a fascinating new

---

17. The water team is a collaboration of Circle of Hope (*www.circleofhope.net/venture*) and the Mennonite Central Committee.

dimension. Some business folks found that in industrialized countries, we spend enough money buying bottled water that if we reallocated that money, it would be enough to provide water for the entire world. So they started a bottled water business whose profits go to dig wells with indigenous labor. And on every bottle of water, it says, "When I was thirsty, you gave me something to drink." Later they met some engineers who designed playground equipment that doubles as water pumps. So as kids play on the seesaw and merry-go-round, they pump water for the village. That's what we mean by taking your passions and connecting them to the world's pain.

A while later, Atom's sister Rachel joined us at the Simple Way. She had gone to one of the leading culinary schools in the country and worked at a fancy restaurant downtown. (She once sneaked Atom and me into a $100 a plate dinner where we fit right in . . . stuffing our pockets full of foods I cannot pronounce the name of.) As she read the Scriptures and hung out with friends in poverty, her gifts began to come to life. She made cookies with kids on the block and made fancy dinners with folks on the street. (It's not every day our homeless friends get lobster.) Both Atom and Rachel are ordinary radicals continuing to discern their vocations and spend their lives for others.

MISSIONARIES TO THE CHURCH

We have never really considered ourselves missionaries to the poor. Traditional thinking about mission and missionary tends to assume that we are taking God to a godless people or a godless place. But God is everywhere, always ahead of us. So missions is more about recognizing where God is at work and joining in. Places cannot be God forsaken, but they can be church forsaken. Our job is to unleash hope, unlock dreams, and help folks have ears to hear and eyes to see God where they are. The movement away from thinking about missions as separate from the rest of our lives is a good one—our whole lives should be missional. Let's refuse to confine missions to a committee or an event or a trip in the summer and integrate that thinking into everything we do. And let's refuse to look at missionaries as God's elite special ops team. We're all missionaries on God's mission. That's what the Bible calls the "priesthood of all believers." One of my friends says, "Let's ordain everyone, call everyone a minister, invite the whole church to be on staff." Every moment holds eternal possibility and is pregnant with potential. Jesus was not simply a missionary to the poor. He *was* poor—born a baby refugee from the badlands of Nazareth, wandered the world a homeless rabbi, died the rotten death of insurrectionists and bandits on the cross, executed by an oppressive empire, buried in a borrowed tomb. Jesus was crucified not for helping poor people but for joining them. That is the Jesus we follow.

A pastor who has been a longtime supporter and friend of the Simple Way (and father to one of the founders!) said, "I used to think you all were missionaries bringing the gospel to your neighborhood, but now I see that it is in your neighborhood that you have learned the gospel, and that you are actually missionaries to the church."

Many of us are disenchanted Catholics, and others are recovering evangelicals. When people used to ask me if we were Protestant or Catholic, I was so discouraged with both that I would just answer, "No. We are just followers of Jesus." Now, as I thirst for God's church to be alive and one, when people ask me if I am Protestant or Catholic, I just answer, "Yes." Chris Haw, whom I first met at Willow Creek and who later moved to Camden and started the Camden community and with whom I wrote *Jesus for President*, has penned a great book about his journey to becoming Catholic. It's titled *From Willow Creek to Sacred Heart*. He is now one of the sharpest, freshest theologians in the country. And when people ask me if we are evangelicals, I usually define it as I did in the introduction to this book and say, "Absolutely, we want to spread the kingdom of God like crazy."

We have never considered ourselves a "church plant." There are congregations on nearly every corner. I'm not sure we need more churches. What we really need is *a church*. I say one church is better than fifty. I have tried to remove the plural form *churches* from my vocabulary, training myself to think of the church as Christ did, and as the early Christians did. The metaphors for her are always singular—a body, a bride. I heard one gospel preacher say it like this, as he really wound up and broke a sweat: "We've got to unite ourselves as one body. Because Jesus is coming back, and he's coming back for a bride, not a harem." So we worship in our neighborhood. A few of us attend the Lutheran congregation, some Iglesia del Barrio (Church of the Neighborhood, which meets in an old, resurrected Methodist building). Many of us are covenanted at a Brethren in Christ cell church called Circle of Hope,[18] where we have renovated a 7,500 square foot abandoned warehouse and gather for worship on Sunday evenings (which we just call PMs, for "public meetings," just one small glimpse of what church really is). Others are Catholic and go to Mass, and still others are not Catholic and go to Mass. We have done our homework club out of the Presbyterian building and have run an Episcopal after-school program. The Lutheran congregation put in showers so we can host larger overnight groups there. Some of us work at the Free Clinic run by the Catholic Workers, and

---

18. *www.circleofhope.net.*

others with a partner community committed to addiction recovery called New Jerusalem.[19] And on and on.

It feels like a body, a big family. Every few months, we gather for Nights of Celebration, or Love Feasts, when we eat some good grub, share stories and songs, and celebrate what God is doing among us. And once a year, we host our Family Reunion, which is an incredible gathering of activist theologians, new monastics, students, old friends, wanderers, revolutionaries, and regular ole Christians (if there is such a thing). It has been a little while since we've had a family reunion. Note to self: it might be time for one. We still have regional and national gatherings from time to time, but some of these grew beyond our capacity to host, so most of the meet-ups these days happen alongside other gatherings, like the Christian Community Development Association and such. But out of these gatherings, things like our project Common Prayer have been born[20]—and lots of new communities and even a marriage or two we helped make happen (with the Lord's help, of course). It is a beautiful organic web of cells within the body. We continually lift one another in prayer, as Jesus prayed, asking that we would be one—one with the faithful disciples of the established church, one with faithful disciples of the underground church, one with the ancient church of our past, one church. What the world really needs is not more churches but a Church.

---

19. *www.libertynet.org/njl*.

20. *Common Prayer* is a collaborative project to weave together ancient prayers and liturgy, connecting those to the world we live in today. There are more than fifty songs, prayers for each day of the year, and prayers for special occasions like dedicating a house and remembering someone who has died. Heck, now there is even a *Common Prayer Pocket Edition* and a *Common Prayer* app for your phone (so those of us who don't sing well can listen and hum along).

A CULT-URE OF SORTS

Any time we make a radical conversion, there is the danger that people will say we are being brainwashed or are joining a cult. The truth is everyone in our culture has been deeply polluted by the noise and garbage of this world, and we all need to be washed clean. We need minds that are renewed and uncluttered so they are free to dream again. And let us not forget that the word *cult* comes from the same root from which we get our word *culture*. So while we are not waiting for a UFO landing, preparing for a mass suicide, or stockpiling weapons, we are forming an alternative culture. It is not simply a counterculture reacting to the dominant culture. (And getting marketed by it. It won't be long before you'll be able to buy gas masks for antiwar protests that are made by Lockheed Martin, or T-shirts that say "Make poverty history" made by kids in sweatshops.) We are forming a new culture. And in many ways, it is broader and more sustainable, much less "tribal" than nationalism and much less dangerous than the cult of civil religion that is infecting the church. And the imperial cult seems to be suspiciously closer to those infamous cults that stockpile weapons and await their suicidal fate while pretentiously fortifying themselves against any truth that would set them free from the illusions that are killing them—those cults who continue to offer blood sacrifices to the gods of Mammon and Violence on the altars of desert sand and jungle soil. The book *Jesus for President* is all about this idea that Christians are meant to be God's holy counterculture, showing the world what a society of love can look like. It is about political imagination and what it means to be the peculiar people of God.

As a community, we have a doctrinal statement so folks know we are not drinking lamb's blood and sacrificing animals (except for that one stray cat that kept coming in . . . just kidding). Most Christian congregations and communities have such a statement of faith articulating their orthodoxy (meaning "right belief"), but that's usually where it ends. For us, belief is only the beginning. What really matters is how we live, how what we believe gets fleshed out, so we also have a statement of orthopraxis (meaning "right living, right practices"). And this is where most belief-oriented faith communities fall short. They tell us only what they believe, but they do not tell us how their beliefs affect their lifestyles. While doctrines alone are not enough, the things that we believe are still very important. Orthodoxy matters, and there is some sloppy theology out there. The language I use these days is that we need to move beyond "belief only" Christianity. I think that's what Jesus meant when he said, "For I tell you that unless your righteousness surpasses that of the Pharisees and the teachers of the law, you will certainly not enter the kingdom of heaven" (Matt. 5:20). Traditionally, many Christian communities have a "rule of life" that articulates both the beliefs and practices of the faith. It is helpful to think about that as we consider what it means to belong to a faith community. This is why it often takes years to grow into full membership in religious communities. In our society, we have focused almost entirely on belief. Our challenge is not just right thinking but right living. We should consider having a rule of life that integrates belief and the practices of the faith as we consider what it means to follow Jesus as a community, family, and individuals. What are the essential beliefs and practices of our faith?

In creating a new culture, we are now a part of what we've come to call a community of communities, a web of relationships between grassroots organizations, intentional communities, and hospitality houses across the country. We have done a bunch of things to try to connect the dots—all trying to build a movement, more than a brand. We set up a directory of communities: www.communityofcommunities. info. For years we did a magazine called Conspire, which ran like a literary co-op with contributors from around the world. You can still get copies at www.thesimpleway.org—lots of wisdom on those pages. Our friend David Janzen has developed a team of elders called the Nurturing Communities Project, which helps new communities get going and helps old communities keep going: http://www.shalommission communities.org/nurturing-communities. And from time to time we do big convergences and reunions where we all get together. Keep in touch by Facebook, Twitter, or our website: www.thesimpleway.org. Many of them are older (and most are wiser) than us, and some are just being born. Nearly everywhere I speak, small groups of young people come forward with fire in their eyes and say, "We have been dreaming the same dreams." A part of what we try to do is make the gospel way of life as accessible as possible.

One of the ways we have begun to understand what is happening is through the lens of the ancient Christian monastic movements. During eras of history when the identity of Christian disciples became all but lost, the Spirit has always led small groups of people into exodus, into the wilderness, the desert, or the abandoned places within the empire. Sister Margaret, one of the wise grandmothers of the movement, likes to say, "The inner city is the contemporary desert." In the abandoned places, we find God and community. We practice resurrection. We see miracles and fight demons. And like the ancient desert, the inner-city desert is filled with saints and villains and misfits of all kinds. It is an enchanted place where good and evil battle every day. Our friends at a sister community called Rutba House in North Carolina organized a gathering devoted to creating a monastic rule of sorts, articulating the many common threads of belief and practice that we see in the contemporary movement of the Spirit.[21] It is not so much fleeing from something as dancing toward something new, "building a new society in the shell of the old," as the Catholic Workers say—creating a culture in which it is easier for people to be good.

SCHOOLS FOR CONVERSION

It's a shame that a few conservative evangelicals have had a monopoly on the word *conversion*. Some of us shiver at the word. But conversion means to change, to alter, after which something looks different than it did before—like conversion vans or converted currency. We need converts in the best sense of the word, people who are marked by the renewing of their minds and imaginations, who no longer conform to the pattern that is destroying our world. Otherwise, we have only believers, and believers are a dime-a-dozen nowadays. What the world needs is people who believe so much in another world that they cannot help but begin enacting it now.

Then we will start to see some true conversion vans— vehicles that run on veggie oil instead of diesel. Then we will see some converted homes—fueled by renewable energy—and laundry machines powered by stationary bicycles and toilets flushed with dirty sink water. Then we will see tears converted to laughter as people beat their swords into plowshares and weld their machine guns into

---

21. The fruit of this conversation can be found in our collaborative book *Schools for Conversion: Twelve Marks of a New Monasticism* and on the website *www.newmonasticism.org*. I have included a summary of these marks in appendix 1.

saxophones, and as police officers use their billy clubs to play baseball. The prophets (Isaiah 2 and Micah 4) offered this poignant image of conversion in which God's people "beat their swords into plows and spears into pruning forks" and nations stop fighting and "study war no more." It's such a powerful vision, we decided, why wait? A few years ago, we rallied some blacksmiths and welders and started doing some weapons conversions—turning weapons into tools, converting the instruments of death into instruments of life. We started with an AK47 and have now done all sorts of weapons conversions. You can see pictures and videos here: *www.rawtools.org.* And, by the way, RAW tools is all about turning WAR around. Send us some guns, and we'll send you some tools we made from them: *https://www.youtube.com/watch?v=dWH4R0_-4hg.*

For even if the whole world believed in resurrection, little would change until we began to practice it. We can believe in CPR, but people will remain dead until someone breathes new life into them. And we can tell the world that there is life after death, but the world really seems to be wondering if there is life before death.

There is the kind of conversion that happens to people not because of how we talk but because of how we live. And our little experiments in truth become the schools for conversion, where folks can learn what it means for the old life to be gone and the new life to be upon us, no longer taking the broad path that leads to destruction. Conversion is not an event but a process, a process of slowly tearing ourselves from the clutches of the culture.

NOT JUST GOOD SAMARITANS

As we practice hospitality, there comes a point where the suffering around us drives us to ask what it would take to reimagine the world. We've all heard the saying, "Give someone a fish and they'll eat for a day, but teach them to fish and they'll eat for the rest of their life." But our friend John Perkins challenges us to go farther. A few years after writing this book, Dr. Perkins and I wrote a book together called *Follow Me to Freedom*. He says, "The problem is that nobody is asking who owns the pond." As we consider economics, some of us will give people fish. Others will teach people to fish. But still others must be looking at who owns the pond and who polluted it, for these are also essential questions for our survival. We must storm the fence that has been built around the pond and make sure everyone can get to it, for there are enough fish for all of us. Not all of us are going to feed people, teach people to fish, and storm the gates of the pond, but I have found it crucial to keep these integrated. If all I did was feed people each week, I'd start to grow weary if I wasn't doing something to address why people are hungry. And if all I did was fight for social change, policies, and legislation, I'd grow tired if I didn't sit on the stoop with a neighbor, wipe someone's tears, or help a kid with homework. The macro level and the micro level are like yin and yang or like Oreos and milk: they go well together.

A homeless mother once told us that there is a big difference between managing poverty and ending poverty. "Managing poverty is big business. Ending poverty is revolutionary." Too often, the church has chaplained the corporate global economy, caring for the victims of the systems. As long as we uncritically manage the collateral damage of the market economy, the world can continue to produce victims. But as Dietrich Bonhoeffer said during his age of injustice, "We are not to simply bandage the wounds of victims beneath the wheels of injustice, but we are to drive a spoke into the wheel itself." It's like in community when the toilet floods, which happens when you have a dozen people sharing one toilet. When it starts to pour out water, you don't just start cleaning up the mess. You also have to shut off the water that is causing the flood.

That's the sort of thing that requires working together and the humility of admitting that we can do together what we cannot do alone. When we did so poorly at helping folks recover from drug addiction, we stepped back and said, "Duh, no wonder. None of us are heroin addicts." So we have surrounded ourselves with friends who have so much to teach us. Alone we see only in part, but together, as the Bible says, "love is made complete among us" (1 John 4:17). One of our sister communities here in Philly is New Jerusalem, which is made up of people recovering from addictions to drugs and alcohol. They have taught us so much about drug addiction, as well as our own addictions and recovery. They have taught us that we cannot look at the sick without looking at what is causing the sickness, that sin is both personal and social. (They teach about "the politics of drugs" and the complexity of the drug industry.) People are poor not just because of their sins; they are poor because of *our* sins (and people are rich because of our sins). On the wall of New Jerusalem is a sign that reads, "We cannot fully recover until we help the society that made us sick recover."

When you see so many of your friends waste away in drug addiction, you start to ask where the drugs are coming from, and it's not just from kids on the corner. When we are staring in the face of the largest prison buildup in the history of civilization, with two million citizens in prison (Mass incarceration has become one of the most pressing justice issues of our time, even more so during the years after I wrote this book. Now here's where we are. The US has 5 percent of the world's population, but 25 percent of the world's prison population. There are more African-Americans in prison or under judicial constraint than there were slaves in 1850. It costs four times more to keep a person in jail than to send a child to school. It costs $69 billion a year to maintain the prisons system. At the time Philadelphia schools were going bankrupt and closing dozens of schools with a $300 million dollar budget, a $400 million prison was being built just outside the city. Here's a good link: *https://www .aclu.org/prison-crisis)*, and one in every three black men under judicial constraint, we start to wonder what good the Thirteenth Amendment is if slavery is illegal *unless a person is convicted of a crime.* Many great books like Michelle Alexander's *The New Jim Crow* and Douglas Blackmon's *Slavery by Another Name* show that slavery did not end— slavery evolved. We now have folks in prison, half of whom are in for crimes related to economics or the drug industry, who are hired to do work that pays twenty-three cents an hour (compared to twenty dollars an hour for union labor). Business experts point to prisoners as the most profitable workers because they work for nearly nothing. It is entirely possible that prisoners could be contracted to do sanitation jobs and other work, at the cost of hundreds of people's livelihood. It is already happening—corporations like AT&T, Starbucks, Microsoft, Eddie Bauer, Revlon, Boeing, Target, Nordstrom, and Victoria's Secret have hired prisoners. One of the more disturbing facts is that the military is one of the largest contractors of prison labor. Prisoners make war supplies, even parts for Patriot missiles (used in Iraq) and helmets, ammunition belts, uniforms, and—get this—even the vestments for chaplains. (A good book on this is *Prison Profiteers: Who Makes Money from Mass Incarceration*.)

So prisoners have done everything from making Victoria's Secret undies to packaging coffee for Starbucks. Filmaker Michael Moore pointed out the sickening trend in his film *Downsize This*. We close the factories down (we have seven hundred abandoned factories in Philly), and people will have no work, and many inevitably will turn to crime or replacement industries like drugs or prostitution or underground markets. Then we'll lock them up and open the factories back up as prisons and hire them to do the jobs they could have had before, but now we can pay them a dollar a day. Scary. And not that far from reality.[22]

When we are trying to teach kids not to hit each other and they see a government use violence to bring about change, we start to consider what it means to give witness to a peace that is not like the world gives (John 14:27). When we live in the wreckage of an old industrial neighborhood that has lost over two hundred thousand jobs and now has seven hundred abandoned factories, we start to ask questions about the corporate global economy, especially when we see the same companies abuse

22. Here are a few other articles on the prison industry:

Mother Jones: *http://www.motherjones.com/politics/2008/07/what-do-prisoners-make-victorias-secret*

Huffington Post: *http://www.huffingtonpost.com/2012/12/10/prison-labor_n_2272036.html*

Global Research: *http://www.globalresearch.ca/the-prison-industry-in-the-united-states-big-business-or-a-new-form-of-slavery/8289*

Ella Baker Center for Human Rights: *http://ellabakercenter.org/blog/2013/06/prison-labor-is-the-new-slave-labor*

Prisoners' Wage: Maximum of $1.15/hour: *http://www.prisonpolicy.org/prisonindex/prisonlabor.html*

UNICOR's 2014 Annual Report: *http://www.unicor.gov/information/publications/pdfs/corporate/2014%20FPI%20Annual%20Management%20Report_C.pdf* other "neighbors" overseas. Dr. Martin Luther King put it like this: "We are called to play the Good Samaritan on life's roadside . . . but one day we must come to see that the whole Jericho road must be transformed so that men and women will not be constantly beaten and robbed. True compassion is more than flinging a coin to a beggar. It comes to see that a system that produces beggars needs to be repaved. We are called to be the Good Samaritan, but after you lift so many people out of the ditch you start to ask, maybe the whole road to Jericho needs to be repaved."[23]

23. Martin Luther King Jr., "A Time to Break the Silence" (sermon, Riverside Church, New York, April 4, 1967).

CHAPTER 6

ECONOMICS OF REBIRTH

Not long ago, a few friends and I were talking with some very wealthy executives about what it means to be the church and to follow Jesus. One businessman confided, "I too have been thinking about following Christ and what that means, so I had this made." He pulled up his sleeve to reveal a bracelet engraved with WWJD (What Would Jesus Do?). It was custom-made of twenty-four karat gold. Maybe each of us can relate to this man—both his earnest desire to follow Jesus and, bound up in the materialism of our culture, his distorted execution of that desire.

BEYOND BROKERAGE

Layers of insulation separate the rich and the poor from truly encountering one another. There are the obvious layers like picket fences and SUVs, and there are the more subtle ones like charity. Tithes, tax-exempt donations, and short-term mission trips, while they accomplish some good, can also function as outlets that allow us to appease our consciences and still remain a safe distance from the poor. Take this poignant example you may have caught wind of: it was revealed that Kathie Lee garments, which have earned Wal-Mart over $300 million in sales annually, were being produced by teenage girls working in abysmal conditions in Honduran sweatshops. These girls, as young as thirteen, worked fifteen-hour shifts under the watch of armed guards and received thirty-one cents an hour. But the great irony is that the garments they were making for Kathie Lee were sold under a label that promised that "a portion of the proceeds from the sale of this garment will be donated to various children's charities." More recently, Kathie Lee has been an advocate for workers' rights. Charity can be a dangerous insulator.

It is much more comfortable to depersonalize the poor so we don't feel responsible for the catastrophic human failure that results in someone sleeping on the street while people have spare bedrooms in their homes. We can volunteer in a social program or distribute excess food and clothing through organizations and never have to open up our homes, our beds, our dinner tables. When we get to heaven, we will be separated into those sheep and goats Jesus talks about in Matthew 25 based on how we cared for the least among us. I'm just not convinced that Jesus is going to say, "When I was hungry, you gave a check to the United Way and they fed me," or, "When I was naked, you donated clothes to the Salvation Army and they clothed me." Jesus is not seeking distant acts of charity. He seeks concrete acts of love: "you fed me . . . you visited me in prison . . . you welcomed me into your home . . . you clothed me."

With new government funds and faith-based initiatives, the social-work model can easily entangle the church in the efficiency of brokering services and resources in a web of "clients" and "providers" and struggling to retain God's vision of rebirth, in which we are all family. I have immense respect for social workers. But I also think Jesus would have failed some of his social work classes on "professional distance." I find some of the most redemptive, life-giving moments happen around dinner tables and in our homes, where we cross the line and actually become a friend, not just a service provider. I know there is a place for boundaries and for wisdom. I also know I just talked to one of the best social workers I know about how she takes her "clients" on family vacation—and that has changed lives more than a hundred therapy sessions ever could. Faith-based nonprofits can too easily be the mirror image of secular organizations, maintaining the same hierarchies of power and separation between rich and poor. They can too easily merely facilitate the exchange of goods and services, putting plenty of professionals in the middle to guarantee that the rich do not have to face the poor and that power does not shift. Rich and poor are kept in separate worlds, and inequality is carefully managed but not dismantled.

When the church becomes a place of brokerage rather than an organic community, she ceases to be alive. She ceases to be something we are, the living bride of Christ. The church becomes a distribution center, a place where the poor come to get stuff and the rich come to dump stuff. Both go away satisfied (the rich feel good, the poor get clothed and fed), but no one leaves transformed. No radical new community is formed. And Jesus did not set up a program but modeled a way of living that incarnated the reign of God, a community in which people are reconciled and our debts are forgiven just as we forgive our debtors (all economic words). That reign did not spread through organizational establishments or structural systems. It spread like disease—through touch, through breath, through life. It spread through people infected by love.

Often wealthy folks ask me what they can do for the Simple Way. I could ask them for a few thousand dollars, but that would be too easy for both of us. Instead, I ask them to come visit. Writing a check makes us feel good and can fool us into thinking that we have loved the poor. It's the same with folks on the street who ask for money. We can give them a few bucks to get them off our backs, but that's not love. If it is love, it's cheap love. Love requires relationship and comes with responsibility. It's more than passing a buck. Love means we get involved. However, I will say for this ten-year edition, if you have a million bucks (or a hundred dollars) and want to give it to us, we'll accept your generous gift. We'd like to have a relationship with you, but we're not one to rob anybody of the joy of giving. So we'll accept your donation, but more than money, we want your heart (*www.thesimpleway.org/donate*). But seeing the squat houses and tent cities and hungry children will transform our lives. Then we will be stirred to imagine the economics of rebirth and to hunger for the end of poverty.

Almost every time we talk with affluent folks about God's will to end poverty, someone says, "But didn't Jesus say, 'The poor will always be with you'?" Even though there are more than two thousand Scriptures that mention God's concern for the poor, this is one of the most quoted. We'll look at this closely in a few pages, but it is important to note that Jesus is quoting Deuteronomy 15 here. The passage begins with God saying, "There should be no poor among you," and then moves to, "If you find that there are poor among you . . .," and finally it says, "There will always be poor in the land." God moves from what should be to what is reality in our sin-plagued world. But then the entire passage that follows is about how we are to care for the poor, hold our possessions with open hands, create systems that insure the poor are taken care of. It is clear that God's will is for none to be poor, and until then, we must be among the poor, as Christ was among the poor. Many of the people who whip out this verse have grown quite insulated and distant from the poor and feel defensive. I usually gently ask, "Where are the poor? Are the poor among us?" The answer is usually a clear negatory. As we study the Scriptures, we see how many texts we have misread, contextualized, and exegeted to hear what we want to. Like this one about the poor being among us, which Jesus says in the home of a leper and after a poor marginalized woman anoints his feet with perfume. The poor were all around him. Far from saying in defeat that we should not worry about the poor, since they will always be among us, Jesus is pointing the church to her true identity—she is to live close to those who suffer. The poor will always be among us, because the empire will always produce poor people, and they will find a home in the church, a citizenship in the kingdom of God, where the "hungry are filled with good things and the rich sent away empty."

I heard that Gandhi, when people asked him if he was a Christian, would often reply, "Ask the poor. They will tell you who the Christians are." Mother Teresa once said, "It is fashionable to talk about the poor, but not as fashionable to talk to the poor." One of the challenges I see is that it can be fashionable to talk about justice and still not know, personally, many of the people affected by injustice. We can have conferences where we care about justice from a safe distance, but still may not have the voices of those most affected by injustice among us. It's possible to care about human trafficking and still not have any authentic relationships with folks on the margins. It's possible to talk about racial justice and still worship in segregated congregations. Real justice goes deeper—it changes us, it keeps us up at night, it causes us to ache in our guts and to weep from the depths of our souls because we know by name the people being abused. It might even mean we go to jail or suffer with them for trying to put our bodies in the way of whatever is about to run over them.

COMPLEXITY OF SIMPLICITY

The old saying goes "Live simply that others may simply live." Simplicity is very popular nowadays. All the time, I get invited to speak at conferences on simple living, and I'm offered nice honorariums to do it! People write books on simplicity and make lots of money. It's a weird thing. There are plenty of liberals who talk about poverty and injustice but rarely encounter the poor, living detached lives of socially responsible but comfortable consumption. And there are plenty of Christians who talk about how much God cares for the poor but don't know any poor folks. There is nothing more sickening than talking about poverty over a fancy dinner. Or how about this one: I once saw an advertisement for a dialogue on global starvation, and the sign boldly read, "Refreshments will be served."

It's too bad that living simply has to be so complicated. Responsible living is a paradox, as it often stirs up questions of privilege. It takes a lot of money or land to "tread lightly on the earth." My neighbors don't eat organic; most of them can't afford to shop at the trendy natural foods stores (if there were one anywhere near us). One elderly African-American woman shared with a group of young progressives (I was one of them), "My ancestors all used to eat organic and grow their own food. It was not radical, it was just what we did before we made such a mess of things." Among all the militant vegetarians and vegans (who eat no meat or animal products), some of us jokingly call ourselves "freegans," because we'll eat anything that's free. It's hard to figure out how to weigh lifestyle questions that can often entrench us in guilt and privilege. We have to have grace with each other and a little humor. (By the way, how much did you pay for this book?) It's also noteworthy that there is a place for beauty and art and imagination. After living with rats and boxes of donations in the living room for many years, we made some adjustments. There is a place for good food and beautiful art; what matters is who you share it with. What's just as important as what you eat is who you are eating with. One of my favorite sayings these days is "Simple living does not mean ugly living." We can live in ways that are simple and responsible— and beautiful.

When we talk of materialism and simplicity, we must always begin with love for God and neighbor, otherwise we're operating out of little more than legalistic, guilt-ridden self-righteousness. Our simplicity is not an ascetic denunciation of material things to attain personal piety, for if we sell all that we have and give it to the poor, but have not love, it is meaningless (1 Cor. 13:3). And there are many progressive liberals who have taught me that we can live lives of disciplined simplicity and still be distant from the poor. We can eat organic, have a common pool of money, and still be enslaved to Mammon (the personification of the money god that Jesus named in the Gospels). Rather than being bound up by how much stuff we need to buy, we can get enslaved to how simply we must live.

Simplicity is meaningful only inasmuch as it is grounded in love, authentic relationships, and interdependence. Redistribution then springs naturally out of our rebirth, from a vision of family that is larger than biology or nationalism. As we consider what it means to be "born again," as the evangelical jargon goes, we must ask what it means to be born again into a family in which our sisters and brothers are starving to death. Then we begin to see why rebirth and redistribution are inextricably bound up in one another, as a growing number of evangelicals have come to proclaim. It also becomes scandalous for the church to spend money on windows and buildings when some family members don't even have water. Welcome to the dysfunctional family of Yahweh.

So it's important to understand that redistribution comes from community, not before community. Redistribution is not a prescription for community. Redistribution is a description of what happens when people fall in love with each other across class lines. When the Bible tells the story of the early church in the book of Acts, it does not say that they were of one heart and mind because they sold every-thing. Rather, they held all in common precisely because they were of one heart and mind, as rich and poor found themselves born again into a family in which some had extra and others were desperately in need. Redistribution was not systematically regimented but flowed naturally out of a love for God and neighbor. I am not a communist, nor am I a capitalist. As Will O'Brien of the Alternative Seminary here in Philly says, "When we truly discover love, capitalism will not be possible and Marxism will not be necessary." A few years ago, the American Enterprise Institute (the "think tank for American capitalism," as it has been called) hosted a debate between me and my friend Peter Greer titled "Was Jesus a Communist or a Capitalist?" You can read about it on CNN (*http://religion.blogs.cnn.com/2010/11/23/was-jesus-a-communist-or-a-capitalist/*) and watch it here: *https://www .youtube.com/watch?v=52nCgezeDjU*. Don't worry—Jesus was nothing that ends in -ist. He defies our categories and transcends our -ists and -isms. We've done that debate a few times and have a blast every time.

FASTING AND FEASTING

Generosity is a virtue not just for those with a special spiritual gifting or an admirable philanthropic passion. It is at the very heart of our rebirth. Popular culture has taught us to believe that charity is a virtue. But for Christians, it is only what is expected. True generosity is measured not by how much we give away but by how much we have left, especially when we look at the needs of our neighbors. We have no right not to be charitable. The early Christians taught that charity is merely returning what we have stolen. In the seventeenth century, St. Vincent de Paul said that when he gives bread to the beggars, he gets on his knees and asks forgiveness from them.

The early Christians used to write that when they did not have enough food for the hungry people at their door, the entire community would fast until everyone could share a meal together. What an incredible economy of love. The early Christians said that if a child starves while a Christian has extra food, then the Christian is guilty of murder. One of the fathers of the church, Basil the Great, writing in the fourth century, put it this way: "When someone strips a man of his clothes, we call him a thief. And one who might clothe the naked and does not—should not he be given the same name? The bread in your cupboard belongs to the hungry; the coat in your wardrobe belongs to the naked; the shoes you let rot belong to the barefoot; the money in your vaults belongs to the destitute." Or in the words of Dorothy Day, "If you have two coats, one of them belongs to the poor." No wonder John the Baptist[1] used to

---

1. John was a wild locust-eating, camel-skin wearing prophet of the desert who probably toted a few dreadlocks and would get a few funny looks from some contemporary Christians. He was a cousin of Jesus and helped

connect redistribution with repentance, as he declared, "Repent, for the kingdom of heaven has come near" (Matt. 3:2), and, "Anyone who has two shirts should share with the one who has none" (Luke 3:11).

People who experiment in sharing may begin out of burden or guilt, but they are sustained by the matchless joy it brings. What delight it is to see others receive the gifts of God, especially when they have been deprived of them for far too long. One of the beggars in Calcutta approached me one day, and I had no money on me, but I felt a piece of gum in my pocket, so I handed it too her. I have no idea how long it had been since she had chewed gum, or if she had ever even had the chance. She looked at it and smiled with delight. Then she tore it into three pieces and handed one to me and one to my friend so we could share the excitement. When those who have gone without life's simple pleasures are given a gift, they are so overjoyed that their instinct is often to share rather than hoard. Kids I got ice cream for in India would run and grab their friends and make everyone take a bite. I remember speaking to a large group of school children about inequality of resources, and we did a simulation that demonstrated how 80 percent of the world has 20 percent of the stuff, and 20 percent of the world is hoarding 80 percent of the stuff. (We divided up school supplies, clothing, and food into piles.) Before we had finished, just after we gave the kids the Dorothy Day quote about how if you have two coats, you've stolen one, one of the kids in the front row tore off his jacket and

---

prepare the way for him. Some call him John the Baptist, and I used to think that meant he was the first Baptist preacher, but now I choose to join with many scholars in referring to him as John the Baptizer, since he passed on this mystical sign of rebirth and baptized Jesus himself in the Jordan River. All before ole Herod cut his head off.

threw it onto the stage with a huge smile, yelling, "Give it to the kids with no coats!" That's the joy of giving. Giving is a joy, not a burden. If we can't give our possessions away, then they possess us. If we aren't careful, the things we own begin to own us. The way we give money and possessions power is by holding them with clenched fists. On the flip side, the way we take away their power is by holding them with open hands and giving them away winsomely. If love fuels us, then our impulse becomes sharing. When we get something wonderful, like ice cream, our instinct is to share it with others. We give stuff away not because it is so bad but because it is so good—we want others to experience the gifts of God.

There's an old story from the desert fathers and mothers, people of deep faith who found it necessary to go into the desert to find God. They lived in little clusters of communities (much the way many of our communities now live, only our desert is the inner cities and abandoned places of the empire). Someone had brought one of the communities a bundle of grapes as a gift. That was quite a delicacy, maybe sort of like giving someone chocolate truffles today. They got so excited, and what happened next is fascinating. Rather than devour them all, they didn't eat a single one. They passed them on to the next community to enjoy. And that community did the same thing. And eventually, those grapes made it through every community and back to the first community without being eaten. Everyone simply wanted the others to experience the joy of the gift. I'm not sure what ever ended up happening with those grapes. I think maybe they had a big party, or maybe they made some wine. But no doubt God was happy. One of the quotes on my wall reminds me of this daily: "The best thing to do with the best things in life is to give them away."

Mother Teresa was one of those people who sacrificed great privilege because she encountered such great need. People often ask me what Mother Teresa was like. Sometimes it's like they wonder if she glowed in the dark or had a halo. She was short, wrinkled, and precious, maybe even a little ornery, like a beautiful, wise old granny. But there is one thing I will never forget—her feet. Her feet were deformed. Each morning in Mass, I would stare at them. I wondered if she had contracted leprosy. But I wasn't going to ask, of course. "Hey Mother, what's wrong with your feet?" One day a sister said to us, "Have you noticed her feet?" We nodded, curious. She said, "Her feet are deformed because we get just enough donated shoes for everyone, and Mother does not want anyone to get stuck with the worst pair, so she digs through and finds them. And years of doing that have deformed her feet." Years of loving her neighbor as herself deformed her feet.

This is the kind of fasting that creates the divine longing for justice, where our feet become deformed by a love that places our neighbors above ourselves, where our own stomachs groan with the hungry bellies of the world. Maybe this is what Jesus meant when he said, "Blessed are those who hunger and thirst for righteousness" or justice (Matt. 5:6).[2] How many of us are really starved for justice? As we saw in the text in Romans 8 about creation's groaning, the closer we get to that groaning, the more we ourselves join it. Perhaps this is the mystery of fasting. Isaiah tells us, "Is not this the kind of fasting I have chosen: to loose the chains of injustice and untie the cords of the yoke, to set the oppressed free and break every yoke? Is it not to share your food with the hungry and to provide the poor wanderer with shelter—when

---

2. In the Hebrew, the same word is used for righteousness and justice.

you see the naked, to clothe them, and not to turn away from your own flesh and blood?" (Isa. 58:6–7). True fasting is not just depriving ourselves of privilege but also sharing sacrificially to bring an end to the cycles of inequality, an end to creation's groaning and the groaning of hungry bellies.

One thing fasting does is sacrifice privilege. Some of us will need to fast to connect us not only to God but to our hungry neighbors. Others of us are hungry and will now be able to dine in the abundance of the Lord's feast. Certainly the thirty-five thousand children starving to death today need not fast to connect to God. Rather we need to fast in order to connect to them and to God. No wonder the Corinthian church is scolded for disgracing the Lord's Supper by allowing some people to come to the table hungry while others are stuffed (1 Cor. 11:21–22). They were not reconciled with one another and needed first to leave the altar to care for their neighbors.

THEOLOGY OF ENOUGH

In addition to rooting simplicity in love, it also seems crucial that economic practices be theologically grounded. I am convinced that most of the terribly disturbing things that are happening in our world in the name of Christ and Christianity are primarily the result not of malicious people but of bad theology. (At least, I want to believe that.) And the answer to bad theology is not no theology but good theology. If this stuff gets you excited, you'll love a couple of other resources that came out since the first edition of this book. One is a project called *Animate: Practices*, in which I teach about sharing—with some sweet animation from my pal Paul Soupiset. Another is a video and study called *Economy of Love*. Bad theology is dangerous. It leads to things like the "prosperity gospel"—with preachers like Creflo Dollar, who recently announced a $60 million fundraising campaign for a private jet. Bad theology can also legitimize violence, something we'll look at later. Eighty-five percent of executions have happened in the Bible Belt. The death penalty has succeeded not in spite of Christians but because of Christians. And we have bad theology to thank. Even the KKK on their website have an entire section on theology. We need to counter bad theology with good theology. So rather than distancing ourselves from religious language and biblical study, let's dive into the Scriptures together, correcting bad theology with good theology, correcting distorted understandings of the warrior God by internalizing our allegiance to the slaughtered Lamb, correcting the health-and-wealth gospel by following the Homeless Rabbi.

I'm convinced that God did not mess up and make too many people and not enough stuff. Poverty was created not by God but by you and me, because we have not learned to love our neighbors as ourselves. Gandhi put it well when he said, "There is enough for everyone's need, but there is not enough for everyone's greed." One of the first commands given to our biblical ancestors (even before they had the Big 10) while they were stuck in the middle of the wilderness somewhere between Pharaoh's empire and the Promised Land was this: each one was to gather only as much they needed (Exod. 16:16). In the story of the exodus, God rains down manna from heaven and assures the Israelites that there will be enough. When they save some for the next day, God sends maggots to destroy their stockpile. (Maybe we need some maggots today.) They are ordered to carry with them one omer of manna (about three pounds) as a symbol of their daily providence of bread. Of course, we hear the subtle echoes of this in the Lord's Prayer as we are taught to pray for our daily bread. (To pray for "my" daily bread is a desecration; we are to pray for "our" daily bread, for all of us.) Over and over, we hear the promise that if we take only what we need, there will be enough. (The apostle Paul quotes from the Exodus passage in 2 Cor. 8:15 as he corrects the young church to stay true to God's economy.)

Deuteronomy 15 gives us another glimpse of the source of poverty. God goes from saying, "There should be no poor among you" to "If there are poor" to "There will always be poor." Even though there is enough for everyone, greed and injustice will always create poor people in the land, so God teaches us personal responsibility to our poor neighbors. God also establishes rhythms of rest for the land and structures of providence such as gleaning, where the poor are able to gather food from the fields. And God sets in place a plan for Jubilee, regular intervals when inequality is dismantled.[3] God systematically interrupts the human systems that create poverty—releasing debt, setting slaves free, redistributing property. Folks always say the Israelites never fully lived out the Jubilee. But our friend Ched Myers says, "That's no excuse to ignore God's commands. That's like saying we don't need to worry about the Sermon on the Mount since Christians have never fully practiced it."

There is deep wisdom in the early desert monastic asceticism and the vow of poverty of centuries-old monastic

---

3. The Levitical Jubilee is God's comprehensive unilateral restructuring of the community's assets to remind Israel that all property and land belong to God, and that they were an exodus people who must never return to a system of slavery (Lev. 25:42). It was to take place every fiftieth year, preceded by a "Sabbath's Sabbath," or the forty-ninth year (Lev. 25:8–12). The Jubilee (named after the jovel, a ram's horn that sounded to herald the remission) aimed to dismantle structures of social-economic inequality by releasing each community member from debt (Lev. 25:35–42), returning encumbered or forfeited land to its original owners (vv. 13, 25–28), and freeing slaves (vv. 47–55).

movements, and yet whenever I talked to my neighbors and homeless friends about a "vow of poverty," they either laughed or gave me a puzzled stare. "Have you ever been poor?" some asked. I began to see how myopic my vision was, and how narrow my language. It reeked of privilege. So I would suggest we need a third way, neither the prosperity gospel nor the poverty gospel but the gospel of abundance rooted in a theology of enough. As Proverbs says, "Give me neither poverty nor riches, but give me only my daily bread. Otherwise, I may have too much and disown you and say, 'Who is the LORD?'" (30:8–9). And after seeing plenty of poor folks forced into economic crimes by their poverty, and after seeing plenty of rich folks so content in their riches that they forget that they need God or anyone else, I think we are all ready for something new.

GOD'S ECONOMY

I have grown to love biblical study. In Philadelphia, there is something called the Alternative Seminary, which is a loose network of people studying the Scriptures together.[4] The Alternative Seminary here in Philadelphia is going stronger than ever thanks largely to my friend, and theological Yoda, Will O'Brien. There are classes, webinars, and events happening all the time. Some are one-day intensives, and others are six-week courses. From time to time we'll even have a year-long course. Check it out here: *http://www.alternativeseminary.net/.* Whether people have knowledge from academia or wisdom from the streets, everyone is valued

---

4. There is now a national movement of underground seminaries called Word and World, which is a nomadic popular school committed to "bridging the gulf between the seminary, the sanctuary, and the street" (*www.wordandworld.org*). Another great underground seminary resource is convened by my friend Ched Myers. Check it out here: *http://www.bcm-net.org/.*

as a teacher and as a learner. In one of our classes, we studied Scriptures that dealt with economics—in an abandoned house on our block. In the class, we had homeless folks, business executives, Bible scholars, young radicals, Catholics, and Protestants, and I had a glimpse of how challenging and invigorating it must have been in Jesus' day for tax collectors, peasants, Zealots, and prostitutes to sit around the same table.

In the Gospels, we see rebirth and redistribution bound up in one another. As we saw earlier, as John the Baptizer prepared the way for Jesus, he preached repentance but in the same breath told people to give away their extra shirt. Of course, Jesus' own teaching is packed with stories of debt, workers' wages, redistribution, and caring for the poor, and his two accounts of the afterlife have unmistakable economic dimensions (the rich man and Lazarus, and the sheep and the goats). All through the New Testament, we are told of how rebirth and redistribution are bound up in one another. We cannot say we love God and pass by our hungry neighbor. No one has seen God, but as we love one another, God lives in us. One of the signs of Pentecost was that there were no needy persons among them, for they shared everything.

So while the Scriptures are laced with teaching on economics, I won't assume that you are interested in a meaty analysis of biblical economics or that everyone gets strange kicks out of Bible study like I do. But there is one passage in particular that reveals the secrets of God's abundance, and I'd like to continue in a healthy tangent if you will allow me. (If you won't, skip to the next chapter, but don't expect to pass the exam.) The passage is in Mark 10, particularly verses 29–31, which reads, "'Truly I tell you,' Jesus replied, 'no one who has left home or brothers or sisters or mother or father or children or fields for me and the gospel will fail to receive a hundred times as much in this present age: homes, brothers, sisters, mothers, children, and fields— along with persecutions—and in the age to come eternal life. But many who are first will be last, and the last first.'" I think this text gives us one of the clearest glimpses of why redistribution is necessary and to be celebrated.

Right before these verses, Jesus had his infamous encounter with the rich ruler (which we already looked at; I sneaked that Bible study in), a story that is not so much about whether rich folks are welcome as it is about the nature of the kingdom of God, whose economy is diametrically opposed to that of the world. Rather than accumulating stuff for oneself, followers of Jesus abandon everything, trusting in God alone for providence. The disciples start to get it, saying, "We have left everything to follow you." And then we come to verses 29–31.

A couple of things strike me about the text: Mark's Gospel assures us that as we leave our possessions and family in allegiance to God's kingdom, we enter a new economy of abundance. But if you look closely, you'll notice a difference between the two almost-identical lists. First, you have a "bonus" item in the second list—persecutions. Yes! Persecutions will come to us when we choose an economic order different from the pattern of the world. And there is also an omission from the second list, which scholars think Mark intentionally left out: fathers. As we are reborn, we leave our biological families. Now we have sisters and brothers and mothers all over the world. And yet the omission of fathers is consistent with Christ's teaching in Matthew that we should call no one father but God (23:9). In an age in which fathers were seen as the lifeline of the family, the seemingly indispensable authority and providential centerpiece, this statement is God's final triumph over patriarchy. Only God is worthy to be seen as father, the Provider and Authority (and of course, King).[5]

Here's the incredible clincher in these verses: the multiplication is not just in the age to come—streets of gold, mansions in heaven, Cadillacs, and crowns. The multiplication of resources begins "in this present age." As I have contemplated these verses with friends and scholars like Ched Myers[6] and Christine Pohl,[7] and as I have lived in community with folks sharing possessions with one another, I have come to see that the divine multiplication begins now, literally and pragmatically. Both the health-and-wealthers and the penitent ascetics miss the deepest reality of these verses, which teach us a radically new economic vision. As we abandon our possessions and biological families, we trust that others too are abandoning their possessions and families, and that there will be an abundance that begins now and lasts for eternity.

MYSTICAL MULTIPLICATION

I used to always say, "Jesus was homeless." And while there is truth in that, I believe the deeper reality is that Jesus had

---

5. Just a note to say that the women in our community meet regularly to talk and study everything from theology to women's health. A book they studied and presented to us all is Paul R. Smith's *Is It Okay to Call God "Mother"?* (Hendrickson, 1993). And while we believe that God is Father, the book was helpful in expanding our minds, even for the skeptics in the house, to all of the biblical characteristics of and names for God.

6. Ched Myers (*http://www.bcm-net.org*) has been an influential scholar and friend. His book *The Biblical Vision of Sabbath Economics* (Tell the Word, Church of the Saviour, 2001) was our text for the Alternative Seminary class on God's economy.

7. Christine Pohl is a professor at Asbury Seminary and has done great work to chaplain intentional communities, and, in her book *Making Room* (Grand Rapids: Eerdmans, 1999), to revive a vision of Christian hospitality.

homes everywhere he went. He impressed this reality on the disciples as he commanded them not to take anything for their journey—no bag, no extra food, no clothes, no money, no shoes. (Except in Mark he did allow them to take shoes, so maybe they got shoes.) The fact that he ordered them not to take these items implies that some of them had access to those things. But they are sent out not in the simple poverty of ascetic life but with a new vision of interdependence, trusting that God would provide for them. As they went into a town, others would open their homes to them. And if not, they were to shake the dust from their feet and move on. The incredible thing is that this ensured not only that the church practiced hospitality but that it would be dependent on hospitality. The line between "us" and "them" was dissolved. All were dependent on God and one another in a new economy.

While theologians and scholars may debate the essence of the feeding miracles in the Gospels, I think one thing is hard to miss: God's economy is one of abundance. When the disciples point out to Jesus that the people are hungry, he tells them to feed them. When they complain about the price, still thinking with the mindset of the market economy, Jesus tells them to take what they have—a little kid's lunch of fish and loaves—and there will be a mystical multiplication.[8] That is the miracle: when we give up our possessions, we are doing it in faith, knowing that other people too are giving up their possessions. In fact, one of the great temptations in the desert was for Jesus to use his power to turn stones into bread and

---

8. For the record, this idea of mystical multiplication is not confined to the world of economics. We are more than the sum of our parts, and we can do together what we cannot do alone. There's the old well-lived truth "Many hands make light work." This is a gift of community. When a truck full of donations shows up that would take me hours to unload, we rally the family and kick it out in a few minutes.

feed the starving.[9] But he insists on trusting the body of Christ to provide "this day our daily bread."

Now we have homes everywhere. When Jesus' followers travel into a town, they can stay with family. These days there are all sorts of experiments in sharing. A lot of cities have car shares or bike shares—just a step up from carpooling (also a good idea). I even heard about an internet-based car share where one person parks at the airport and someone arriving at that airport uses their car instead of renting one. The internet creates all kinds of new possibilities for sharing and ways of maintaining good quality control. (Both guests and hosts can be rated or reported so you can see their track record.) People have created ways to loan their houses, and stuff like couch-surfer networks have arisen to organize hospitality in phenomenal ways. Pretty fantastic stuff. This generation seems to dig collaboration. A lot of companies have even built collaboration into their DNA, knowing that we can do more together and be smarter together than we can as a bunch of isolated individuals. When I go on speaking engagements, I always request to stay in homes rather than hotels, dependent not on the market economy but on the hospitality of the church. I usually say to folks who ask me to speak, "If you can't find a home for me to stay in, then I won't be able to make it." And it is much more beautiful to spend an evening with a family in a home than alone in a hotel flipping channels, trying not to be seduced by dirty movies and dirty advertisements.

---

9. Anybody remember the miniseries about Jesus that aired on CBS a few years back? While I found much of it wanting (better off reading the book!), the part about the desert temptation entails a starving little girl pleading with Jesus to turn stones into bread, and he says to the Tempter, "I will trust my church." It must have been hard.

WHISPERS OF ANOTHER ECONOMY

We need the imagination to dream what this sort of radical interdependence could look like. In our community, one question we continually revisit is health insurance. Many of us feel uneasy living without it, especially as we have kids entering our communal life. And yet it is difficult to use that privilege when many of our neighbors go without health care. It conflicts my spirit to take assistance from the government when I believe it is the primary responsibility of the new community to care for one another. A few years ago, I came across a collective of thousands of Christians who pool their money each month in order to cover one another's medical bills. This feels much more in harmony with the spirit of the early church, the sense of being a big family with a parent with a big wallet. So I am now a part of that community, and each month I get a letter telling me who's in the hospital, where my money is going, and how to pray for my sisters and brothers. Over and over, I have seen the divine multiplication meeting people's needs. And a few years back, I had an accident and racked up a $10,000 medical bill. I brought that need before the community and it was met in full. There are many great medical collectives. The one I am part of has been around for thirty-five years, and we've shared more than $500 million in medical bills. (That's half a billion bucks!) We share about $15 million a year in medical expenses. And every month we still get a newsletter reporting who is in the hospital so we can pray for each other, and so we know where our common pool of money is going—not to yachts and private planes for executives but to pay the bills of brothers and sisters.

In Philly, we have an ongoing dialogue about creating a village of communities, bartering with one another, sharing things we need—even creating a new currency where people exchange hours of work and are valued not because they have money but because they are willing to contribute to others and offer their time to service.[10] One community may have a plumber but need a gardener; another may have a gardener but need blankets; and yet another may have blankets but need a plumber. It is miraculous how the abundance of God and the gifts of the children of God are able to provide mystically for people's needs.

Others of us have been trying to think responsibly about how to create alternative economic possibilities—like with clothing, for instance. Any time we have heard disturbing news about who is making our clothes, we've tried to respond, and not all in the same ways. One friend is working toward a global living wage, translating what it costs to live in different areas of the world, and trying to ensure that corporations are paying wages that will allow people to live. Some folks respond to oppression by shopping in thrift stores so that companies rarely see our money; more likely it goes to a family or a charity like the Salvation Army. Other folks cover up brand names so we don't advertise unless we know that what we advertise incarnates the values of the kingdom. Some of us make our own clothes. In addition to hitting the streets in protest, we can point people to alternatives that are more life-giving, fun, and sustainable. An entire youth group wrote me once to tell me they were making clothes together. And my pants have special holsters for bubbles and sidewalk chalk, and one of my housemates wears a tutu. Where else can you find that?

10. I've even bartered with friends who are helping me with this book, since I obviously cannot offer them any money because we're giving all that away.

RADICAL INTERDEPENDENCE

The reality of divine multiplication is realized only when we allow ourselves to be dependent on God and live in radical interdependence with one another. I caught a glimpse of that back in the leper colony in Calcutta, and now I see it in my neighborhood. Kensington is one of the poorest districts in Pennsylvania and is deliberately neglected by the city. The streets often pile up with trash and the walls are covered with graffiti. Some folks feel a sense of degradation, a feeling that they are not worth as much as people in other neighborhoods. But for others, this neglect is a catalyst to organize ourselves. When the city refuses to plow our streets, we get out and have snowball fights and shovel our streets together. When trash piles up, it's a good excuse to have a block party, so we rope off the street, clean the trash, and open the fire hydrant to play in the water. One of my most vivid experiences of community here in my neighborhood happened in 2007. A seven-alarm fire (that means *big*) started in one of the abandoned factories owned by the city, and it burned down an entire block of houses and badly damaged dozens more. More than a hundred families were affected. Many were evacuated; most lost electricity. What was remarkable, though, was watching our neighborhood come together. Folks opened their homes to each other. One family took all the homeless pets. Another started cooking for everyone. We all pulled together like a big family. The Red Cross set up an emergency shelter, since dozens of families and children were displaced, but a few hours later, the volunteers came to us, stunned. "You've gotta hear this," they said. "No one ended up needing to stay in the shelter. Your neighborhood rose to the occasion and all took care of each other." Beautiful. I have learned an important lesson from my neighborhood. Many neighbor-hoods that are economically poor are rich in community. And the flip side is also true: many neighborhoods that are well off financially are poor when it comes to community. Folks don't know each other and may even think they don't need each other. In the years since the fire, we have rebuilt the whole block that burnt down. And now we're reclaiming the land (still owned by the city) where the factory used to be. We call it Phoenix Park, because it rose from the ashes.

A family very dear to our hearts owns the Josefina minimart across the street from our house. Over the years, we have become inseparable. Their kids come over for homework, to do our theater camp, and to beat us at Uno (though they cheat sometimes). We helped rehab their house, and they helped teach us Spanish. Oftentimes they need transportation to restock the store or pick up the kids. We found that we could insure them (and actu-ally at no extra cost) under our policy. So we share cars, and they never take our money for groceries. We are not Good Samaritans, nor are we an efficient nonprofit pro-vider. We are family with them, and money has lost its relevance. This family no longer owns the store, but are still dear friends. The kids are all grown up now. I'm thankful for all the memories. Now there is a new family who owns the store, so we're starting from scratch, which is going well. A while back, the store was robbed and the whole neighbor-hood took up an offering to help replace some of what was lost. Community. Not long ago, we had to take our car in to the mechanic, and after it was repaired, it was returned without a bill. When I asked about it, our mechanic told me we were taking care of a family he cared deeply for, so the repairs were a gift to us, since we all have to take care of each other. Funny how money loses its power. As one of the early Christians said, "Starve Mammon with your love." I hope Mammon goes hungry around here.

No wonder it is easier to fit a camel through the eye of a needle than for a rich person to enter the kingdom, as Jesus said to that rich ruler. That doesn't mean rich people are excluded or not welcome. It means that it is nearly impossible for them to catch the vision of interdependent community, dependent on God and one another. Rich folks, while they may be spiritually starving for God and community, still believe the illusion that they are self-sufficient autonomous individuals, and that belief is incompatible with the gospel that says wherever two or more are gathered, God is among us. And yet "nothing is impossible," as the text in Mark 10 says. Rocks can cry out, donkeys can talk, dead people can come to life, and rich people can release their riches and enter the kingdom of God. Yes!

One of the communities I have bumped into is a bunch of middle-aged families in the suburbs who had decided to do a little experiment in community. They started sharing garden tools and lawn mowers. They would do laundry together and share machines. They found it was more fun to do their laundry together, spending time with each other while they waited (which poor folks have known for a long time). Before long, they had a community garden and had set up cooperative childcare. A few of them even moved in together. It felt so natural. Eventually, they made the front page of the newspaper, and one of the folks who had started it said to me, "Isn't that weird? What we are doing is front-page news. It just seemed to make sense." A lot of things like credit unions and insurance collectives started with a similar vision of sharing money, bearing each other's burdens, and collectively resisting the drive for individual profit and the isolating loneliness inherent in that. The common good is a wondrous idea. But it's always a challenge to love our neighbors as ourselves and to seek the common good as much as our own good. We have to be more innovative than the credit-card companies and payday lenders (and it does take imagination to get people to spend money they don't have). Love compels us to care about people more than profits. So we have to devise ways of getting people out of debt that are just as powerful as the ways credit card companies devise to get people into debt. But we can do it! In Philly we even have a Debt Annihilation Team (at Circle of Hope) whose mission is to collectively free people from their debts, and there is a science to it. Their motto is straight from the Bible: "Do not owe anything to anyone besides love" (Rom. 13:8). Here's a link: *http://www.circleofhope.net/compassion-teams/*. We also have all sorts of land trusts and a new land bank—all with a similar goal of working together for the good of our city. Heck, Pennsylvania began as a commonwealth, and some of us still hope that we can live into the original dream of the Quakers (and others), who believed they could create a society where the common well-being of every person was a core value.

There are so many experiments in community living and hospitality in different economic and social contexts that the best I can do is give you glimpses of them. But there is one more beautiful story I cannot help but mention. A married couple who were unable to have children happened to meet a woman who had found herself six months pregnant and homeless, so they invited her into their home. It proved to be such a beautiful experience that they decided to continue living together to help raise the new baby girl while the mother pursued her dream of going back to school to become a nurse. They have been living together over a decade now. They are a family, and the baby is now a teenager and the mom a nurse. A heart-wrenching twist to the story is that the wife of the married couple is now very ill with multiple sclerosis, but now the nurse living in her home is caring for her, just as she had cared for the nurse. This is the divine gift of mystical providence and radical interdependence. The woman of the married couple who opened their home died shortly after the original release of this book. And yes, the formerly homeless mom was her nurse as she died.

Another group of folks I've grown to love are some jewelers in the UK. Many of them had been business folks in the world's market economy. The jewelry industry is notoriously wicked, often called the "blood diamond" market, and is responsible for significant human suffering around the world as workers shed blood, tears, and their very lives working to mine the gems and precious metals that they can't even afford to buy. But these business folks in the UK experienced a collision of their faith with the industry, the ole "can't serve God and Mammon" thing. Rather than just altogether abandon the industry, they decided to try transforming it, "practicing resurrection," as we say. They traveled to Bolivia, Columbia, and across Africa, finding the people who work in the diamond industry. They built personal relationships with them and now are pioneering an incredible jewelry business called Cred. As we met in their store in England, one of the founders said to me, "Can you imagine the feeling of satisfaction when you put your wedding band on and know that from the moment that diamond was mined until the ring goes on your finger, every worker was treated with dignity and respect?" My pal Greg Valerio is a legend now in the jewelry industry. He's won all sorts of awards for his work as a fair-trade jewelry activist. He's written a book, *Making Trouble*, and if you're looking for bling, he's the man. No blood will be spilled. And his wife is a theologian, so she puts into words the theology and philosophy that drive their vision. Ruth Valerio is a gem (pun intended). She's an eco-warrior-activist-theologian (http://ruthvalerio.net/). That gives such integrity to the gospel we preach. Having encountered the sacredness of Jesus and of their global neighbors, these people are a different breed of jeweler now.

THEOLOGICAL PRANKSTER

I love how Jesus deals with money, such shrewdness and imagination. First of all, he's really careful: "Judas, you carry the money." (Of course, Judas sells the brotha out for thirty pieces of silver, but that's for another day.) Jesus is always so clever when they come to try to trap him in their schemes. At one point in the Gospels (Matt. 22:15–22), the religious elite try to trap Jesus by seeing if he pays taxes. They give him a coin and ask him, "Who does this belong to?" And Jesus very carefully says, "Give to Caesar what is Caesar's." I love that he shrugs and tells them it's got Caesar's image stamped on it, so give it back to him. Caesar can have his coins, but Caesar has no right to take what is God's. And life is God's. Caesar can put his stamp on the stuff of earth, which moths and rust will destroy, but Caesar has God's stamp on him. God made Caesar. And that means Caesar is not God. I wrote a sermon titled "God's Image and Caesar's Counterfeit" exploring this coin thing a little deeper, building on the teaching of a rabbi named Arthur Waskow. Caesar's image is branded on lifeless metal, while God's image is placed on life itself. We are God's coins, divine image-bearers. Caesar's coins are all the same, but people are not. Caesar is about uniformity, mass production, sameness. God is about diversity, every person with unique DNA and no one with the same fingerprint. Another thing about coins, it was said that you could tell the expanse of an empire by how far the emperor's coins reached. What if that's God's plan in commanding us to "fill the earth, and reproduce like the locusts," that we carry God's image with us everywhere we go, to the ends of the earth, and anytime a life is lost, we lose part of God's image in the world? God's empire is very different from Caesar's. You can hear the full sermon here: *https://www.youtube.com/watch?v=AymaUg3quJ4.*

Another time (Matt. 17:24–27), the authorities come and ask Peter if Jesus pays the temple tax, and Peter instinctively says that yes, he does. But when Peter sees Jesus a bit later, Jesus does something crazy (as usual). He tells Peter to go get a fish and it will have "a four drachma coin in its mouth"—the exact amount required for the tax. Does that strike anyone else as odd?[11] Fish don't usually have money in their mouths. The whole scene is blown up into this big lampoon, a street theater.[12] Who cares about the taxes, a stinking fish had money in its mouth! That's cool. I think Jesus is saying, "You can have your money. I made that fish!" God created Caesar, and God created the heavens and the earth. Caesar cannot do that. Give to Caesar what is Caesar's. Well, Caesar can have his coins, but life is God's and Caesar has no right to take that. Once we've given to God what's God's, there's not much left for

---

11. A first-century historian adds some depth to the significance of the fish when he points out that it was believed that the emperor (he was speaking of Domitian) controlled the animals and all of nature and that even the fish would jump to lick his hand.

12. There's an old peasant proverb that captures the humor and irony of what Jesus is up to: when the emperor passes, the peasant bows . . . and farts. With revolutionary subordination, we give the empire what it asks, but not on its own terms. Caesar may have his coins, which rust will destroy, but life and nature are God's. And if Caesar takes our lives from us, we will rise from the dead.

Caesar. I get asked sometimes if Christians should pay their taxes, and folks often cite this text ("Give to Caesar . . ."). I've written more about taxes and "revolutionary subordination" in both *Jesus for President* and *Red Letter Revolution*. And I wrote a piece titled "Give to Uncle Sam What Is Uncle Sam's" here: *http://www.huffingtonpost.com/shane-claiborne/give-to-uncle-sam-what-is_b_837785.html*.

I think that when we talk about economics, we have to have that sort of imagination and creativity to get out of the messes we've created. Until we have the sort of imagination Jesus had to upstage hoarding and to celebrate a dream more liberating than the American dream, nothing will change. Until we have the courage to risk and scheme ways of redistribution with the same passion and fervor with which people scramble after wealth, the market will overpower God's vision of Jubilee.

A couple of years ago, two things happened. First, we won a lawsuit for police misconduct in New York City. The police had been arresting homeless people for sleeping in public, and charging them with disorderly conduct. Hundreds of folks rallied to bring attention to this situation, and many of us slept outside to express our feeling that it should not be a crime to sleep in public. I was arrested one night as I slept. Through a long legal process, I was found not guilty, and then I filed a civil suit of wrongful arrest, wrongful prosecution, and police misconduct. And we won, in addition to a legal precedent, around $10,000, though we felt the money didn't belong to me or to the Simple Way but to the homeless in New York for all they endure. It was their victory.

The second thing that happened was that after our study of biblical economics, we received an anonymous gift of $10,000, which had been invested in the stock market and now was being returned to the poor.

So $20,000 was enough to stir up the collective imagination. What would it look like to have a little Jubilee celebration today? The idea rippled far beyond the Simple Way, and before long, friends from all over were thinking about it, with smiles on their faces. Where should we have it? Where else but on Wall Street, in the face of the world's economy. We also decided that this was not a one-time celebration but an ancient celebration, going back to Leviticus 25, and an eternal celebration of the New Jerusalem. We decided to send $100 to a hundred different communities that incarnate the spirit of Jubilee and the economics of love. Each $100 bill had "love" written on it. And we invited everyone to Wall Street for the Jubilee.

After months of laughter and dreaming, it really happened. It was a big day. And we were ready (though we still had butterflies in our bellies). About forty people brought all the change they could carry, over thirty thousand coins in bags, coffee mugs, briefcases, and backpacks. Another fifty people would be meeting us on Wall Street. A dozen "secret stashers" ran ahead hiding hundreds of two-dollar bills all over lower Manhattan—in parks, napkin holders, phone booths. At 8:15 we started trickling into the public square in front of the main entrance to the New York Stock Exchange. We deliberately dressed to blend in; some of us looked homeless (some were), others looked like tourists, and others business folks. Word of the redistribution had spread throughout New York, and nearly a hundred folks from the alleys and projects had gathered. We had choreographed the celebration like a play production, making Wall Street the stage of our theatrics of counterterror. At 8:20, Sister Margaret, our seventy-year-old nun, and I stepped forward to proclaim the Jubilee.

"Some of us have worked on Wall Street, and some of us

have slept on Wall Street. We are a community of struggle. Some of us are rich people trying to escape our loneliness. Some of us are poor folks trying to escape the cold. Some of us are addicted to drugs, and others are addicted to money. We are a broken people who need each other and God, for we have come to recognize the mess that we have created of our world and how deeply we suffer from that mess. Now we are working together to give birth to a new society within the shell of the old. Another world is possible. Another world is necessary. Another world is already here."

Then Sister Margaret blew the ram's horn (like our Jewish ancestors used to) and we announced, "Let the celebration begin!" Ten people stationed on balconies above the crowd threw hundreds of dollars in paper money, filling the air. Then they dropped banners which read, "Stop terrorism," "Share," "Love," and, "There is enough for everyone's need but not enough for everyone's greed—Gandhi."

The streets turned silver. Our "pedestrians," "tourists," "homeless," and "business people" began pouring out their change. We decorated the place with sidewalk chalk and filled the air with bubbles. Joy was contagious. Someone bought bagels and started giving them out. People started sharing their winter clothes. One of the street sweepers winked at us as he flashed a dustpan full of money. Another guy hugged someone and said, "Now I can get my prescription filled."

It worked. We had no idea what would happen.[13] We knew it was dangerous, intentionally bringing God and

---

13. The police had come in full force but were quite disarmed by the fun (hard not to smile at bubbles and sidewalk chalk). One of them later told me he was ordered to "get rid of them," but he couldn't tell who "they" were. Laughing, he said next time we have a Jubilee, we could do it outside his station.

Mammon face to face. But this is precisely what we have committed our lives to. It is risky, and yet we are people of faith, believing that giving is more contagious than hoarding, that love can convert hatred, light can overcome darkness, grass can pierce concrete . . . even on Wall Street. This was ten years before Occupy Wall Street and the language of the 99 percent and the 1 percent. Now the disparity between the superrich and superpoor is even more pronounced. *Forbes* magazine says that the richest eighty-six people in the world now own the same amount of wealth as half the world (3.5 billion). Maybe it's time for another Jubilee on Wall Street.

Here's a marvelous video of the original Wall Street Jubilee: *https://www.youtube.com/watch?v=4ETBMhEzYKU.*

CHAPTER 7

PLEDGING ALLEGIANCE WHEN KINGDOMS COLLIDE

I have become well acquainted with the dualism in the North American church. Once, after taking a trip to Iraq to protest the war, I went to Willow Creek and gave a talk titled "The Scandal of Grace." Afterward, they explained to me that the pulpits are not for political messages. I thought about what would have happened if Reverend King hadn't allowed the gospel to get political. My heart sank as I walked into the foyer and noticed something I had never seen before: the American flag standing prominently in front of the auditorium. And never before was I so heartbroken that the cross was missing. For the flag and the cross are both spiritual. And they are both political. It is a dangerous day when we can take the cross out of the church more easily than the flag. No wonder it is hard for seekers to find God nowadays. It's difficult to know where Christianity ends and America begins.[1] Our money says, "In God We Trust." God's name is on America's money, and America's flag is on God's altars.

---

1. Two of the more troubling signs I've seen are a red, white, and blue T-shirt that says "jesUSAves" (Jesus Saves, emphasis on the USA), and a new line of old-school Christian fish symbols you can put on your car, but instead of "Jesus" in the middle of the fish, it has "Bush." Truth is stranger than fiction: see *www.bushfish.org*.

POLITICS SHMOLITICS

For those of us who grow instantly nauseated at the mention of the word *politics*, maybe we can break it down a little bit. And for those of you who like thinking about politics and want to go deeper, check out *Jesus for President*. I wrote it with my friend Chris Haw, and it is all about political imagination, allegiance, and what it means to be the peculiar people of God in the belly of an empire. The English word politics derives from the Greek word *polis*, as in "metropolis" or "Indianapolis." The word is rooted in the concepts of "city," "civil," "citizen," "civic," basically what it means to be a society of people. Anything involving humans living together purposefully is political, a *polis*. As the people of God, we are building a new society in the shell of the old, a new *polis*, the New Jerusalem, the city of God. This is essentially a political act. Without a doubt, envisioning the radical countercultural values of God's kingdom is by its essence political. Imagine the Gospels with every mention of king, kingdom, Lord, Savior, crowns, banners, and thrones (all words from the imperial lexicon) all edited out. A gospel that is not political is no gospel at all. The root of the word *allegiance* means "Lord"; that's exactly what the early Christians were executed for, for pledging an allegiance to another kingdom, another Lord—treason. In 2004, as the presidential election rolled around, many of us studied the Scriptures[2] and considered what it means to claim Jesus as Lord, or as president. When people asked who I was voting for, I would say, "My President has already ascended the throne and has already delivered his

---

2. Dozens of us gathered around Scripture for studies that we called Kingdom Night, seeking to understand how to pledge allegiance when our kingdoms collide.

State of the Union address. I don't believe that God needs a commander-in-chief or a millionaire in Washington, and I have little faith that either of the likely options will incarnate the Beatitudes, the Sermon on the Mount, and the fruit of the Spirit. I will declare my allegiance from the mountaintops, joining the chorus of the saints and martyrs. And I will raise the banner of love above all flags." After all, we vote every day by how we live, what we buy, and who we pledge allegiance to, so I just resolved to write in my vote, as I did not find it on the national ballot. And I was determined not to let my vote be confined to a private booth, secret ballot, or taboo conversation.

PULLING OUT OF BABYLON

Besides *politics*, there are other words that sometimes give folks trouble. Christian jargon includes words like faith, faithful, and faithfulness that are not easy to wrap your hands around. These are complex words, especially for folks outside Christendom. If you look up faith in the dictionary, most of the definitions revolve around "complete trust, unquestioned loyalty, confident allegiance." Though it may be a little bit of a stretch for those of us with entrenched Christian minds, let's try thinking of faith as loyalty (as in a faithful husband). What are we loyal to? Many are loyal to political parties, and most folks are faithful to their friends. Patriots are faithful to their countries. What are Christians loyal to?

Faith in the Roman Empire was a central virtue for first-century Mediterraneans. The Greek word for faith, *pistis*, was used to describe loyalty to Caesar. People had faith in Caesar, and reciprocally, Caesar was faithful to preserve peace and prosperity. People were killed for being faithless. It was precisely his faithlessness to Rome and his faithfulness to Jesus for which John, the writer of Revelation, was persecuted and exiled by Emperor Domitian. It's not surprising that the early Christians were labeled by imperial officials as "the faithless." Over and over, early Christian writings tell us of how Christians were branded atheists by the imperial courts and executed for this capital crime. They had lost all faith in the empire and had become faithful to God alone as the one who could preserve peace and prosperity. They claimed Jesus as their only emperor (Acts 17:7), they preached the kingdom of their God, and they pledged allegiance to the slaughtered Lamb. Today, there are many things I love about "America the Beautiful," and yet the book of Revelation sounds a clear warning that any glory we give to Babylon is glory that belongs only to God. As my friend Tony Campolo says, "We may live in the best Babylon in the world, but it is still Babylon, and we are called to 'come out of her.'"

John warns the church in Asia Minor to be "faithful unto death" (Rev. 2:10). He describes a marriage between God and God's people. They are to be loyal to their lover, Yahweh, their faith remaining in God alone, adorned as a bride, the New Jerusalem. Describing Rome as the whoring seductress Babylon the Great, John warns the Christians that the empire will entice them with a counterfeit splendor, and he warns against flirting with her pleasures and treasures, which will soon come to ruin. They are not to be shocked and awed by Babylon's power nor dazzled by her jewels. Rather than drinking humanity's blood from her golden cup of suffering (17:6), they are to choose the eucharistic cup filled with the blood of the new covenant. We are faithful not to the triumphant golden eagle (ironically, also an imperial symbol of power in Rome) but to the slaughtered Lamb.

WHEN KINGDOMS COLLIDE

Shortly after September 11th, I traveled to speak to a large congregation in the Midwest. (And no, it wasn't Willow Creek.) Before I got up to preach, a military color guard presented the US flag at the altar. The choir filed in one-by-one, dressed in red, white, and blue, with the "Battle Hymn of the Republic" playing in the background. I knew I was in big trouble. The congregation pledged allegiance to the flag, and I wished it were all a dream. It wasn't. I got up to speak, thankful I was standing behind a large podium lest anyone try to pelt me with a pew Bible. I went forward to preach the truth in love with my knees knocking and managed to make it out okay with a bunch of hugs and a few feisty letters. This is a dramatic (though painfully true) illustration of the messy collision of Christianity and patriotism that has rippled across our land. I thought this was an exceptional and dramatic example, but I've had some zingers since this. I spoke at a military academy where they had a full-on procession of military vehicles and weaponry. They fired cannons and saluted the flag, and then I got up to speak. I felt compelled to speak on the fruit of the Spirit (love, joy, peace, patience, kindness, gentleness, goodness, faithfulness, and self-control), the things Scripture says God is like and we should hope to be more like. I talked about how the fruit of the Spirit take training and discipline and are not always cultivated by the culture around us. Afterword, one young soldier came up to me, nearly in tears, and told me that as he heard the list of the fruit of the Spirit, it became clear to him that these were not the things he was being trained to become. We prayed together, and I think of him often. I know that young man is not alone.

I saw a banner hanging next to city hall in downtown Philadelphia that read, "Kill them all, and let God sort them out." A bumper sticker read, "God will judge evildoers; we just have to get them to him." I saw a T-shirt on a soldier that said, "US Air Force . . . we don't die; we just go to hell to regroup." Others were less dramatic—red, white, and blue billboards saying, "God bless our troops." "God bless America" became a marketing strategy. One store hung an ad in their window that said, "God bless America—$1 burgers."[3] Patriotism was everywhere, including in our altars and church buildings. In the aftermath of September 11th, most Christian bookstores had a section with books on the event, calendars, devotionals, buttons, all decorated in the colors of America, draped in stars and stripes, and sprinkled with golden eagles.

This burst of nationalism reveals the deep longing we all have for community, a natural thirst for intimacy that liberals and progressive Christians would have done much better to acknowledge. September 11th shattered the self-sufficient, autonomous individual, and we saw a country of broken fragile people who longed for community—for people to cry with, be angry with, to suffer with. People did not want to be alone in their sorrow, rage, and fear.

But what happened after September 11th broke my heart. Conservative Christians rallied around the drums of war. Liberal Christians took to the streets. I've received a few letters from self-identifying "liberal Christians" who thought this sentence was unfair, or at least unclear. And I think they are right. I did not intend to say that it was wrong to protest in the streets or that the protestors of the war were trampling on the flag. To be clear, the Iraq war is listed as one of the most protested wars in history, and it should

---

3. And I saw another sign that the "b" had fallen off of so it just said "God less America." I guess they had another audience in mind. Ha!

be. It's estimated that more thirty-six million folks protested in three thousand official protests across the globe. Most everybody in my community went to jail for nonviolent protests. And as we look back and consider what the past ten years of war have left us with, one can't help but think we should have protested even more. Nonetheless, the point I wanted to make, and still believe to be true, is that many Christians missed the opportunity to validate both the horror of September 11th and outrage at war as a response to September 11th. In the aftermath of September 11th, many congregations missed the chance to bear witness of God's concern for the victims of the attack and God's concern for the victims of the imminent war. Many of us hunkered down into familiar camps rather than finding a more creative way of standing with all who suffer. Many of the antiwar activists would do well to visit the memorial in NYC. And many of the war hawks would do well to visit the Ameriyah shelter in West Baghdad. Every life lost is reason for grief and outrage. The cross was smothered by the flag and trampled under the feet of angry protesters. The church community was lost, so the many hungry seekers found community in the civic religion of American patriotism. People were hurting and crying out for healing, for salvation in the best sense of the word, as in the salve with which you dress a wound. A people longing for a savior placed their faith in the fragile hands of human logic and military strength, which have always let us down. They have always fallen short of the glory of God.

NONTRADITIONAL FAMILY VALUES

Feeling desperate in the aftermath of September 11th, I asked Steven, one of the kids in my neighborhood, what we should do. Steven has grown up in the inner city and has seen some hard things and is well acquainted with violence. He is about thirteen now and has always been one of my teachers. When he was eight, he told me he had been trying to figure out who invented the gun. One day he ran up and said, "Hey, hey, I figured it out. I know who invented the gun."

"Who?" I asked.

"Satan . . . because Satan wants us to destroy each other, and God wants us to love each other."

So when I asked him two days after September 11th, when he was ten, what we should do, he thought pensively and said, "Well, those people did something very evil."

I nodded.

He went on, "But I always say [he was ten years old!], 'Two wrongs don't make a right.' It doesn't make sense for us to hurt them back. Besides we are all one big family."

Then his face brightened and he looked at me wide-eyed and said, "Shane, that means you and me are brothers!"

We laughed, and I thought to myself, Steven, tell that to the world.

Jesus offers a new vision of family. Jesus tells a guy named Nicodemus that in order to enter the kingdom of God, he has to be reborn (John 3:1–8). At one point in the Gospels, someone tells Jesus that his biological mother and brothers are outside, and Jesus says, "Who are my mother and my brothers? . . . Whoever does God's will is my brother and sister and mother" (Mark 3:31–35). He had a new definition of family, rooted in the idea that we are adopted as orphans into the family of God and that this rebirth creates a new kinship that runs deeper than biology or geography or nationality. Rebirth is about being adopted into a new family—without borders. With new eyes, we can see that our family is both local and global, including but transcending biology, tribe, or nationality, a renewed vision of the kingdom of God with brothers and sisters in Afghanistan and Iraq, Sudan and Burma, North Philly and Beverly Hills. Any vision short of that is too myopic for a Jesus whose own biological family called him crazy for saying things that disrupted traditional family values.

There is the passage where Jesus says that unless you hate your own family, you are not ready to be his disciple (Luke 14:26). That was one of my favorite verses in high school. Some folks try to explain it away by saying that Jesus meant that our love for our family should look dismal compared to our love for God, and there is some truth in that, but particularly in Luke's Gospel, the word used is "hate," just like when Jesus talks about hating enemies. It's true that Jesus is not shunning a love for our families; he loves his momma so much that when he is dying on the cross, he tells John that now she is his momma (again the new sense of kinship, as they were not biologically related). It is also clear that Jesus is using some strong language to stretch our vision of family and kinship, extending rather than stifling our love. Perhaps the most infinite love we can experience is that of a momma for her little baby or of a husband for his wife, and Jesus is saying that same love must be extended in our rebirth. The same desperate love a mother has for her baby or that a child has for his or her daddy is extended to all of our human family. Biological family is too small of a vision. Patriotism is far too myopic. A love for our own relatives and a love for the people of our own country are not bad things, but our love does not stop at the border. We now have a family that is much broader than biology, that runs much deeper than nationalism. Jesus is telling us that we have family in Iraq, in Afghanistan, in Palestine. We have family members who are starving and homeless, or dying of AIDS, or in the midst of war.

The reality of our rebirth should mess with us. There are times when it does, as in the deep groaning that swept our nation after the tsunami in 2004. People waited in line to adopt children orphaned by the disaster, and a sense of solidarity and family extended across the planet. Or consider the hundreds of families who opened their own homes to those suffering from Hurricane Katrina in 2005. People across the country made tremendous sacrifices in order to bring their displaced neighbors into their families, knowing the burden was too big to bear alone. And it got a little lighter as more and more people decided to carry it together.

But back in Jesus' age, just as in our own, family is one of the most significant barriers to potential risk-takers who would leave everything for the way of the cross. This might explain why Jesus has some hard things to say about our earthly ties, such as not burying our dead or leaving behind our mothers and fathers and all that is "born of the flesh." These earthly allegiances create a myopia that stands in the way of God's vision and justice, which are larger than tribe, clan, or nation. Violence is always rooted in a myopic sense of community, whether it be nationalism or gangs. We long for people to fight with, mourn with, and celebrate with. In my neighborhood, kids talk about their "fam," referring to the people in their cliques whom they would go great distances to protect. Graffiti murals and veterans walls help us remember people in our tribes who have died. Martin Luther King sensed this myopia both in the ghettos and in the Vietnam War and longed for our vision to be broader than our "fam" or our country. As King said, we are "bound by allegiances and loyalties which are broader and deeper than nationalism. . . . This call for a worldwide fellowship that lifts neighborly concern beyond one's tribe, race, class, and nation is in reality a call for an all-embracing and unconditional love for all."[4]

There is now a global movement of friends without borders: www.friendswithoutborders.net. The vision of a border-free world has resonated with folks around the world. One of my inspirations has been the young people of Afghanistan known as the Afghan Peace Volunteers. This movement started among the youth of Afghanistan, after thirty years of nonstop war. They began to study Gandhi and Dr. King and before long launched their own peace movement. Their motto is "A little bit of love is stronger than all the wars in the world." The blue scarf is their symbol. It serves as a reminder that there is one blue sky that connects us all around the world, as brothers and sisters. We've seen entire elementary schools in the States, inspired by these Afghan youth, decorate their buildings with blue scarves and declare themselves border-free friends. Check them out here: http://ourjourneytosmile.com/blog/. And jump on one of their monthly conference calls where folks around the world call in and listen to each other: www.globaldaysoflistening.org.

One of my favorite memories was when we were able to do a Skype call with the kids on my block and these youth in Afghanistan, and they shared common hopes, fears, and pain, and dreams of a world free of violence. And when I visited Ferguson after the killing of Michael Brown, the Afghan Peace Volunteers had me take a blue scarf to lay at the memorial.

---

4. Martin Luther King Jr., "A Time to Break the Silence" (speech, meeting of clergy and laity concerned about Vietnam, Riverside Church, New York, April 4, 1967).

Over the years they have started a nonviolent training center, an intentional community house, a women's collective, and micro businesses like their duvet project, where they make blankets for refugees.

It had been a dream of mine to visit them in Kabul. In 2012 that dream came true.

The tragedy of the church's reaction to September 11th is not that we rallied around the families in New York and D.C. but that our love simply reflected the borders and allegiances of the world. We mourned the deaths of each soldier, as we should, but we did not feel the same anger and pain for each Iraqi death, or for the folks abused in the Abu Ghraib prison incident. We got farther and farther from Jesus' vision, which extends beyond our rational love and the boundaries we have established. There is no doubt that we must mourn those lives lost on September 11th. We must mourn the lives of the soldiers. But with the same passion and outrage, we must mourn the lives of every Iraqi who is lost. They are just as precious, no more, no less. In our rebirth, every life lost in Iraq is just as tragic as a life lost in New York or D.C. And the lives of the thirty thousand children who die of starvation each day is like six September 11ths every single day, a silent tsunami that happens every week.

TO IRAQ

I began to hear other voices echoing my friend Steven's. We met a man named Bob McIlvaine. His twenty-six-year-old son, Bobby, was killed in the September 11th attacks. I have spoken alongside Bob at several peace vigils and demonstrations, and he has become a good friend of our community. When he speaks, he wears Bobby's baseball cap and always has tears in his eyes. He shares his pain and anger at the loss of his son. And then he says, "But there has not been a moment that passed when I believed that more violence will solve anything. I do not want any father to feel what I feel right now." He has a strong sense that the people of Iraq are dads, families, and children. He and others who lost family members started a group called the Families for Peaceful Tomorrows, whose slogan has become "Our grief is not a cry for war." Several of them have gone to Iraq to be with families there. They share the stories of ordinary Iraqi people who would flood them with hugs and flowers and gifts to bring back to families who lost their loved ones in the September 11th attacks. These are the stories that should have made the news, stories that were drowned out by all the noise of war. I've had the honor of doing several events together with Families for Peaceful Tomorrows. On the tenth anniversary of September 11th, my friend Ben Cohen (founder of Ben and Jerry's) and I hosted an event called Jesus, Bombs, and Ice Cream. Terri Rockefeller (who lost her sister in the September 11th attacks) is among the all-star cast of that event. It was powerful to hear how she and other survivors of September 11th use their pain to work for reconciliation rather than retaliation. (Don't worry if you missed it; it's all caught on tape: *http://store.thesimpleway .org/collections/dvds.*)

Heavy on my heart during this time were the children in our neighborhood, whom we are trying to teach not to hit each other. I have felt the ethos of violence in our neighborhood, and I have seen the bitter fruit of the myth of redemptive violence. I heard a kid declare war on another kid, calling him a terrorist. I think I just got tired of people hurting each other, in my neighborhood and in our world. The words of Reverend Martin Luther King echoed in my spirit. As he continually taught rejected, angry urban youth that violence and weapons would not solve their problems, he came to realize they were receiving contradictory messages: "I have told them that Molotov cocktails and rifles would not solve their problems. But they asked, and rightly so, what about Vietnam? They asked if our own nation wasn't using massive doses of violence to solve its problems. Their questions hit home, and I knew that I could never again raise my voice against the violence of the oppressed in the ghettos without having first spoken clearly to the greatest purveyor of violence in the world today—my own government."[5] Every time our government chooses to use military force to bring about change in the world, it once again teaches our children the myth of redemptive violence, the myth that violence can be an instrument for good. This is precisely the logic we are trying to rid ourselves of, especially here in the inner city, and even more so for those of us who have pledged allegiance to the cross rather than the sword, and heed Jesus' rebuke to Peter that "all who draw the sword will die by the sword" (Matt. 26:52). Violence infects us. We begin to believe that violence can bring peace in our world, in our neighborhoods, in our homes, in our hearts. I think of the memorial garden a few blocks from my house, near the inner-city school with the most graduates who died in Vietnam; it's no coincidence that it is in one of the poorest neighborhoods in our city. Here's a video I shot in the memorial garden: *https://www.youtube.com/watch?v=IOwDeoeNLeo*. One of my friends who is a veteran of the Iraq war talks about how many young people who struggle economically are compelled to join the military because it promises to pay for education and an income. He says, "We don't have a draft in America,

---

5. Ibid.

but we do have an economic draft." In our neighborhood, recruiters give out flyers that say, "They told you to go to college; they just didn't tell you how to pay for it. Join the Navy." This is one thing that motivated us to start our scholarship fund—each year we work with Eastern University to provide a full-tuition scholarship for a young scholar from our neighborhood. I've written more about the economic draft here on CNN: *http://religion.blogs.cnn.com/2010/06/25/my-take-the-economic-draft/.* There are plenty of times I'd like to bust out a sword and cut someone's ear off like Peter. But . . .

I began to consider what it means to pledge allegiance to Jesus and his cross. After nearly a year of discernment, seeking the wisdom of God and close friends, I decided to join the chorus of peacemakers, the incredible witness of Voices in the Wilderness[6] and the Christian Peacemaker Teams[7] and Peaceful Tomorrows.[8] After counting the cost of going to Iraq and the cost of not going to Iraq, I went to Baghdad in March 2003 with the Iraq Peace Team, a team of clergy, priests, veterans, doctors, journalists, students, and concerned citizens. I put together a statement articulating why I was going,[9] and I headed to Iraq, where I ended up living through the most beautiful and horrific month of my life. I realize many of you reading this don't remember the "shock and awe" bombing of Baghdad, the war in Iraq, or September 11th. Some of you weren't even born yet. This bombing in March 2003 was unprecedented and horrific. On

---

6. *www.vitw.org.*

7. *www.cpt.org.*

8. *www.peacefultomorrows.org.*

9. The statement is included in appendix 2. And my full journal from Iraq can be read and copied from our website, *www.thesimpleway.org.*

average, 941 bombs a day were dropped during Operation Shock and Awe. Estimates on the number of war-related deaths during the invasion range between 600,000 to one million. It's also estimated that more than seven thousand of those were civilians killed in the initial bombing. I was there during the bombing of Baghdad, visiting homes, hospitals, and families—and going to worship services with the hundreds of Iraqi Christians I met there.

Essentially, I went to Iraq because I believe in a God of scandalous grace. I have pledged allegiance to a King who loved evildoers so much he died for them, teaching us that there is something worth dying for but nothing worth killing for.

I went to Iraq in the footsteps of an executed and risen God. The Jesus of the margins suffered an imperial execution by an oppressive regime of wealthy and pious elites. And now he dares me and woos me to come and follow, to take up my cross, to lose my life to find it, with the promises that life is more powerful than death and that it is more courageous to love our enemies than to kill them.

I went to Iraq to stop terrorism. There are extremists, both Muslim and Christian, who kill in the name of their gods. Their leaders are millionaires who live in comfort while their citizens die neglected in the streets. But I believe in another kingdom that belongs to the poor and to the peacemakers.

I went to Iraq to stand in the way of war. Thousands of soldiers have gone to Iraq, willing to kill people they do not know because of a political allegiance. I went willing to die for people I do not know because of a spiritual allegiance.

I went to Iraq as a missionary. In an age of omnipresent war, it is my hope that Christian peacemaking becomes the new face of global missions. May we stand by those who face the impending wrath of the empire and whisper, "God loves you, I love you, and if my country bombs your country, I will be right here with you." Otherwise, our gospel has little integrity. As one of the saints said, "If they come for the innocent and do not pass over our bodies, then cursed be our religion."

I went to Iraq hoping to interrupt terrorism and war, in small ways and in large ways, in moments of crisis and in everyday rhythms. I went to Iraq as an extremist for love. Christian Peacemaker Teams is still in Iraq and nearly every troubled region in the US. Here's the original statement of my friend Ron Sider, speaking in 1984 at the Mennonite World Conference, that was catalytic in the birth of CPT: "Unless we are prepared to risk injury and death in nonviolent opposition to the injustice our societies foster, we don't dare even whisper another word about pacifism to our sisters and brothers in those desperate lands. Unless we are ready to die developing new nonviolent attempts to reduce international conflict, we should confess that we never really meant the cross was an alternative to the sword. Unless the majority of our people in nuclear nations are ready as congregations to risk social disapproval and government harassment in a clear call to live without nuclear weapons, we should sadly acknowledge that we have betrayed our peacemaking heritage. Making peace is as costly as waging war. Unless we are prepared to pay the cost of peacemaking, we have no right to claim the label or preach the message."

FAMILY IN IRAQ

Looking back now, I am embarrassed at how surprised I was to find friends and family in Baghdad. It was as if I thought Iraq was filled with Osama bin Ladens and Saddam Husseins, and not with families and children just like ours.[10] I grew especially close to one of the "shoeshine boys," a homeless boy about ten years old named Mussef, who shined shoes to survive. The first day I met him, he was begging me for money to buy something to eat. I had been forewarned not to get in the habit of giving money to the boys who lined the streets in front of our apartments. When I stubbornly said no to his relentless attempts on my wallet, he turned away and muttered a string of obscenities. I whipped my head around in shock, and he took off running. Not the best first impression. Day after day, though, we grew on each other. We went for walks, turned somersaults, and yelled at the airplanes, "Salaam!" (Peace!) Every day when I walked outside, he would run at me full speed, jump into my arms, and kiss me on the cheek. And I had the shiniest shoes in Baghdad.

One day, Mussef joined our group on a walk into the center of town carrying pictures of Iraqi children and families suffering from the war and sanctions. Journalists took pictures and talked to us as we stood in one of Baghdad's busiest intersections. Mussef had begun to internalize what was happening. His shining face became bleak. Nothing I could do made him smile. As the group went home, and the cameras left, Mussef and I continued to sit. He mimicked with his hand the falling of bombs and made the sound of explosions, as tears welled up in his eyes. Suddenly, he turned and latched onto my neck. He began to weep; his body shook as he gasped for each breath of air. I began to cry. I was glad the cameras were gone as we wept as friends, as brothers, not as a peacemaker and a victim. Afterward, I took him to eat, banquet style, tipping everyone

---

10. In fact, the Iraqi population is very young. UNICEF reports that nearly half of the population is under the age of twenty.

extravagantly so my guest would be welcomed. Every five minutes, he would ask me, "Are you okay?" I would nod and ask, "Are you okay?" And he would nod.[11]

In Iraq, we were considered guests and received such warm hospitality—meals that were on the house, free rides from taxi drivers. In their minds, ordinary people separated us from our government. The Iraq people were incredibly strong. In the midst of the bombing, they still had weddings, music festivals, and soccer matches in the streets.

One day, we had a birthday party for a young girl named Amal, who was turning thirteen. We had a feast, grilling out in a park nearby. We played all kinds of crazy games, blew bubbles, juggled, turned flips, and ran in circles until we couldn't stand up anymore. As we were playing a little game of balloon volleyball, bombs began to explode in the background. The adults all looked uneasily at each other, but we kept playing. Then one explosion hit very close. A couple of us huddled down with the little children. I looked at this young teenager who had courage I could only dream of; she looked deep into my timid eyes and said, "It's okay; don't be scared." And she smacked me on the head with the balloon. These children were raised hearing bombs—in 1998, in 1991—and yet they will still play in the park with people whose country is destroying theirs. Amal joked about how she might think differently about the war if Bush would bomb her school. When we asked her what she wanted for her birthday, she said, "Peace." And it wasn't because we told her to. She really believed that someday people might not kill each other. As bombs continued to thunder in the background, I was

---

11. To be honest, we were both scared out of our minds, but we each wanted to ensure that the other would not start weeping again.

reminded once again that life is more powerful than death, that children can teach old tyrants and cynics how to love. I was reminded of the verses in Isaiah that prophesy the coming of a reconciled creation and people, where "the wolf will live with the lamb, the leopard will lie down with the goat, the calf and the lion and the yearling together." The last words in the verse are "and a little child will lead them" (Isa. 11:6).

I was invited to worship services nearly every day while in Iraq. The Christians in Baghdad gave me so much hope for the church. One of the most powerful worship services I've ever experienced was just a few days before I headed home. Hundreds and hundreds of Christians from all over the Middle East had gotten together—Catholic, Protestant, Orthodox. They read a statement from the Christian church directed to the Muslim community, declaring that they love them and believe they were created in the image of God. Then we sang familiar songs like "Amazing Grace." We said the Lord's Prayer in several languages. They led us to the cross and prayed a prayer similar to the one Jesus prayed when he was on the cross: "Forgive us, for we know not what we are doing." Hundreds and hundreds of people continued to try to get into the service and ended up gathering outside with candles. It was holy.

Afterward, I was able to meet with one of the bishops who had organized the gathering, and I explained to him that I was shocked to find so many Christians in Iraq. He looked at me, puzzled, and then gently said, "Yes, my friend, this is where it all began. This is the land of your ancestors. That is the Tigris River, and the Euphrates. Have you read about them?" I was floored—by my ignorance and by the ancient roots of my faith. It is the land of my ancestors. Christianity was not invented in America . . . how about that?

The bishop went on to tell me that the church in the Middle East was deeply concerned about the church in the United States. He said, "Many Americans are for this war."

I nodded.

And he asked, "But what are the Christians saying?"

My heart sank. I tried to explain to him that many of the Christians in the US are confused and hope that this is a way God could liberate the Iraqi people.

He shook his head and said, very humbly, "But we Christians do not believe that. We believe 'blessed are the peacemakers.' We believe if you pick up the sword, you die by the sword. We believe in the cross." Tears welled up in my eyes as he said, "We will be praying for you. We will be praying for the church in the US . . . to be the church."

ROAD OF ANGELS

I left Baghdad with other members of our peace team in a three-car convoy heading for Jordan through the western Iraqi desert. Bridges were down, debris covered the streets, and destroyed vehicles were strewn along the road. A few hours into the trip, we began looking for gas. One gas station was bombed, another abandoned. Then another. With tanks on empty, we stopped at a final gas station, also vacant. We were joined by a van filled with students from the University of Baghdad who were headed for the refugee camp in Jordan. Before long, they had hooked the battery of their van up to the gas pump, and using the energy from the battery, they filled our car with gas. And we headed off with renewed vigor. The roads became increasingly treacherous. There were bombed-out buses and inciner-ated ambulances. We swerved out of the way of light posts, car parts, and shrapnel. Soon we could see the gigantic smoke clouds from bomb hits, only seconds old on the near horizon. One of the bombs hit only about a kilometer away. The drivers became increasingly tense, speeding up to about 80 mph to minimize the likelihood of our becoming "collateral damage" in this war.

We began to lose sight of each other, and suddenly one of the tires on our car, the last in the convoy, burst with a loud pop and we spun out of control. The car plunged into a ditch and flipped onto its side. We were able to climb out of the doors on the top side of the car and pull everyone out. The five of us were all injured and badly shaken, and two had life-threatening injuries—one person was bleeding profusely from his head. The first thing I noticed was a car of Iraqi civilians that had stopped to help us. (It was the first car to pass, and within one minute of the accident.) Without a second thought, they piled all of us into their car and headed to the nearest town, waving a white sheet out the window as the war planes continued to fly overhead. Miraculously, only minutes away, there was a little town called Rutba, a city of approximately twenty thousand people located about 150 km east of the Jordan border. As they drove us to the hospital, many thoughts went through my mind, including the worry that we would become hostages. So I handed them a sheet that explained in Arabic who we were, and they nodded with smiles.

As we drove into the town, we were deeply disturbed to see that it was devastated by bombing. Before we could get out of the car, doctors greeted us, and the town began to gather. When they learned that several of us were from the US, the head doctor asked loudly, "Why this? Why? Why is your government doing this?" We had frequently asked this question ourselves. With tears in his eyes, he explained that only a couple of days earlier, one of the bombs had hit the hospital, the children's ward. So they could not take us to the hospital. He added with a dignified smile, "But you are our brothers, and we will take care of you. We take care of everyone—Christian, Muslim, Iraqi, American . . . it doesn't matter. We are all human beings. We are all sisters and brothers." And they set up a little clinic with four beds and saved my friend's life, apologizing for the scarcity of supplies due to the sanctions. The townspeople began to bring blankets and water. When we inquired about going back to the car to get our passports and bags, they looked at us like we were crazy, explaining that even their ambulances had been hit by the bombs, but they smiled and invited us to live in Rutba. A gifted journalist named Greg Barrett wrote a book titled *The Gospel of Rutba*, and he traveled back to Rutba with us on the return trip we made in 2010. For a while the US denied bombing the hospital in Rutba and other atrocities, but Greg did an amazing job snooping around, turning over stones, and telling the truth—the sad, haunting truth. And he also did an amazing job recounting the beautiful story of hospitality, a modern rendition of the Good Samaritan story Jesus told.

By that time, the other cars in our convoy had returned and found us, having been told by the van of university students that the car had crashed. And we had a lovely reunion. (After passing the car, they weren't sure we were still alive.) We finished the tenuous journey through the war zone, stopping briefly by the car to get our belongings and heading for the border. As we left, the townspeople and doctors gave us hugs, kissed us, and placed their hands on their hearts. We offered the doctors money, but they insisted that they were caring for us as family. They did have one request: "Tell the world about Rutba." And we have. My close friends Jonathan and Leah Wilson-Hartgrove, who were in that convoy with me, started a community just a few weeks after returning from Iraq. Their community in Durham, North Carolina, is called the Rutba House, and they do their best to practice the hospitality that we received in that little town.

The doctors told us to "tell the world about Rutba," and we did. We told the story hundreds of times, and the Rutba House in Durham is a living witness to how that experience moved us. But it was always a dream of ours to visit Rutba again.

Seven years later, in 2010, we got to go back. The five of us who were in the car accident in 2003 were all able to go, and we were joined by several friends, one of whom was a soldier in Fallujah who wanted to return to Iraq as a peacemaker, and another was Greg Barrett, who wrote *The Gospel of Rutba*.

We drove that treacherous desert road from Jordan to the Anbar Province and into the little town of Rutba. When we got there, it was like something out of a movie. The whole town had gathered to greet us like royalty. They had found the doctors who had saved our lives, and we embraced with tears flowing freely. We laughed together as they explained that when they first heard we were coming back, they thought we had forgotten something valuable like a computer or a camera! But when they heard we were coming back just because we wanted to visit and rekindle the friendship, they were deeply moved. Someone did mention that there are a few militants who might want to kill us, but it was "only a few." And they slept beside our beds with AK47s to protect us. (I often laugh about how this did not fit into my theology of nonviolence, but I was grateful for their hospitality!)

And then they insisted that we had to meet the mayor of Rutba. As we met with this kind man with a warm smile, he spoke of how stories like this, and friendships like the ones we were all forging, move the world. It is not war but love that brings peace.

Then he said that he would like to see Rutba create a more permanent partnership with a city in the United States and become "sister cities." I ambitiously made the pitch for Philly. "It's the City of Love," I said. But the mayor nixed it quick: "No, Philadelphia is too big. Rutba is small. We need a small city in the US." Then he explained to us that he had been to one city in the US and he loved it. It was a little town in North Carolina that reminded him of Rutba. That town was Durham.

It was a Pentecostal moment! I started weeping, in utter shock. And I explained to him that a community had started in Durham, inspired by Rutba's hospitality, and that the community was called Rutba House.

Gleaming, the mayor declared with all the official clout warranted by his position as mayor, "Then it is done. We will be sister cities with Durham." Then he added, "And we will start a community of peace and reconciliation in Rutba, and we will name it Durham House."

This was one of the most moving and surreal experiences I have ever had. It is also one of those stories that ends with "to be continued." Rutba and the Anbar Province continue to be one of the most troubled corners of the world, making communication next to impossible and travel there equally difficult. So keep it all in your prayers. And if you meet someone who has $100,000 lying around, we'd love for them to help rebuild the hospital that was bombed. Until then, we'll keep telling the story of Rutba, and we'll keep living out the love they showed us in that magical little town.

The story is a testimony to the tremendous courage and generosity of the Iraqi people. They have also reminded us not to tell it in a way that makes the experience seem extraordinary or exceptional. And they are right. Arab hospitality is something we experienced over and over again. I am convinced that had we wrecked in another town, there would have been another "Rutba" around the corner. It exemplifies our time in Baghdad, in all its beauty and in all its horror. When the people of Rutba put their hands over their hearts as a sign of respect, it struck me how similar it looked to saluting the flag to pledge allegiance. It was as if they touched their hearts to pledge to love and care for us, a beautiful sign of an allegiance that runs deeper than family and biology, an allegiance whose only banner is love.

It was refreshing to find family in Iraq and to bring the stories of those sisters and brothers back home.

It was also refreshing to bring to the Iraqi people the stories of the hundreds and hundreds of creative and prophetic actions for peace being taken in the United States. People back home began to vigil, lobby, and cry out in the streets and in the federal buildings. Over a hundred people were arrested for blocking the doors of the federal building in Philadelphia. They had gathered not in the polarizing anger of street protest but in the quiet, revolutionary subordination that influential Mennonite theologian John Howard Yoder speaks of.[12] Revolutionary subordination exposes the evils of power and violence without mirroring them, by gently allowing them to destroy themselves and then rising above the ruins. This approach, of course, is exemplified by Jesus, who was led like "a lamb to slaughter"; it was with revolutionary subordination that Jesus "disarmed the powers and authorities" and made a "public

---

12. John Howard Yoder, *The Politics of Jesus* (Grand Rapids: Eerdmans, 1972).

spectacle of them, triumphing over them by the cross" (Col. 2:15). His was a humble redemptive suffering that flew in the face of the arrogant myth of redemptive violence. The protesters in Philly were not pointing fingers and thanking God that they were "not like the evildoers." They were simply beating their chests and saying, God have mercy on us sinners, for the mess we have made of your world. In fact, many of them duct-taped their mouths shut to symbolize the silenced voices. I remember hearing about it while I was in Iraq. Alexa, the first little child to live in our community at the Simple Way, held a sign reading "Toddlers for peace." And I remember seeing a picture of my community partner Michelle with a button that said, "I have family in Iraq." I knew she was thinking about me. And I knew she was thinking much more broadly—about the Iraqi children and the US soldiers, a family suffering far too much because we know not what we do, as a wise man once perceived.

There was a beautiful moment right after I returned from Iraq when the kids in the ghetto cried out against the violence on our streets and in our world. The kids on my block had decorated the street with sidewalk chalk and a slogan that read "No war—forever." Once again the grass pierces concrete, love overcomes hatred, and nonviolence breaks through the ghetto streets. We were learning the Way of the Prince of Peace, and we were teaching the Way to our kids.

One of the things that became painfully clear to me in Iraq is that what's at stake today is the reputation not just of America but of Christianity, and that's what keeps me up at night. I heard people in Iraq call leaders in the US "Christian extremists," just as leaders here speak of "Muslim extremists." Everyone is declaring war and asking for God's blessing. One beautiful Iraqi mother threw her hands in the air and said, "Your country is declaring war in the name of God and asking God's blessing, and that is the same thing my country is doing. What kind of God is this? What has happened to the God of love, to the Prince of Peace?" Her question haunts me.

A woman in the US came up to me after I had spoken about my time in Iraq and told me with deep sincerity that she wasn't really very political, she just wanted Muslim folks in Iraq to come to know the love and grace of Jesus. I told her that that is exactly what I want. We considered together the ethos of our world and asked the question, Are Muslim people any closer to understanding the gospel of peace and the God of love? And the answer was quite clear to us as we sat in a prayerful silence. In addition to the great work of Christian Peacemaker Teams, Muslim Peacemaker Teams, Voices for Creative Nonviolence, Mennonite Central Committee, Doctors without Borders, and all the other groups that have been working for peace and resurrection in Iraq for decades, there are some magnificent new organizations on the scene, like the Preemptive Love Coalition, whose fantastic motto is "Love now, and ask questions later." They have organized a host of international doctors who work alongside Iraqi doctors to save lives. Working from a list of more than thirty thousand children who will die without surgery, they provide surgeries for kids no matter who their parents are. And they have some of the most redemptive stories I have ever heard. Hardened hearts have melted as they watch folks from "enemy" countries save their family members' lives. Muslim leaders have had visions and dreams in which Jesus visits them in their sleep. Amazing stuff. You can read more in my friend Jeremy Courtney's book *Preemptive Love*.

Too often we just do what makes sense to us and ask

God to bless it. In the Beatitudes, God tells us what God blesses—the poor, the peacemakers, the hungry, those who mourn, those who show mercy—so we should not ask God's blessing on a declaration that we will have no mercy on evildoers. We know all too well that we have a God who shows mercy on evildoers, for if he didn't, we'd all be in big trouble, and for that, this evildoer is very glad. Rather than do what makes sense to us and ask God's blessing, we'd do better to surround ourselves with those whom God promises to bless, and then we need not ask God's blessing. It's just what God does.

When I returned from Iraq, I was speaking everywhere, from megachurches to activist rallies to the United Nations. I've heard so many beautiful stories of courage. Congregations that have caught the vision for God's borderless love and erected the Iraqi and Afghan flags alongside the US flag at their altars. Originally, I thought that I went to Iraq for the Iraqi people and for the kids in my neighborhood. But as I have traveled, I have come to see that I also went to Iraq for our friends and family members in the military. Over and over, soldiers have come to me with tears in their eyes, pouring out their inner conflict as they feel their spiritual and national allegiances collide. Soldiers have come to the altar to ask for forgiveness for what they did in Iraq. One young soldier came forward for an altar call in which I invited people to "disarm" and lay their burdens on the altar. He said that he was on one of the ships that fired the Tomahawk missiles into Baghdad while I was there, and now he was living with that. And we prayed and cried out to God. Another older soldier came up to me and said, "I have been all over the world with the military. I was in Afghanistan. I was in Iraq." With tears in his eyes, he told me about his struggle with his identity, and he handed me his dog tags from around his neck. Over and over, we have had soldiers visit our community and live with us; we have helped some of them leave the military. Others have returned missionally, leading Bible studies in the military like they were in a little Christian underground. Another friend still in the air force told me about Bible studies they were doing in the military, reading books by authors like Walter Wink and John Howard Yoder, prophets of Christian peacemaking.[13]

One of the folks I was in Iraq with is Charlie Liteky. In 1968 Charlie Liteky was given the highest award in the US, the Medal of Honor by President Lyndon Johnson. In the movie *Forrest Gump*, they dubbed Tom Hanks over Charlie as he is given the award. What is not as well known is that in 1986, Charlie joined some of the most decorated veterans in the US as they returned their Medals of Honor and renounced all war.

Charlie and I got to be in Iraq together in 2003 with the Iraq Peace Team. One of the things he taught me is that veterans often know the horrors of war better than anyone. We can see it in the suicide rate (one a day for soldiers, twenty-two a day for veterans) and in the rate of homelessness and addiction (there are fifty thousand homeless veterans).

When we fight for peace, we are fighting for them. We honor the men and women in uniform by trying to put an end to war. I remember Charlie holding a sign while we were in Iraq that said, "I hate war as only a veteran can." It reminded me of the words of Ernest Hemingway: "Never

---

13. In fact, he helped me edit this book, making sure I'm not just preaching to the choir. After reading the manuscript, he sent me an e-mail saying he is torn by his military duties, as he is a highly respected soldier, and he's not sure what to do next.

think that war, no matter how necessary, nor how justified, is not a crime. Ask the infantry and ask the dead."

I now have a pile of dog tags from veterans who have told me they want to be "free of their chains." And I am so grateful for the courageous witness of veterans for peace like my friend Logan and Ben Corey. There are countless resources for vets out there, but one of the newest is Centurion's Guild, which is led by current and former service members. They have taught me that the person who pulls the trigger feels a part of themselves die. Perhaps that helps explain the soaring suicide rate among the military. *Time* magazine had a cover story titled "One a Day" that reported that one active-service soldier a day commits suicide, and that number goes up to nearly twenty-two a day when you include veterans. Let's recommit ourselves today to honor the infantry and the dead by committing to build a world without war.

PLEDGING ALLEGIANCE

Rebirth means that we have a new paradigm of "us" and "them." Our central identity is no longer biological. And our central allegiance is no longer national. Our pronouns change. Our new "us," as Jesus teaches, is the church, the people of God doing the will of the Father. Certainly, there are times when America is that. And there are times when America is not. When we hear that "we" were attacked, do we think "we" the church or "we" as Americans? What is our primary identity? When the Bush administration said that a way of life was being attacked, it was true, but it was not the gospel that was being attacked. It is no coincidence that what was attacked wasn't the World Council of Churches but the symbols of the corporate global economy and the arms that would protect it. More than ever, we must be asking what will create a safer, more sustainable world. And I believe God has given us a vision for that, a vision that looks very different from the dream of America. One soldier I met returned from Iraq deeply disturbed. He said, "I just risked my life for the American dream, and I am not even sure I believe in it anymore. And I am pretty sure that the world cannot afford it." No wonder Jesus began to weep as he overlooked Jerusalem, crying out, "If you had only known what would bring you peace" (Luke 19:42).

Over the past couple of years since I was in Iraq, the drums of war have died down and the desperate cries of lonely survivors have rippled across the globe. And in these raw moments of pain, I have seen so many signs of hope that history will not again repeat itself with more precious blood shed. Nearly every denomination in the World Council of Churches declared that the war in Iraq was not God's will and not in line with any Christian tradition, including just-war theory.[14] The pope spoke out and sent a convoy to Baghdad while we were there. Evangelical theologians from all over the earth have written extensively about the war in Iraq and its alternatives (like my friend Rene Padilla in Argentina, author of *War and Terror: A Latin Perspective*), and this broad voice gives credibility to the speck of Christianity we see here in the US. After traveling internationally, I have been refreshed to see a global church

---

14. I just met with a Methodist conference and heard bishops voice their deep concern for the Christian identity and the Methodist tradition in particular (since the president professes Methodist faith). In line with Matthew 18:15–20, they have asked to meet with the president and have sent him a letter to express grave concern, declaring that what is being done in Iraq is not Wesley's teaching, Methodist theology, or just-war practice. These are tremendous signs of hope.

with such integrity, a church which for the most part does not suffer the polarization and dualism of evangelicalism in the United States. Prominent scholar and evangelical thinker (and dear friend!) Ron Sider has written two new books that are immensely helpful in thinking about war and militarism. The first is *The Early Church on Killing*, in which Ron has carefully documented what the early Christians had to say about war and military service, and other issues of life. It blows your mind to see how consistently the earliest Christians stood on the side of life, and against the taking of life in every way—abortion, capital punishment, violence in all forms. None of them ever condoned killing in any form, even in war. There was a small debate about whether a Christian could serve in the military if they refused to kill (keep in mind in ancient Rome the military was not just a war machine but it was also how bridges and roads were built, making it much more conceivable that you could be in the military in a noncombat role). But certainly Christians could be in the military only if they refused to kill. Ron's second (recent) book is *Nonviolent Action*, a close look at how nonviolent movements have worked to change history. His fundamental thesis for this book is that nonviolence works when we try it. The problem is not that we have tried the way of Jesus and it failed but that we haven't really tried the way of Jesus very often.

CHAPTER 8

JESUS MADE ME DO IT!

When I got home from Iraq, a woman came up to me, pointed her finger in my face, and said, "How dare you be so careless with your life and put your mother through all that? Jesus would be shaking his finger in your face, saying, 'How dare you be so reckless?'" I listened, silently, wondering what Jesus she was talking about. The Jesus who died on a Roman cross and invited his disciples to do the same? The Jesus who taught his disciples that if they wanted to find their lives, they should lose them? (And most of them did, perhaps leaving behind some angry parents.) For centuries, Christians have been jailed, beaten, and executed for preaching that Jesus. I recently heard a preacher say, "It's a good thing Jesus wasn't too worried about his safety, or he would have never left heaven." We live in a safety-obsessed society, held hostage to fear. Fear robs us of all sorts of miracles and experiences. Fear often leads to violence. But Scripture says that love casts out fear. As you read the stories of the early Christians and martyrs, you find that they laughed at death. They stared fear in the face without flinching. But they were also human. I'm sure they got scared at times. I remember when I was in Afghanistan visiting the Afghan Peace Volunteers. One of the folks I was with was Maireed Maguire, who is one of the most courageous people I've ever met. She won the Nobel Peace Prize for her work in Northern Ireland. As she was speaking about her experiences, one of the Afghan women asked her if they ever got scared as they stood in the way of the violence that was taking the lives of their children. And in her charming Irish accent, she said, "Of course, we got scared! There is nothing wrong with being scared. But fear is something different. Fear is when we let being scared stop us from doing what love requires of us." Brilliant. It is natural to be scared. But fear should never stop us from what love calls us to do, even if love calls us to give up our lives for another person. How was I to tell this lovely lady that Jesus was actually the one responsible for my traveling to Iraq in the heat of the bombing, not a decision that I would rationally make, even on my worst days?

I had a college professor who said, "All around you, people will be tiptoeing through life, just to arrive at death safely. But dear children, do not tiptoe. Run, hop, skip, or dance, just don't tiptoe." In my youth-group days, I had seen all too many wild would-be Jesus radicals fall by the wayside because they had never been trusted with the adventure of revolutionary living. When I was a youth leader, one of the high school kids who had "given his life to Jesus" got busted only a few weeks later for having acid in school. I remember asking in disappointment, "What happened, bro? What went wrong?" He just shrugged his shoulders and said, "I got bored." Bored? God forgive us for all those we have lost because we made the gospel boring. I am convinced that if we lose kids to the culture of drugs and materialism, of violence and war, it's because we don't dare them, not because we don't entertain them. It's because we make the gospel too easy, not because we make it too difficult. Kids want to do something heroic with their lives, which is why they play video games and join the army. But what are they to do with a church that teaches them to tiptoe through life so they can arrive safely at death?

THE DANGER OF SAFETY

I'm not sure where we get the notion that Christianity is safe or that Christians should play it cool. Growing up, I always thought that Christians were good upstanding citizens, but the more I get to know Jesus, the more trouble he seems to get me into. Søren Kierkegaard puts it well: "To want to admire, instead of follow, Christ is not an invention of bad people; no it is more an invention of those who spinelessly want to keep themselves detached at a safe distance from Jesus."[1]

Some Christians take so few risks, it's no wonder folks have a hard time believing in heaven. Most of us live in such fear of death that it's as if no one really believes in resurrection anymore. Sometimes people ask me if I am scared, living in the inner city. I usually reply, "I'm more scared of the suburbs." The Scriptures say that we should not fear those things which can destroy the body, but we are to fear that which can destroy the soul (Matt. 10:28). While the ghettos may have their share of violence and crime, the suburbs are the home of the more subtle demonic forces—numbness, complacency, comfort—and it is these that can eat away at our souls.

My dear mother (bless her heart) has some things to say about safety. Again, I'm her only child, so there's a lot at stake for her. As she has watched me go to jail and travel to Iraq, with God's hand evidently in it all, my mom has learned a lot about faith, safety, and risk. It has not been easy, but recently

---

1. Søren Kierkegaard, *Provocations: Spiritual Writings of Kierkegaard*, ed. Charles E. Moore (Farmington, PA: Plough, 2002), 86.

she told me, "I have come to see that we Christians are not called to safety, but we are promised that God will be with us when we are in danger, and there is no better place to be than in the hands of God." Perhaps the most dangerous place for a Christian to be is in safety and comfort.

In his book *The Lion, the Witch, and the Wardrobe*, C. S. Lewis portrays this dangerous encounter with the God that should make all of us shiver. Lucy is about to meet Aslan, the lion, and she asks, "Is—is he a man?"

> "Aslan a man!" said Mr. Beaver sternly. "Certainly not. I tell you he is the King of the wood and the son of the great Emperor-beyond-the-Sea. Don't you know who is the King of the Beasts? Aslan is a lion—*the* Lion, the great Lion."
>
> "Ooh!" said Susan, "I'd thought he was a man. Is he—quite safe? I shall feel rather nervous about meeting a lion."
>
> "That you will, dearie, and no mistake," said Mrs. Beaver; "if there's anyone who can appear before Aslan without their knees knocking, they're either braver than most or else just silly."
>
> "Then he isn't safe?" said Lucy.
>
> "Safe?" said Mr. Beaver; "don't you hear what Mrs. Beaver tells you? Who said anything about safe? 'Course he isn't safe. But he's good. He's the King, I tell you."[2]

That's the God I have come to know, a God who is not at all safe, but a God who is good.

---

2. C. S. Lewis, *The Lion, the Witch, and the Wardrobe* (New York: HarperCollins, 1950), 79–80.

A DANGEROUS LOVER

These days, not many people stand before God with their knees knocking. The Scriptures say that the demons believe in Jesus and they "shudder" (James 2:19), but even most Christians don't shudder anymore when they think of Jesus; it has all grown so ordinary and stale. For most of my life, there wasn't much to shudder over, except hell. And now the tables have turned. It's God who makes the demons of hell shudder. I'm not scared of hell. Hell's a hard thing to grasp, but I know how much I want folks to experience God's love and grace, and I know how much more good God is than me, so that helps me rest pretty confidently. Besides, Jesus assures Peter that "the gates of hell will not prevail against the church."[3] So it's not hell that makes me shudder but God, because I have no idea what in the world God's going to dare me to do next.

On the one hand, the shuddering is like that of new lovers—giddy, obsessed, infatuated. Any portrait of or story about our new lover that we can get our hands on, we cling to. Whenever someone mentions his or her name, our eyes twinkle and our hearts jump—that kind of shudder. Jesus, the one I long to fall asleep cuddling with, run off into the woods with, live and die with—my lover.

On the other hand, it is a shiver of awestruck wonder. I have no idea what's going to happen next—just throw my hands in the air and hold on, like riding a good roller coaster. Have you ever seen *The Lion King*? It's like that part

---

3. Gates were built in the walls around cities to fortify them from outsiders. They were for defensive, not offensive, purposes, so many theologians suggest that when Jesus says that the gates of hell will not prevail, he was pointing to the fact that he and the church will storm the gates of hell to rescue those held inside.

where the hyenas are talking about Mufasa, and one of them says his name and they all shake and say, "Ooh! Say it again, say it again . . . Mufasa . . . ooh!" That kind of shudder. "Jesus . . . ooh, say it again." Just the thought brings butterflies to my stomach. That's the Jesus I love. And that's the Jesus who scares me to death. There are plenty of other options for living that will not get you jailed, mocked, or nailed to a cross. And there are much easier ways of being cool than by trying to follow Jesus. I'm just not so sure the cool thing is all it's cracked up to be.

REMEMBERING COOL

I guess everybody's just trying to be cool. I remember the cool days. I used to be cool, chilling with the in-crowd of respectable United Methodists, sporting my bow tie and khaki shorts (oh yes, I did), and toting my Confederate flag. (Okay, that was cool only in East Tennessee in the 1980s.) But everything cool came to an abrupt end, my coolness ruined by a God who has everything backward. I heard that disturbing whisper of Jesus telling me that even the pagans hang out with their cool friends, that instead we are to be extraordinary and hang out with the not-so-cool, the people sitting in the lunchroom alone, folks who talk to themselves and have distinct aromas. In fact, Revelation warns that we must be either hot or cold, because if we are lukewarm (an old-school way of saying "cool"), we will be spit out of God's mouth (Rev. 3:16). The end of cool—left in the smoke of people set on fire by God. I started to think maybe I should beware of things that are cool and normal, because Jesus didn't seem to be either of those.

A few years back, when I had multicolored dreadlocks, I got up to speak to several hundred young people after being introduced as "the coolest Christian ever." Startled and a bit distressed by the intro, I asked for a pair of scissors. I stood on the stage, took my cherished dreads in my hand, and said, "Dear ones, I am afraid I've become too cool. Christians are not called to be cool. We are called to be extraordinary." And then I cut them all off. (And of course, the kids thought that was cool.)

As French theologian Jacques Ellul once said, "Christians should be troublemakers, creators of uncertainty, agents of a dimension incompatible with society." After all, we follow one who certainly had lots of adjectives attached to his reputation, but cool was not among them. (For one thing, it's not Aramaic.) Not to mention ole John the Baptist wearing his camel skin and eating locusts, worse than any thrift-store suit or *Fear Factor* dare. You don't get crucified for being cool; you get crucified for living radically different from the norms of all that is cool in the world. And it's usually the cool people who get the most ticked off, since you are disturbing their order, for it was indeed the cool religious leaders and the cool politicians who killed the Lover from Nazareth. Some things never change. I was speaking at an event and met some high school kids who told me a great story inspired by some of these challenges to coolness. They told me they had been thinking about prom and how it seemed to celebrate the people who were most popular and most attractive, the cool kids. And then they said, "We're not sure how excited Jesus would be about prom." As a prom king myself, I found that a little offensive but decided to hear them out. They went on to explain how they had organized an alternative prom where they invited all the folks in town and from their school who had special physical and mental challenges, and they threw an epic party called Dancing with Disability! Their faces lit up as they told me what it was like to crown one of the kids with Down syndrome as king. In fact, they decided to crown everybody there as kings and queens. A whole room full of folks the world might easily overlook were recognized as royalty that day. Love it.

CITY OF BROTHERLY SHOVE

Jesus teaches that it is nothing extraordinary to love our friends and relatives, people who think and look like us. He says that even the pagans and sinners love their friends (Matt. 5:46–47). But we are to be extraordinary; we are to love people who don't think and look like us, even our enemies.

One of my favorite passages is in Luke 14, where Jesus tells us how to throw a party. Only he doesn't actually call it a party. He's talking to a bunch of religious folks, so he calls it a banquet, but he's talking about a party. He says, "When you give a luncheon or dinner, do not invite your friends, your brothers or sisters, your relatives, or your rich neighbors; if you do, they may invite you back and so you will be repaid. But when you give a banquet, invite the poor, the crippled, the lame, and the blind, and you will be blessed" (vv. 12–14). I had never been to a party like that. All the parties my friends threw, Christian or not, were ones where you invite people who are like you—friends, relatives, rich neighbors, yep. We must not have highlighted that verse. Here's Jesus telling us not to throw parties like that.

A few years ago, I caught a glimpse of the kind of party Jesus wants us to throw, although it got us into some trouble. Philadelphia had begun to pass antihomeless legislation, making it illegal to sleep in the parks, illegal to ask for money, illegal to lie down on the sidewalks. (They even chose to implement it on Dr. King's birthday!) Ironically, the reason for many of these laws was Love Park, which is a historic site in Philly known as a great place for skate-boarding (which was also made illegal). Love Park was a place where homeless folks hung out. It was visible, safe, and central. Folks knew they could go there to give out food or clothing to people on the street. We used to go there back when we were in college, and there are some nice steam vents that kept people (and some big rats) warm. One of the city's boldest moves was passing an ordinance that banned all food from the park. Specifically, it reads, "All persons must cease and desist from distributing food." And they began fining those of us who continued to share food. We started wondering what in the world it meant to love our neighbors as ourselves when they were being jailed for sleeping and eating. As St. Augustine said, "An unjust law is no law at all." What did it mean to submit to authority and yet uphold God's law of love? Either we had to invite them into our home (which reached capacity), or we wanted to be out with them, in solidarity. So we threw a party in Love Park.

About a hundred of us gathered in Love Park with homeless friends. We worshiped, sang, and prayed. Then we served communion, which was illegal. But with clergy and city officials there supporting us, and with police and the media surrounding us, we celebrated communion. Most of the police sat back and watched, not daring to arrest any-one, especially during communion. Then we continued the "breaking of the bread" by bringing in pizzas. It was a love feast, and then we slept overnight in the park with our homeless friends. We did that week after week, with the police watching over us and the media standing by. And then one night after worship, as we slept under the "Love" sign, which we had covered with a big question mark, the police circled the park and arrested all of us. Not the best wake-up call. We were taken to jail in handcuffs. But over and over, many of us slept out, and over and over, we were arrested, though sometimes the police were sympathetic and agreed that we should not be arrested for sleeping. A bunch of bigwig lawyers even called, offering to represent us. We were very thankful and invited them to come and support us, but we decided to be represented by a homeless friend, who wouldn't be able to have fancy lawyers if he were alone. So our buddy Fonz agreed to be our spokesperson.

As we stood before the judge, I wore a shirt that read, "Jesus was homeless." The judge asked me to step forward, and I did. He read my shirt aloud and said, "Hmm. I didn't know that."

I said, "Yes sir, in the Scriptures, Jesus says that 'foxes have holes and birds have nests but the Son of Man has no place to lay his head.'"

The judge paused pensively and said, "You guys might stand a chance."

And we did.

Before we went to court, we read all of the Scriptures where Jesus warns the disciples that they will be dragged before courts and into jails, and they had new meaning for us. He warned them not to worry about what to say, so we didn't. When the time came for us to testify, Fonz stood up in court and said, "Your Honor, we think these laws are wrong." We said, "Amen. What he said."

The district attorney[4] had her stuff together. She was not joking around. We faced numerous charges, jail time, thousands of dollars in fines, and hours and hours of community service. (Imagine that!)

---

4. Honest to goodness, when we were in court once, I accidentally called the district attorney the persecutor instead of the prosecutor. Oops.

The judge said to the court, "What is in question here is not whether these folks broke the law; that is quite clear. What is in question is the constitutionality of the law."

The DA shot back, "The constitutionality of the law is not before this court." And the DA threw her papers on the table.

The judge retorted, "The constitutionality of the law is before every court. Let me remind the court that if it weren't for people who broke unjust laws, we wouldn't have the freedom that we have. We'd still have slavery. That's the story of this country, from the Boston Tea Party to the civil rights movement. These people are not criminals; they are freedom fighters. I find them all not guilty, on every charge."

The papers called it a "Revolutionary Court Decision." And the judge asked us for a "Jesus was homeless" T-shirt.

Those same laws resurfaced again recently, so pray that we get the same judge if we get arrested again! Philadelphia's mayor passed an executive order banning all "outdoor feeding," which means you can't share food with more than four people in public without a permit. But this time we were ready. We even had the same T-shirts from ten years ago. And we had new ones printed that read, "If Jesus had done the fish and loaves miracle in Philly, he would've gone to jail!" People came out of the woodwork to protest this ordinance. (It was almost as if we hadn't missed a beat from ten years ago.) And it was incredible to see people of faith take a courageous stand against injustice.

During the public hearings, one older Pentecostal woman said, "Fifteen years ago, God told me to start making casseroles and taking them out to the street to share with the homeless. I haven't missed a week in fifteen years. If the mayor wants to stop that, then the mayor better talk to God, 'cause he started it all!"

Then a Catholic theologian testified, and it was equally beautiful. He argued that when we share food with the hungry, it is a sacrament. We are not just feeding a pitiful homeless person, but we are feeding Christ. According to Matthew 25, when we do something to the least of these, we do it to Christ. When God asks us if we fed him when he was hungry, we will not say back to God, "Sorry, our mayor wouldn't let us." Our Catholic friend then declared that to say we cannot feed the homeless is to say we cannot feed Christ, and that is a violation of our religious freedom. A federal judged backed that up, declaring that it is indeed a violation of religious freedom to make it illegal to share food with those on the streets. Hallelujah!

Nonetheless, across the United States, laws like these are being passed. More than fifty cities have passed anti-homeless legislation that discriminates against those who do not have homes. These laws have made it illegal to sleep in public, share food with the homeless, ask for spare change, even look for food in the trash. (One city made all trash city property.) One story made national news recently when a ninety-year-old man, Arnold Abbott, in Florida faced charges for feeding the homeless (*http://www.cnn.com/2014/11/04/justice/florida-feeding-homeless-charges/*). Abbott said police confronted him and told him to "drop that plate." It was as if he had a weapon instead of a platter.

What is just as beautiful as the laws are disturbing is to see people of faith and conscience rise up across the country to challenge these laws. One of my favorite stories is from our dear friends at Open Door Community in Atlanta. Folks without permanent housing often have a hard time finding a place to use the restroom, and Atlanta police arrested folks who were caught using the restroom in a park or alleyway. And there were even cases where folks were charged with public indecency and registered as sex offenders. Their lives would be stigmatized by this offense, all because they couldn't find a bathroom. So our friends at Open Door organized a "PEE for FREE with DIGNITY" campaign, calling for public bathrooms in Atlanta. They marched to city hall carrying toilets and insisting that you can't arrest people for not finding a public restroom if there are no public restrooms. And it is part of the momentum that led to public toilets in Atlanta. We need this kind of courage and creativity to expose injustice and change bad laws.

We caught a glimpse of what Paul and Silas saw as they sang and prayed in that jail cell until "the prison doors flew open, and everyone's chains came loose" (Acts 16:26). I began to believe that maybe Jesus really meant that's how we are to throw a party. And I knew that he meant it when he said, "If the world hates you, keep in mind that it hated me first. . . . In this world you will have trouble. But take heart! I have overcome the world" (John 15:18; 16:33). In fact, I remember thinking that if the world does not hate us, perhaps we should question whether we really are part of another kingdom. And of course, the prayer "forgive us our trespasses" has a new ring to it when you're sitting in jail charged with defiant trespassing.

To this day, I hold on to a little saying I had with me in that court, the words of Dr. King: "There is nothing wrong with a traffic law which says you have to stop for a red light. But when a fire is raging, the fire truck goes through that red light, and normal traffic had better get out of its way. Or when a man is bleeding to death, the ambulance goes through those red lights at top speed. There is a fire raging . . . for the poor of this society. Disinherited people all over the world are bleeding to death from deep social and economic wounds. They need brigades of ambulance drivers who will have to ignore the red lights of the present system until the emergency is solved."[5]

And I remember what one of those police officers said one night as we were taken to jail. As he was searching me, he found my Bible in my pocket. "We're going to have to take this," he said. They had never taken my Bible before, so I asked him why. Smiling, he said, "It's a dangerous book. We can't have you reading that." I laughed. His comment lent new meaning to the phrase "sword of the Spirit." As I thought more about it, though, it's true; this is a dangerous book. For centuries, it has gotten people killed, beaten, jailed.

CONSPIRING WITH GOD

It's funny, I've never thought of myself as dangerous, nor do people who know me. But I found out that some people think I might be. After I got back from Iraq, I participated in a gathering in the Bahamas called La Mesa,[6] where a bunch of theologians and pastors and old friends get together to talk trash and get a tan. We had a delightful time. Heading back to Philly, I was, as usual, significantly early arriving at the airport. (I've become accustomed to getting "randomly" searched every time.) But this time, things were a little different. I was asked by the officers at the checkpoint to step aside for questioning, which I willingly did. They asked me what I do (which is hard to explain). They asked me what I was in the islands for. I told them to talk with friends. They asked me what we were

---

5. This is from Dr. King's book *The Trumpet of Conscience*. I found it in my favorite collection of Dr. King's writings: *A Testament of Hope*, ed. James M. Washington (San Francisco: HarperSanFrancisco, 1986), 647.

6. If you ever have to suffer for Christ down in the Bahaman islands, make sure you visit our friends at New Providence Community Church (*www.npcconline.org*).

talking about, and I decided to play it safe and answered, "Jesus." That may not have been the best idea, since they sat me down and interrogated me. They dug through all of my stuff—pictures, articles, books—and went page by page through all of my folders. They asked me about my trip to Iraq, which I did not try to skirt around. (They seemed to have Orwellian knowledge of it anyway.) But I was glad to tell them all about Iraq, and about the gospel that was getting me in so much trouble. They seemed genuinely interested. And then they blasted me with questions for the next two hours, after which they told me I would have to come back the next day and do it all again. By this point, obviously, I had missed my plane. So I lethargically agreed. (There are worse places to get stuck.)

The next day, we did it all again, with a few more officers. It went a little quicker this time, but they confiscated all of my buttons[7] before they sent me on.

I was glad to finally be on that plane and thought I was home free. As we were preparing to land, though, there was an announcement on the intercom: "Would passenger Mr. Shane Claiborne please hit your call button." So I looked around, a little embarrassed, and hit it. The attendant came to me and said that there were a couple of officers who needed to talk with me, and they would be meeting me upon arrival. I started to wonder if I was on one of those hidden-camera shows.

When we landed, two casually dressed plainclothes officers escorted me off the plane, flashing their Department of Homeland Security badges. They were suspiciously friendly

---

7. The buttons were handmade at the Simple Way and were inscribed with such threatening slogans as, "If terror is the enemy, then love is the hero," "God bless everyone," and "Jesus is my president."

as we sat down to talk. I hesistate to say it, since it seems uncannily like Hollywood, but I kid you not, they opened up a thick file with my name on it. I could see pictures and articles and pieces of the Simple Way website. And we talked. I shared with them the gospel and warned them that it could get them in trouble or cost them their jobs, but that it was all worth it. With a twinkle in their eyes, they let me go. I said, "Bye . . . until we meet again." So I really do think they were just being overly cautious, since apparently some of the September 11th terrorists had gone through the Bahamas. And I enjoyed getting to share my experiences and the gospel with them.

As I think about it all, I cannot help but giggle that a handful of folks going to Iraq to love their enemies and take medications to Iraqi children could be perceived as potential threats.[8] But I've started to read some more parts of the Scriptures a little differently now. When the Bible speaks of "principalities and powers," I used to think about demons and exorcisms. But when you look a little closer, it reads, "For our struggle is not against flesh and blood, but against the rulers, against the authorities, against the powers of this dark world and against the spiritual forces of evil" (Eph. 6:12).[9] I know a few good police officers and now a

---

8. Not to mention that the US government has now initiated a suit against the group I went to Iraq with, and some of us could face prison sentences. We're not too worried, though. Even the Bush-appointed judge has said that the government's case does not look too good and that the prosecutors have a long road ahead of them.

9. It is widely held that Paul wrote these words during his two-year prison term in Rome. It's interesting that the word he uses here for the authorities we wrestle with is the same word he uses in the notorious verses in Romans that folks use to prooftext atrocities committed by world leaders. When folks use Romans 13:1, "Let everyone be subject to the governing authorities, for there is no authority except that which God has established," to say that we should not do anything that collides with government leaders, I invite them to hear that with the ears of Iraqi

couple of DHS officers well enough to see that they are not the enemy. But there is something going on in the world, and very real powers stand in the way of God's Spirit. I am developing the eyes with which to see them.

John Dominic Crossan is one of the leading contemporary scholars of the historical Jesus and early Christianity, and a controversial figure. Whether it's with the Jesus Seminar or the religious right, Crossan catalyzes debate as people seek to understand Jesus. I will shrewdly avoid the delicate theological issues he stirs up, but one of his books[10] begins with a fascinating story, a fantastic dream Crossan recounts in which Jesus comes to him and says, "I've read your book and it's quite good. So now are you ready to join me and my vision?" Crossan pauses and replies, "I don't think I have the courage, Jesus, but I did describe it well, didn't I?" Jesus thanks him for his contribution to biblical scholarship and in a whisper dares him, "That's not enough . . . Come and follow." After writing hundreds of pages about this Jesus, Crossan stands bewildered, knowing all too well that it will cost him everything he has and believes in, maybe even his very life.

A few years back, a friend and I had dinner with Dominic Crossan. As we shared with him our feeble attempts to follow after the peasant revolutionary he wrote about, his eyes gleamed with excitement. You could almost smell the fresh aroma of the gospel as it rose above the suffocating pages of academia. He told me he had met plenty of

---

Christians. Was Saddam Hussein established by God? There is much more going on than we have time for here. I would suggest reading Walter Wink's book *The Powers That Be* (Galilee Trade, 1999) and checking out the site *http://Jesusradicals.com* if you are looking for some lively discussion.

10. John Dominic Crossan, *Jesus: A Revolutionary Biography* (San Francisco: HarperSanFrancisco, 1995).

evangelical Christians, but not too many that still believed that ole rabbi really meant the stuff he said.

So if the world hates us, we take courage that it hated Jesus first. If you're wondering whether you'll be safe, just look at what they did to Jesus and those who followed him. There are safer ways to live than by being a Christian. And there are cooler ways to live than by trying to follow the gospel. But look on the bright side, if you end up in jail, historically, you will be in very good company. Jail has always been an important place for Christians. In eras of injustice, it becomes the Christian's home. So live real good, and get beat up real bad. Dance until they kill you, and then we'll dance some more. That's how this thing seems to work.

A note on going to jail for Jesus. I've had many young 'uns ask me, "How many times have you gone to jail?" with a smile on their faces as if they are looking for an excuse to go themselves. It's important to say that our goal was never to go to jail; our goal was to do what is right no matter the cost. I tell the kids in my neighborhood, "You can go to jail for doing something wrong. And you can also go to jail for doing something right. When you see us going to jail [usually on TV], we are doing something we believe is right."

Civil disobedience, as it is often called, has held an important place in history. We think of the civil rights movement, the sit-ins, Rosa Parks on the bus in Montgomery, Harriet Tubman and the underground railroad, and so many of the movements that have changed history. Dr. King said he was uncomfortable at first going to jail, but then he looked at history and saw that he was in good company. Jesus for starters. And so many of the saints and heroes of history have gone to jail. And still do. Even as I write this, one of my friends, Kathy Kelly, with whom I was in Iraq, is in jail for an extended period of time. This time I think she was delivering a loaf of bread and a petition to one of the centers where militarized drones are operated (*http://www.democracynow.org/2014/12/29/peace_activist_kathy_kelly_heads_to*).

The whole idea of civil disobedience—or as we like to call it, "holy mischief"—warrants a little more reflection. So I have included a new appendix in the back of the book for your reading enjoyment. Oh, and Henry David Thoreau also wrote a pretty sweet piece titled "Civil Disobedience." And Leo Tolstoy has a whole book: *Writings on Civil Disobedience and Nonviolence*. But for now, appendix 4 can suffice.

CHAPTER 9

JESUS IS FOR LOSERS

A few years back, I was talking with a homeless guy in an alley downtown, and he started sharing with me about God. He was familiar with the Bible but kept talking about "the Christians" in the third person. A little confused, I finally asked him, "Are you not a Christian?" "Oh no," he said, "I am far too messed up." I asked him what he thought a Christian is, and he said, "Someone who's got their stuff together and has things figured out." I confessed that I must not be a Christian either and that I wasn't sure I had ever met one, and we laughed.[1] We read together the passage where Jesus tells the Pharisees (the ones who "had things together"), "It's not the healthy who need a doctor, but the sick. . . . I have not come to call the righteous, but sinners" (Matt. 9:12–13).

The gospel is good news for sick people and is disturbing for those who think they've got it all together. Some of us have been told our whole lives that we are wretched, but the gospel reminds us that we are beautiful. Others of us have been told our whole lives that we are beautiful, but the gospel reminds us that we are also wretched. The

---

1. In fact, one of the best cardboard signs for panhandling that I've come across was one made by a dear friend who found himself in hard times standing on a street corner. The sign simply read "In need of grace."

church is a place where we can stand up and say we are wretched, and everyone will nod and agree and remind us that we are also beautiful.

One thing I've learned from believers and from activists alike is that community can be built around a common self-righteousness or around a common brokenness. Self-righteousness comes in many forms. There are self-righteous fundamentalist Christians who say, "I would never drink alcohol or listen to secular music or go to a casino." And there are self-righteous progressive activists who say, "I would never drive an SUV or use styrofoam or eat meat or wear Nikes." We must take our convictions seriously, but sometimes our righteousness comes by pointing out others' wrongness. Jesus came not only to make us moral but also to give us life. And you can be moral but not alive. Hopefully, we can be both. Both are magnetic. People are drawn toward folks who have it all together, or who look like they do. People are also drawn toward folks who know they don't have it all together and are not willing to fake it.

Christianity can be built around isolating ourselves from evildoers and sinners, creating a community of religious piety and moral purity. That's the Christianity I grew up with. Christianity can also be built around joining with the broken sinners and evildoers of our world crying out to God, groaning for grace. That's the Christianity I have fallen in love with.

In Luke 18:10–14, Jesus tells a remarkable story about two folks praying. "Two men went up to the temple to pray, one a Pharisee and the other a tax collector. The Pharisee stood by himself and prayed, 'God, I thank you that I am not like other people—robbers, evildoers, adulterers—or even like this tax collector. I fast twice a week and give a tenth of all I get.' But the tax collector stood at a distance. He would

JESUS IS FOR LOSERS

not even look up to heaven, but beat his breast and said, 'God, have mercy on me, a sinner.' I tell you that this man, rather than the other, went home justified before God."

The Pharisee, a member of one of the sects of Judaism that made up the religious elite in Rome's empire, boasts of his religious devotion and moral obedience, thanking God that he is not like the "evildoers." Then there is the tax collector who stands at a distance and dares not even look up to heaven. He just beats his chest and says, "God, have mercy on me, a sinner," and it's that ole tax collector, rather than the Pharisee, who goes home justified before God. I'm convinced that the world is looking not for Christians who are perfect but for Christians who are honest. And the problem is that we haven't been honest, and we have pretended that we are perfect. The church should be a place where imperfect people can fall in love with a perfect God.

THE PROBLEM OF EVILDOING

Taken to its extremes, the infection of Pharisaic self-righteousness (the Pharisees were obsessed with purity), which Jesus compares to a yeast that creeps its way through dough, would lead us to deem it our duty to rid the world of losers and evildoers (whether we define evildoers as warmongers or anarchists), like pulling weeds out of a garden. Only a few stubborn anarchists or Jerry Falwell[2] are going to argue that September 11th was what America deserved.

---

2. Here's the exact quote from Jerry Falwell's response to September 11th two days later on *The 700 Club,* with Pat Robertson nodding in agreement: "I really believe that the pagans, and the abortionists, and the feminists, and the gays, and the lesbians who are actively trying to make that an alternative lifestyle, the ACLU, People for the American Way, all of them who have tried to secularize America. I point the finger in their face and say 'you helped this happen.'" Falwell later issued a well-warranted apology (see *http://archives.cnn.com/2001/US/09/14/Falwell.apology*).

And only a few articulate speechwriters are going to call America unequivocally good. After all, even Jesus warns us that "no one is good—except God alone" (Mark 10:18).

Many of us want the same things. We want the world to be rid of evil. We want justice. We want to liberate the oppressed. The question is, How do we do that? Ironically, most violence comes from a deep desire for justice. No one likes weeds in their garden. And no one likes evil in the world. We all would like to rid the world of evil (and have gardens free of weeds), which is probably why all the talk of good and evil is so attractive. But the problem, says Jesus, is that if we try to pull up the weeds from the garden, we will rip the wheat up too. In Matthew 13:24–30, he gives a firm command to let the wheat and the weeds grow together, and to let God sort them out at the harvest. And we are not God. Rich Mullins used to say, "I know, '"Vengeance is mine," saith the Lord,' but I just want to be about the Father's business." (He was joking, of course.)

If you've seen Mel Gibson's movie *The Passion of the Christ* (if you haven't, I'd recommend just reading the book), you know that you can't help but walk away from that movie with the overwhelming sense of Jesus' love for evildoers. Even while the Roman soldiers are tearing his flesh apart, he cries, "Father, forgive them, for they don't know what they are doing." The big question seems to be what to do with evil. And when it comes to the world's logic of redemptive violence, Christians have a major stumbling block on their hands—namely, the cross.

It goes all the way back to the original sin in the garden of Eden. Adam and Eve are invited to enjoy the fruit of all the trees except one—the tree of the knowledge of good and evil. And the serpent tempts them to eat of that fruit by telling them that if they do, they will be like God. And so Adam and Eve grubbed down on it, and humanity still craves the fruit of that tree. It's darn good fruit, but it's the only fruit reserved only for God; it's not for ambitious young naked couples or for zealous old fully armored military folks.

The Sermon on the Mount and the Beatitudes just don't seem like the best tools with which to lead an empire or a superpower. The truth that we have to lose our lives in order to find them doesn't sound like a good plan for national security. As old troubadour Woody Guthrie sings, "If Jesus preached in New York what he preached in Galilee, we'd lay him in his grave again" (especially if he did it on Wall Street). I guess that's why we hear a lot about God's blessing and about God's expanding our territory but very little about a cross or a love for enemies. There comes a point where we recognize we're trying to serve two masters, and we have to choose which one we will serve. Our arms are just not big enough to carry both the cross and the sword.

We can learn from the bloody pages of history. The more vigorously we try to root out evil by force, the more evil will escalate. For every Muslim extremist killed, another is created. Keep in mind this was written many years before ISIS. Sadly, it seems to be even more true today than when I wrote it in 2006. When we fight fire with fire, we get more fire. Violence begets violence. Hatred begets hatred. And love begets love.

The violent, evil ideology that drives ISIS and other groups like it has spread like a disease, and much of it is a reaction to the violence that has been done to Muslims— historically, and even recently. My veteran peacemaker friend Benjamin Corey says a good slogan for drone warfare is "Drones: creating enemies faster than they can kill them." Studies show the numbers of recruits in extremist groups have skyrocketed since the war and since the drones.

So when Saddam was ousted, it is not that surprising that what filled the vacuum is even more horrific. A passage I often think of when I think of Iraq is Luke 11:24–26: "When an impure spirit comes out of a person, it goes through arid places seeking rest and does not find it. Then it says, 'I will return to the house I left.' When it arrives, it finds the house swept clean and put in order. Then it goes and takes seven other spirits more wicked than itself, and they go in and live there. And the final condition of that person is worse than the first." When I returned to Iraq in 2010, I found many Iraqis wishing Saddam was still in power. He was far from good, but he was better than Al Qaeda and ISIS. At least when Saddam was in power, they told me, they had water and electricity. Likewise, the more passionately we love our enemies, the more evil will diminish. This is also the story of the martyrs—for every Christian killed at the hands of evil, another would rise up, converted by their faithful self-sacrificial love. And historically, Christianity spreads most rapidly when we are killed at the hands of evildoers without retaliating. It's the story of the growth of the church during the great persecutions. They wrote that for every one of them who was killed, there were ten converts. As the saying goes, "In the blood of the martyrs is the seed of the saints." The paradox is that the church is healthiest during eras of persecution, and it gets sick during periods of comfort and ease and power. It is no surprise that statistics show Muslim people are less open to Christianity now than they were a year ago. Pharisaic extremists are alive today in every religion—in Islam, in Christianity, in Judaism.

Church history is filled with movements of piety, like the Puritans, who marked themselves by separating from the unholy and deemed it their duty to destroy all that is not pure in the world. This is also the twisted theology that led Hitler to try to "cleanse" the world of Jews. And the KKK have a entire section of their website dedicated to their toxic theology, which is loaded with troubling language about whiteness and "dispelling darkness"—that's why they set crosses on fire. While I'm on a little tangent, it is both haunting and humbling to see the evil done in the name of Christ, with the Bible in hand. We are quick to denounce the evils of groups like ISIS, and we should be. But we also must confess that horrific things have been done in the name of Christ. We need only read a little of the history of lynching in this country to hear stories of unimaginable evil done by folks who were in church every Sunday. And the pages of church history are filled with the embarrassing bloodstains left by Christian movements that have tried to rid the world of evil by the sword. Martyrs, heretics, the busy guillotine of the English Reformation, and the cruel punishments of the Spanish Inquisition. In such times, the cross always loses.[3]

And yet there is the constant whisper of the cross. Church history is also full of movements that remained faithful to the cross. Even when it appeared that the world would destroy them, Christians knew that God would be faithful even as they remained faithful.

History is also filled with movements of people who cry out to God that they are unholy, who identify and confess their sins—such as Europe's Confessing Church and the college revivals in the United States that began

---

3. I really hesitate to allude to the CBS miniseries on Jesus again, lest you think it's worth your time, but there's a fabulous scene in which the Tempter meets Jesus in the garden of Gethsemane just before he is about to be crucified. The devil tells him, "They do not understand your cross, Jesus. They will never understand your cross." And he shows Jesus glimpses of the Crusades and holy wars, all of the blood shed in the name of God, and he asks Jesus if he still wants to die, for that. Perhaps that was the last temptation.

with humble confession of sins, with people beating their chests before each other and God. Perhaps one of the most powerful things the contemporary church could do is to confess our sins to the world, to humbly get on our knees and repent for the terrible things we have done in the name of God. In his book *Blue Like Jazz*, author Don Miller tells the delightful story of how he and his friends dressed like monks and set up a confessional booth on their notoriously heathen college campus. But instead of hearing other people's confessions, they were confessing their sins as Christians and the sins of Christendom to anyone who was willing to listen and forgive. I think the world would be willing to listen to a church on its knees, a church that doesn't pretend to be perfect or to have all of the answers. I think a mystical, sacramental healing can begin within us and extend into the wounds of our world.

That stuff Jesus warned us to beware of, the yeast of the Pharisees, is so infectious today in the camps of both liberals and conservatives. Conservatives stand up and thank God that they are not like the homosexuals, the Muslims, the liberals. Liberals stand up and thank God that they are not like the war makers, the yuppies, the conservatives. It is a similar self-righteousness, just with different definitions of evildoing. It can paralyze us in judgment and guilt and rob us of life. Rather than separating ourselves from everyone we consider impure, maybe we are better off just beating our chests and praying that God would be merciful enough to save us from this present ugliness and to make our lives so beautiful that people cannot resist that mercy.

CRACKS LET THE LIGHT COME IN

St. John of the Cross, a sixteenth-century Spanish monk and mystic philosopher, understood the emptiness and pain of human existence. (He wrote a book called *The Dark Night of the Soul*, for goodness sake. Goth kids dig him.) He coined the old saying, "The cracks let the light come in." (And yes, Leonard Cohen sings it well in his song "Anthem.") Somehow God likes broken vessels. I am convinced that Jesus came not simply to make bad people good but to bring dead people to life. We can be moral but not alive; a lot of conservatives and liberals have taught me that, and I myself have been a victim of the Pharisaic yeast infection. There are many people who are morally "pure" but devoid of any life, joy, or celebration. For some, this "purity" means that we do not touch anything that is "secular," and for others, it means that we don't eat anything that is not "organic." But if it is not born of relationships, if it is not liberating for the oppressed and the oppressors, if it is not marked by raw, passionate love, then it is the same old self-righteousness that does little more than flaunt our own purity by making the rest of the world see how dirty they are. No matter where it pops up, this yeast hinders us from seeing God's image in every human being, be they a soldier or a centurion, a tax collector or a stockbroker, a Zealot or an anarchist. No one is beyond redemption.

The tax collector knows he is a sinner and just cries out to God for grace. When we are first aware of our own brokenness, our eyes are opened to see our own faces in the faces of the oppressed and to see our own hands in the hands of the oppressors. Then we shall all be truly free.

The tax collector teaches us, as does Jesus, that this gospel is for sick people, not for the righteous. There is another breed of extremist rising up. We are sinners beating our chests, crying out to God, "Have mercy on us." We will beat our chests outside the White House, outside the abortion clinics, in New York on September 11th, in the ghetto of Philadelphia. We will hurt no one (although our own chests may get a little sore). We will love evildoers, even if it costs us our lives. And then we will see evildoers become extremists for grace. This is the story of our faith.

THE GOD OF LOSERS

Whenever someone tells me they have rejected God, I say, "Tell me about the God you've rejected." And as they describe a God of condemnation, of laws and lightning bolts, of frowning gray-haired people and boring meetings, I usually confess, "I too have rejected that God."

I've met a lot of Christians who say, "If people knew about all of my struggles and weaknesses, they would never want to be a Christian." I think just the opposite is true. If people really knew what idiots we are, in all our broken-ness and vulnerability, they would know that they can give this thing a shot too. Christianity is for sick people. Rich Mullins used to say, "Whenever people say, 'Christans are hypocrites,' I say, 'Duh, every time we come together we are confessing that we are hypocrites, weaklings in need of God and each other.'" We know that we cannot do life alone, and the good news is that we don't have to. We are created for community.

Bono, the great theologian (and decent rock star), said it like this in his introduction to a book of selections from the Psalms: "The fact that the Scriptures are brim full of hustlers, murderers, cowards, adulterers, and mercenaries used to shock me. Now it is a source of great comfort."[4] Thank God for grace. Moses killed someone. So did David. And Saul. Half the Bible is written by some pretty messed-up

---

4. Bono, "Introduction," in *Selections from the Book of Psalms*, Pocket Canons (New York: Grove, 1999).

people. But that's why it is a love story. God is bigger than our mistakes. Grace gets the last word. The Bible would be much shorter without grace. Consider King David, whom many Christians remember as a man after God's own heart. Well, David breaks just about every one of the big Ten Commandments in about two chapters of the Bible—he covets, commits adultery, lies, murders (and this is all after he has answered God's call)—and yet he is still one of the losers God trusted and used. Matthew's Gospel gives us the genealogy of Jesus, which could compete with any of our families on the dysfunctionality thermometer. One of my favorite parts is when Matthew gets to the section of the genealogy that involves David's infamous sex scandal with Bathsheba; he writes, "David was the father of Solomon, whose mother had been Uriah's wife." Ha! He names other women in the lineage, but when he gets to Bathsheba, he makes sure we all remember everything that went on there. (David had Uriah killed.) What a mess! So if that is the Son of God's lineage, none of us can be too bad off. No wonder people were always asking about Jesus, "Whose kid is this? Isn't he from Nazareth?" Galilee was the hub of peasant revolts and uprisings. It was notorious, the badlands. Whenever people call our neighborhood the Badlands, as it is commonly referred to by locals, and they imply that nothing good can come from here, I remind them that that's exactly what people said about Nazareth, and look what showed up there.

Consider the fact that Jesus tells parables like the one about the Good Samaritan. Look at the hero—a Samaritan? Jews did not like Samaritans, thought they had some whacked out views about God and worship. They wouldn't even walk through Samaria. But Jesus tells a story in which the Samaritan is the hero and the priest is the loser who passes his neighbor by. That's the kind of thing that ticked the religious elite off. Sister Joan Chittister puts it well: "God consistently challenges the chosen and includes the excluded."

I recently spoke at a large youth gathering. Afterward, a crowd of teenagers came up and asked for my autograph. At first, I laughed at the idea, but then my heart ached as they told me that they rarely got to actually meet the speaker. Each night, I stayed until all the kids were gone. We prayed together, told jokes, sat around and sang songs; it was incredible. And yet some still asked for autographs. So here's what I did. I explained to them that I would write them a note, and this is what I wrote: "This is not an autograph, because there is nothing special about me that is not also special about you. Never forget that you are beautiful, just like everyone else. And never forget that you are a fool, just like everyone else." Yeah, my hand got tired, but I think they began to get it. Rich Mullins used to say, alluding to the Old Testament story in which God speaks through a donkey, "God spoke to Balaam through his ass, and God's been speaking through them ever since." So if God should choose to use us, we shouldn't think too highly of ourselves. And we should never assume that God cannot use someone, no matter how ornery or awkward they appear to be. Rich Mullins was known for his winsome honesty about his own struggles and contradictions. One of my favorite stories of Rich was when he and a friend were on a train ride and began to have some "bro time." They got really honest about some of their struggles and sins. As the train arrived at the final stop, a woman sitting in front of them recognized Rich and said, "Are you Rich Mullins?" Retelling the story, Rich laughed and said, "In that moment, I thought of all the things she might have heard me confess, and I had to decide—am I Rich Mullins?" He smiled, and owning his own darkness, he said confidently, "Yes . . . I am Rich Mullins." There is something liberating about being honest and owning our struggles.

A buddy of mine who is a fairly prominent youth minister just told me about a trip he took with a bunch of teenagers to one of those "mountaintop" spiritual retreats with lots of tears, confessions, and spiritual goose bumps. On the way up, the van had a flat tire of the worst kind—in the rain, no tools, a bad spare. As all the kids stared out the window, his temper escalated and went beyond the tipping point. He lost it and started yelling, cussing, and kicking the blessed thing. Finally, he was able to get the van going, climbed back in, and told everybody to shut up and leave him alone for a bit. A little embarrassed, they headed on to the retreat, with a few snickers coming from the back of the van. He said the retreat was the same as it was every year, with the worship, preaching, and altar call. But that year, something crazy happened. One of his toughest kids from the ghetto told him the week after they returned that he had given his life to Jesus. My friend was a bit stunned and asked him to explain how it happened. "Was it the messages, the altar call?" The young man said, "No, it was on the way up when I saw you cussing at the van. I thought, If he can be a Christian, I can give this thing a shot too."

There are so many people who are longing to be brought to life, who know all too well that they have done evil and long to hear not only of a God who embraces evildoers but also of a church that does the same.

OVERCOMING DARKNESS

In the early days of our community, Michelle, a founding partner of the Simple Way, and I headed out to get a loaf of bread. We walked underneath the El tracks just a block from our house, a strip notorious for its prostitution and drug trafficking, where the air is thick with tears and struggle. We walked past an alley, and tucked inside was a woman, tattered, cold, and on crutches. She approached me, asking if I wanted her services. Our hearts sank, but we scurried on to get our bread. Then we headed quickly home, nodding at the woman as we passed. When we got home and opened the bread, we noticed the bag had a large gash in the side and the bread had gone bad. We would have to go back, and we both knew what that meant. We would have to walk by that woman again. We walked by the alley and saw her in there crying, shivering. We got our bread, and as we saw her yet again, we could not just pass by. We stopped and told her we cared for her, that she was precious, worth more than a few bucks for tricks on the avenue. We explained that we had a home that was a safe place to get warm and have a snack. So she stumbled onto her crutches and came home with us.

As soon as we entered the house, she started weeping hysterically. Michelle held her as she wept. When she had gained her composure, she said, "You all are Christians, aren't you?" Michelle and I looked at each other, startled. We had said nothing about God or Jesus, and our house doesn't have a cross in the window, a neon "Jesus saves" sign, or even a little Christian fish on the wall. She said, "I know that you are Christians because you shine. I used to be in love with Jesus like that, and when I was, I shined like diamonds in the sky, like the stars. But it's a cold dark world, and I lost my shine a little while back. I lost my shine on those streets." At that point, we were all weeping. She asked us to pray with her that she might shine again. We did; we prayed that this dark world would not take away our shine.

Days, weeks went by, and we did not see her. One day, there was a knock at the door, and I opened it. On the steps there was a lovely lady with a contagious ear-to-ear smile. We stared at each other. We see a lot of people, so I was going to try to fake recognizing her, but she called my bluff and beat me to it. "Of course you don't recognize me, because I'm shining again. I'm shining." Then I knew. She went on to explain how deeply she had fallen in love with God again. She said she wanted to give us something to thank us for our hospitality but sadly confessed, "While I was on the streets, I lost everything I owned. Except this." She pulled out a box and apologetically confessed that she smoked a lot and always collected the Marlboro Mile points from the cigarette packs. "So this is all that I have, but I want you to have it." And she handed me a box bursting at the seams with hundreds of Marlboro Miles. It's one of the most precious gifts I've ever been given, like receiving the widow's last pennies. And they make good Bible markers. Now whenever I am speaking somewhere and open up the Word, I see a Marlboro Mile (and the elders raise their eyebrows), and I am reminded of all the broken lives that have lost their shine a little while back. Not too long ago, I got a phone call, and it was my friend! She had heard a sermon of mine in which I told this story, her story. And she got all excited. "I'm a resurrection story! I'm a resurrection story!" That's what we get to do—love people back to life.

THE SCANDAL OF GRACE

There's another person who felt the world killed the good in him, a young man who was a decorated army veteran in the 1991 Gulf War. I remember reading the letters he wrote home from the war, in which he told his family how hard it was to kill. He told them he felt like he was turning into an animal because day after day it became a little easier to kill. His name was Timothy McVeigh. He came home from serving in the Army Special Forces, horrified, crazy, dehumanized, and became the worst domestic terrorist we have ever seen. His essays cry out against the bloodshed he saw and created in Iraq: "Do people think that government workers in Iraq are any less human than those in Oklahoma City? Do they think that Iraqis don't have families who will grieve and mourn the loss of their loved ones? Do people believe that the killing of foreigners is somehow different than the killing of Americans?"[5] No doubt his mind had been tragically deranged by the myth of redemptive violence. He bombed the federal building in Oklahoma City in hopes that complacent Americans could see what "collateral damage" looks like and cry out against bloodshed everywhere, even in Iraq. Instead, the government that had trained him to kill, killed him, to teach the rest of us that it is wrong to kill. Dear God, liberate us from the logic of redemptive violence.[6]

One of the people I have grown to love is a man named Bud Welch. He lost his twenty-three-year-old daughter, Julie Marie, in that Oklahoma City bombing at the hands of Timothy McVeigh. He says he went through a period of rage when he wanted Timothy dead. "I wanted him to fry," he says. "I'd have killed him myself if I'd had the chance." But there was a moment when he remembered the words of his daughter, who had been a courageous advocate for reconciliation. She used to say, "Execution teaches hatred."

---

5. Timothy McVeigh, "Essay on Hypocrisy" (federal prison, Florence, CO, March 1998).

6. Before he was killed, I wrote Timothy McVeigh several letters hoping that he could hear through all of the noise the gentle whisper that he is beautiful and not beyond redemption.

It wasn't long before Bud decided to interrupt that cycle of hatred and violence and arranged a visit with McVeigh's dad and family. As they met, Bud says he grew to love them dearly and to this day says he has "never felt closer to God" than amid that union. He decided to travel around the country speaking about reconciliation and against the death penalty, which teaches that some people are beyond redemption, and pleading for the life of Timothy McVeigh. And he says he felt "a tremendous weight had lifted" from his shoulders.

As he worked through his anger and pain and confusion, he began see that this evil spiral of redemptive violence must stop with him. And he began to look into the eyes of Timothy McVeigh, the murderer, and see the image of God. He longed for him to experience love, grace, and forgiveness. Bud is one who still believes in the scandal of grace.[7] As I wrote my book on the death penalty, I found story after story of grace. There are countless other folks like Bud Welch—victims' families against execution. They inspire me. For starters, check out Journey of Hope, Murder Victims' Families for Reconciliation, Murder Victims' Families for Human Rights, and the Forgiveness Project—all victims of violence who have found better ways forward than killing to show how wrong it is to kill.

Ironically, when I was giving that talk titled "The Scandal of Grace," I told the story of Bud Welch as I talked about how God's love extends to all losers, whether Usama bin Laden, Saddam Hussein, Saul of Tarsus, Timothy McVeigh, or me. The program team showed a PowerPoint presentation using the "visual edition" of Philip Yancey's

---

7. To read Bud's story and other stories of reconciliation and grace, see *http://www.theforgivenessproject.com.*

work *What's So Amazing about Grace?* In the PowerPoint, different images pop up behind the words "amazing grace that saved a wretch like me," and different people's faces are branded with the words "like me"—Mother Teresa, sports stars, celebrities—and one of them was Timothy McVeigh. It created such discomfort that the program team was told to remove the image of Timothy from the presentation before the second service. There *is* something scandalous about grace. It's almost embarrassing that God loves losers so much. It flies in the face of the world's myth of redemptive violence. No wonder the early Christians had such bad reputations and questionable credibility. No wonder they were called "the scum of the earth, the garbage of the world," as one of the leaders, a former murderer himself, wrote (1 Cor. 4:13). One of my other favorite stories of extreme grace happened shortly after the original printing of *The Irresistible Revolution*. In 2006 a deranged, armed gunman named Carl Roberts entered a one-room Amish schoolhouse in Nickel Mines, Pennsylvania, and shot ten girls, ranging in age from six to thirteen years old, killing five. Then he turned the gun on himself and killed himself.

But what quickly began to steal the headlines was the way the Amish responded. Amish families instinctively built a bridge to the shooter's family and went to visit them—Carl's widow, children, and parents.

People from around the world, moved with compassion, began to send the Amish gifts and money, and the Amish used the money to create a fund for the family of the shooter. As the funerals rolled around, the Amish attended funeral after funeral of their own children who had died, but then they went to the funeral of Carl Roberts, the man who had killed their kids, so they could grieve with his family and hold hands as they found a way forward. Marie Roberts,

Carl's widow, wrote an open letter to the Amish community thanking them for their forgiveness, grace, and mercy, saying, "Your love for our family has helped to provide the healing we so desperately need. Gifts you've given have touched our hearts in a way no words can describe. Your compassion has reached beyond our family, beyond our community, and is changing our world, and for this we sincerely thank you."

I was in Australia speaking when the shooting happened, and I will never forget one of the front-page headlines in the Australian newspaper. It read, "Amazing Grace: Why Would the Amish Do What They Did?" In *Jesus for President*, my pal Chris Haw and I wrote a section called "Amish for Homeland Security," winking at how the world might be different if we had had the Amish imagination after September 11th.

Now, hold on—there's more. Once a week, the mother of Carl Roberts visits Rosanna, one of the girls her son shot and almost killed. Rosanna is now fourteen years old, sits in a wheelchair, eats with a feeding tube, and is unable to talk. But she is not unable to love and be loved. Terri helps bathe her and reads to her and sings with her. Spending time together helps to heal the wounds of this tragedy. Every week when Terri visits Rosanna, she is forced to confront the damage her son caused. But it reminds her that none of us have to be held hostage by the worst moments of our lives. Healing of even the deepest wounds is possible.

I recently had a chance to meet Terri. We got to take a hammer together and beat on a gun and turn it into a tool. Grace gets the last word (*http://www.huffingtonpost.com/2015/03/21/raw-tools-gun-garden-tools_n_6914636.html*).

It's the old eye-for-an-eye thing that gets us. But the more I've studied the Hebrew Scriptures, the more I am convinced that this was just a boundary for people who lashed back. As the young exodus people were trying to discover a new way of living outside the empire, God made sure there were some boundaries. If someone breaks your arm, you cannot go back and break their arm and then their leg too. Just like in old feudal wars or with contemporary gangs, things escalate. A shock-and-awe bombing leads to a shock-and-awe beheading. A Pearl Harbor leads to a Hiroshima. A murder leads to an execution. A rude look leads to a cold shoulder. "An eye for an eye" we have indeed heard before and learned its logic all too well. But Jesus comes declaring in his State of the Union Sermon on the Mount address (Matt. 5:38), "You have heard that it was said, 'Eye for eye, and tooth for tooth,'" but there is another way. And it's a good thing, since as Gandhi and King used to say, "An eye for an eye and a tooth for a tooth leaves the whole world blind" (and with dentures).

The Gospels tell the story of a group of people who are ready to stone an adulteress. (Stoning was the legal consequence of adultery.) They ask Jesus for his support of this death-penalty case. His response is that they are all adulterers. He says, "Let any one of you who is without sin be the first to throw a stone at her" (John 8:7). And the people drop their stones and walk away with their heads bowed. We want to kill the murderers, but Jesus says that we are all murderers: "Anyone who is angry with a brother or sister will be subject to judgment. Again, anyone who says to a brother or sister, 'Raca,' is answerable to the Sanhedrin. And anyone who says, 'You fool!' will be in danger of the fire of hell" (Matt. 5:22). Again the stones drop. We are all murderers and adulterers and terrorists. And we are all precious.

When we look through the eyes of Jesus, we see new things in people. In the murderers, we see our own hatred. In the addicts, we see our own addictions. In the saints, we catch glimpses of our own holiness. We can see our own brokenness, our own violence, our own ability to destroy, and we can see our own sacredness, our own capacity to love and forgive. When we realize that we are both wretched and beautiful, we are freed up to see others the same way.

In his work *I and Thou*,[8] brilliant European thinker Martin Buber speaks of how we can see a person as simply a material object, something you look at, an "it," or we can look into a person and enter the sacredness of their humanity so that they become a "Thou." (And as a Jewish philosopher who immigrated to Palestine to advocate for Arab-Jewish cooperation, Buber knew all too well how easily we objectify and demonize others.) All the time, we look *at* people—hot girls, beggars, pop stars, white folks, black folks, people with suits or dreadlocks. But over time, we can develop new eyes and look *into* people. Rather than looking at people as sex objects or work tools, we can see them as sacred. We can enter the Holiest of Holies through their eyes. They can become a "Thou."

I saw this happen when the dying and the lepers whispered that sacred Hindi word *namaste*. And I saw it in Iraq, when people put their hands over their hearts. In South Africa, I also learned about *ubuntu*, which is a similar idea. It means, "I cannot be all that I am meant to be until you are everything you are meant to be." We do not live in isolation. An injury to one is an injury to all. And until all of us are free, none of us are free. Our humanity is reflected in each other's eyes. It is in such moments that we understand what the Catholic Workers mean when they say, "The true atheist is the one who refuses to see God's image in the face of their

8. Martin Buber, *I and Thou* (Riverside, NJ: Free Press, 1971).

neighbor." Looking into the eyes of people who love us may be the clearest glimpse of God many of us get in this world.

I have an old hippie friend who loves Jesus and smokes a lot of weed, and he's always trying to get under my skin and stir up a debate, especially when I have innocent young Christians visiting with me. (The problem is that he knows the Bible better than most of them do.) One day, he said to me, "Jesus never talked to a prostitute." I immediately went on the offensive: "Oh, sure he did," and whipped out my sword of the Spirit and got ready to spar. Then he just calmly looked me in the eye and said, "Listen, Jesus never talked to a prostitute because he didn't see a prostitute. He just saw a child of God he was madly in love with." I lost the debate that night.

When we have new eyes, we can look into the eyes of those we don't even like and see the One we love. We can see God's image in everyone we encounter. As Henri Nouwen puts it, "In the face of the oppressed I recognize my own face, and in the hands of the oppressor I recognize my own hands. Their flesh is my flesh, their blood is my blood, their pain is my pain, their smile is my smile."[9] We are made of the same dust. We cry the same tears. No one is beyond redemption. And we are free to imagine a revolution that sets both the oppressed and the oppressors free.

---

9. Henri Nouwen, *With Open Hands*, 6th ed. (New York: Ave Maria, 1987), 46.

CHAPTER 10

EXTREMISTS FOR LOVE

Growing up, I was told that good people go to church. And then I looked around and watched the news and found a church full of sick people and a world that had some decent pagans. And I studied sociology. My studies taught me that the higher a person's frequency of church attendance, the more likely they are to be sexist, racist, anti-gay, pro-military, and committed to their local church. And I figured if that's what it means to be a Christian, I wasn't sure I wanted to be one, or whether even Jesus would want to be one, for that matter. I wondered why Jesus didn't take back his religion. As I've heard my old mentor Tony Campolo say, "If we were to set out to establish a religion in polar opposition to the Beatitudes Jesus taught, it would look strikingly similar to the pop Christianity that has taken over the airwaves of North America."

A friend and I prepared a video clip once for a worship service. Our goal was to capture people's responses to the word *Christian*, so we took a video camera and hit the streets, from the trendy arts district to the suburbs. We asked people to say the first word that came to mind in response to each word we said: "snow," "eagles" (it's Philly), "teenagers," and finally "Christian." When people heard the word Christian, they stopped in their tracks. I will never forget their responses: "fake," "hypocrites," "church," "boring." One guy even said, "used-to-be-one" (sort of one word). I will also never forget what they didn't say. Not one of the people we asked that day said "love." No one said "grace." No one said "community." A few years ago, the Barna Group, a prominent research company, went to every state in the US and asked young non-Christians what their perceptions of Christians were. What they found was heartbreaking. The top three answers were: (1) anti-gay, (2) judgmental, (3) hypocritical. And they did not say the number one thing Jesus said we should be known for: loving. Thankfully, over the past decade this has been changing, but maybe not as quickly as I would like it to. The original book my friends Gabe and Dave at Barna did was called *UnChristian*. More recently, they released a follow-up book called *The Next Christians*. I do hope a generation from now when people hear the word *Christians* they do not say anti-gay, judgmental, and hypocritical, but that they say loving. Let's be a part of *that* revolution.

GOD, SAVE THE CHRISTIANS

We live in an age in which people, when they hear the word Christian, are much more likely to think of people who hate gays than people who love outcasts, and that is a dangerous thing. Bumper stickers and buttons read, "Jesus, save me from your followers." Over and over I see people rejecting God because of the mess they see in the church. As contemporary author and ragamuffin Brennan Manning says, "The greatest cause of atheism is Christians who acknowledge Jesus with their lips, then walk out the door and deny him with their lifestyle. That is what an unbelieving world simply finds unbelievable."

But I have tremendous hope that a new kind of Christianity is emerging. I'd just like it to get here sooner than later. We live in a world of dangerous extremes. "These are extreme times," Dr. King said. "The question is not whether we will be extremists, but what kind of extremists we will be. Will we be extremists for hate or for love?"[1] The world has seen Christian extremists who will blow up abortion clinics and dance on the doctors' graves. We have seen Christian extremists who hold signs that say, "God hates fags." The world has seen Christian extremists who declare war in the name of the Lamb. But where are the Christian extremists for love and grace?

IF TERROR IS THE ENEMY, THEN LOVE IS THE HERO

Saul of Tarsus was one of the religious extremists who terrorized the first Christians. Saul was a devoutly religious man, and we are told that he studied "at the feet of Gamaliel." I know church history isn't everybody's thing, but let me just say that Gamaliel was the grandson of Hillel, who was one of the forefathers of the Pharisees. Hillel was a renowned Pharisee; one of few accorded the title Rabboni, which means "our teacher" (in contrast to Rabbi, which means "my teacher"). So that's no small detail. Saul was a distinguished Pharisee, certainly one of those Pharisees who, like in the story in Luke, could stand up and say, "Thank you that I am not like the sinners and evildoers." So he made it his duty to snuff out the radical young Jesus movement. He was an extremist, a terrorist, going house to house trying to "destroy the church," imprisoning the followers of the Way (Acts 8:3). And one of those young Jesus-followers was a kid named Stephen, known to be the first Christian martyr.

---

1. Martin Luther King Jr., "Letter from the Birmingham Jail" (April 16, 1963).

As the Sanhedrin are killing Stephen (Acts 7:54–8:1), the Scriptures say that Saul was there "giving approval to his death" and watching over everyone's coats. I'm not sure exactly what that means, but I have a hunch people said, "Here, Saul, hold my jacket while I go pound on that brotha!" As they are killing ole Stephen, he cries out something extraordinary: "Lord, do not hold this sin against them." He had heard a statement similar to that before from his rabbi, Jesus of Nazareth. Stephen, in the beautiful words of extreme grace, cries out to God on behalf of those who are killing him, and that prayer will be heard over and over from the mouths of the martyrs who come soon after him. It is a prayer that brings redemption. It is a prayer that converts evil rather than destroys evildoers.

I don't think it's a coincidence that the next chapter of Acts (chap. 9) is about Saul's conversion as he goes on to become Paul, a terrorist converted by scandalous grace. And he becomes an extremist for grace, writing so eloquently of God's love for sinners, of whom he counts himself the "chief."[2] The contagion of grace. Grace is contagious, just like violence.

I always say that if we believe terrorists are beyond redemption, we can rip out half of our New Testament, since it was written by a converted terrorist who became an extremist for grace. When my wife prays for the people in ISIS and Al Qaeda and other groups like Boko Haram, she often prays for another "Saul of Tarsus," a radical conversion where an extremist for hatred could be transformed into an extremist for grace. It stretches my faith to even imagine it

---

2. And check this out: several accounts of ecclesial history tell the legend that there was another conversion, of an old man named Gamaliel. Early Christian writings tell us that before his death in AD 50, Gamaliel converted and was baptized by his former student, Paul. I love that.

sometimes. But not only is it possible, it has actually happened before. It's what happens when we discover that God has a desperate love for losers just like us.

A CHURCH OF EXTREMISTS FOR GRACE

Church history is filled with stories of extreme grace. One of my favorites is the story of the apostle James. The story of James's death has been passed down for hundreds of years. To give a little context, James (along with his brother, John) was one of Jesus' cousins, a bit of a zealot. As they were walking through Samaria one day, some Samaritans were giving them a hard time, so James offered to help Jesus take care of them by calling down "fire from heaven" on the Samaritans. I'm not sure exactly what that meant back then, but Jesus was not happy and rebuked him. The story of Jesus' life continued, and James watched Jesus love people and then die. So eventually James faced his own execution for having followed the one who loved his enemies to death. He was imprisoned and was set to be executed. Before his execution, he spoke to his executioner about God's love and grace. The executioner was so deeply moved that he asked for forgiveness and surrendered his life to Christ. James forgave him, and they embraced. Then he and the executioner were killed together.

Then there's the story, centuries later, of Dirk Willems, the famous Anabaptist martyr of the 1500s. He was imprisoned and was set for execution for standing against the corruption of the church during a dark age of ecclesial history. But he managed to escape and was pursued by guards. (Just because the Bible says we are to love our enemies doesn't mean we can't run from them!) He ran through the winter fields of Holland, with one of the guards in hot pursuit. As Dirk crossed over a frozen pond, he heard a deep cracking of the ice behind him, and he looked back to find that the guard had fallen through. In that moment, he faced a critical decision. He turned around and dove into the water, saving his pursuer's life, only to be taken back to prison. Despite the guard's plea for Dirk's release, he was soon burned at the stake. But think about his witness of grace and love!

While I was in Iraq, one of the Christian Peacemakers on our team was a Franciscan priest, and so we contemplated the daredevil grace of St. Francis during one of our devotions. We flashed back to another confusing time of conflict—1219, during the Fifth Crusade. Christians and Muslims were slaughtering each other in the name of God. War had become a necessity and a habit. Centuries of church history, in which followers of the Way renounced their allegiance to the kingdom of the world and its kings, had been perverted by the seduction of gaining the whole world but losing our souls. And then Francis, who had set forth as a soldier to Perugia, had a vision of loving our enemies. He pleaded with the commander, Cardinal Pelagius, to end the fighting. Pelagius refused. Instead, Pelagius broke off all diplomatic relations with the sultan of Egypt, Malik al-Kamil. The sultan in turn decreed that anyone who brought him the head of a Christian would be rewarded with a Byzantine gold piece. Francis, however, pursued his vision in steadfast faith, surmounting all dangers in a journey to see the sultan. He traveled through fierce fighting in Syria and inevitably was met by soldiers of the sultan's army, who beat him savagely and put him in chains, dragging him before the sultan himself.

Francis spoke to the sultan of God's love and grace. The sultan listened intensely and was so moved that he offered Francis gifts and money. Having refused the riches offered him by the sultan (of course), Francis did accept one gift—an ivory horn used in the Muslim call to prayer, which Francis later used to summon his community to prayer. (You can still see the horn in Assisi.) While the sultan refused to become a Christian (or perhaps did not dare), he did undergo a radical transformation. He became known for his extraordinarily humane treatment of Christian prisoners during the war. The transformative power of grace.

More recently, I think of our elders in the civil rights movement. Our friend John Perkins is a visionary leader from the civil rights days who spent much of his life getting beat up by white folks, and he has been one of the most beautiful voices of love and reconciliation in the United States. He's written a bazillion books, but a particularly lovely one is a book he coauthored with a former KKK leader (Thomas Tarrants) titled *He's My Brother*, another story of extreme grace. John's life and work have given birth to a compelling movement called the Christian Community Development Association,[3] one of the most diverse gatherings within the North American church and whose pillars are reconciliation, relocation, and redistribution.

Dr. King was another one of our elders who spoke of God's love and grace amid hatred. King marked Gandhi as one of the great teachers of nonviolence and said this just before he died: "To our most bitter opponents we say: 'Throw us in jail and we will still love you. Bomb our houses and threaten our children and we will still love you. Beat us and leave us half dead and we will still love you. But be ye assured that we will wear you down by our capacity to suffer. One day we shall so appeal to your heart and conscience that we shall win you in the process, and our victory will be a double victory.'"[4]

---

3. *www.ccda.org.*

4. Martin Luther King Jr., "The American Dream" (speech, Ebenezer Baptist Church, Atlanta, GA, July 4, 1965).

EXTREME GRACE IN IRAQ

In Iraq, we were invited to Christian worship services nearly every night. One unforgettable night was at St. Rafael's cathedral in Baghdad, where once again I was reminded of the God of extreme grace. We sang familiar tunes, and the priest got up to give the homily. He had just served six months in prison for his faithfulness to the gospel. What would his message be, at such a crucial moment?

He told the true story of a woman whose son and husband were killed by a police officer. Eventually they caught the police officer and dragged him before the court. In court, as the judge considered the sentence of the police officer, the woman spoke boldly: "He took my family away from me, and I still have a lot of love to give, and he needs to know what love and grace feel like—so I think he should have to come to visit my home in the slums, twice a month, and spend time with me, so that I can be a mother to him, so that I can embrace him, and he can know that my forgiveness is real."

We all sat silently, struck dumb by grace. The priest urged us all to love our enemies. I have heard that a million times. I have traveled across the country preaching it. But now there was a twist: the enemy he spoke of was my country. The boundaries of God's grace were being pushed once again. Somehow it seemed so scandalous to ask these beautiful people, who were about to be attacked by the same enemy who had killed many of their family members and decimated their city only ten years before, to love and forgive—again. We are to love those who bomb us? We are to love George W. Bush and Saddam Hussein? The priest led us to the cross, urging us to say, "Father, forgive them for they know not what they do." He admitted that this action is not based on logic;

it is based on a love that does not make sense, a scandalous grace. And he urged this Iraqi congregation and their international friends to love those who persecute them.[5]

The service ended with the singing of "Amazing Grace." And I sat in tears, wishing I could be the judge of those who decided to go to war. I would sentence them to spend two days a month in the Al Monzer Pediatric Hospital in Baghdad, where I held child after child with pieces of metal in their bodies. Maybe then they would become extremists for grace.

I remember visiting one of the hospitals in Iraq. The doctors walked us by bed after bed of children who had been injured or killed in the bombings. I saw a little girl shaking in her bed, asking over and over, "What did I do to America? What did I do to America?" I saw a father hold his child, whose body was speckled with missile fragments, and heard him say, "What kind of liberation would do this to my child? If this is liberation, then we do not want it. If this is democracy, they can keep it." I could hear the echo of the words of Dr. King (speaking of Vietnam, of course): "They must see us as strange liberators." The doctors had tears in their eyes as they explained that they had not slept in days and had seen over a hundred casualties in the first three hours. Amid all of the horror, the manager of the hospital said something I will never forget: "Violence is for

5. That night in Baghdad, I read Psalm 23. It's the one folks usually read at funerals: "Though I walk through the valley of the shadow of death." And I felt like I was. But I noticed something I had never noticed before. The psalm says that a table is prepared "in the presence of my enemies." I remember thinking, Why are our enemies there? What if after we die, God brings our enemies to the table and asks them how we treated them? What if Jesus asks them, "Shane here claims to follow me. Did he love you? Did he feed you and pray for you like I taught him to?" What would our enemies say? And how awkward would dinner be with Saddam or George W. or the in-laws?

those who have lost their imagination. Has your country lost its imagination?" I will never forget the tears in his eyes as he cried for imagination. A few years back, I met up with Ben Cohen, founder of Ben and Jerry's Ice Cream. He said, "I've read some of your stuff, and I like it." I said, "I've eaten some of your ice cream, and I like it too." And a wonderful friendship was born. He's a good friend to have for a lot of reasons, not the least of which was a lot of free ice cream at our block parties. But we also found that we had similar dreams and imagination—the ability to dream of a world without war. So we conspired to create a project called Jesus, Bombs, and Ice Cream, which is about imagining a world with fewer bombs and more ice cream. Our debut show was on the tenth anniversary of September 11th. We had Terri Rockfeller from September 11th Families for Peaceful Tomorrows, that group of survivors of September 11th who have used their grief to work for peace instead of war. And my Iraq-veteran pal Logan shared his story. We had spoken word, live painting on stage, pyrotechnics, and even heard from our Afghan Peace Volunteers in Kabul. We also had the world's best juggler (really) juggle weapons over Ben's head, and we disguised a watermelon as a bomb, which Josh chopped to pieces and gave out. And we transformed an AK47 into garden tools. As a grand finale, we had ice cream fall from the sky attached to helium-balloon parachutes (which were dropped by soldiers in camo, of course). Yeah, it was pretty fantastic. We captured it all on tape so you can watch it all at home with a pint of Chubby Hubby (*www.thesimpleway.org/store*). Oh, and you can see a couple of Ben's classic clips online. He stacks Oreos that each represent $10 billion of federal spending so you can see how the money stacks up: *https://www.youtube.com/watch?v=YVPG b21oaq8*. And here Ben pours out thousands of BBs representing the 150,000 Hiroshima-size bombs in the US arsenal: *https://www.youtube.com/watch?v=3bJsGJhpZd8*.

The whole project was about imagination, which the world needs more of. What if we used all the brilliant minds that are creating things like military drones to dream up ways of creating peace?

HOLY MISCHIEF

What I love about Jesus is that he always has imagination. Author and professor Walter Wink does brilliant work demonstrating Jesus' creativity in his teaching in the Sermon on the Mount.[6] Talking about the familiar "turn the other cheek" verses, Wink points out that Jesus is not just suggesting that we masochistically let people step all over us. Instead, Jesus is pointing us toward something that imaginatively disarms others. When hit on the cheek, turn and look the person in the eye. Do not cower and do not punch them back. Make sure they look into your eyes and see your sacred humanity, and it will become increasingly harder for them to hurt you. When someone tries to sue you for the coat on your back and drags you before the court, go ahead and take all of your clothes off and hand them over, exposing the sickness of their greed. When a soldier asks you to walk a mile with them and carry their pack (as was Roman law and custom), don't throw your fist in the air like the Zealots, just walk with them two miles instead of one, talk with them and woo them into our movement by your love.

In each of these instances, Jesus is teaching peasants the third way. It is here that we see a Jesus who abhors both passivity and violence, who carves out a third way that is neither submission nor assault, neither fight nor flight. It

---

6. Walter Wink, *The Powers That Be* (New York: Doubleday, 1998).

is this third way, Wink writes, that teaches that "evil can be opposed without being mirrored . . . oppressors can be resisted without being emulated . . . enemies can be neutralized without being destroyed."[7] Then we can look into the eyes of a centurion and see not a beast but a child, and then walk with that child a couple of miles. Look into the eyes of tax collectors as they sue you in court. See their poverty and give them your coat. Look into the eyes of the ones who are hardest for you to like, and see the One you love.

We need more of the prophetic imagination[8] that can interrupt violence and oppression. The biblical prophets are always doing bizarre things to get folks to listen to God. Moses turns a staff into a snake. Elijah hits a rock and fire comes out of it, and he brings fire down on an altar (pyro). Jeremiah wears a yoke to symbolize imperial captivity. (He's eventually arrested.) Ezekiel eats a scroll. Hosea marries a prostitute and stays faithful to her to show God's love for Israel. John the Baptizer eats locusts and makes clothes out of camel skin. Jesus pulls money out of a fish's mouth, flips over tables in the temple, and rides a donkey into Passover (and not because he was a Democrat).[9]

---

7. Ibid., 111.

8. A phrase coined by Walter Brueggemann in his book creatively titled *The Prophetic Imagination*.

9. Passover was an anti-imperial Jewish festival in which the Jews celebrated their ancestors' coming out of Egyptian slavery and "passing over" to a land of promise. With Roman soldiers lining the street, Jews gathered and waved palm branches, symbols of resistance to the empire (a Jewish flag of sorts). Passover was a volatile time, often marked by riots and bloodshed. When Jesus rode a donkey into this festival, it would have been a lampoon, like street theater at a protest. Scholars call it the anti-triumphal entry into Jerusalem. Kings did not ride donkeys. They rode mighty war horses with an entourage of soldiers around them. So here is Jesus making a spectacle of violence and power, riding in on the back of a donkey.

It is this prophetic imagination that we evoke with stunts like blowing the ram's horn and proclaiming the Jubilee on Wall Street, then dumping $10,000 in coins outside the Stock Exchange. Or serving communion in Love Park even though it was illegal to distribute food. In his recent book, *The Beloved Community*,[10] religion professor Charles Marsh calls the Simple Way "theological pranksters." I think the world needs some theological pranksters who open our minds to new possibilities. One of my Princeton Seminary professors, Dr. Mark Taylor, calls it the "theatrics of counterterror" that upstages the theatrics of war, prisons, and racism with extreme acts of disarming love. When someone keeps us laughing, we don't even think to become defensive. We are disarmed by a gentle revolution.

Criminologists teach that one of the quickest ways to diffuse violence is with surprise. Those who commit violence depend on the predictability of the victims. When victims do something that surprises them, it throws the whole plan out of whack. Jesus is always doing weird things in the midst of conflict, like when the men are about to kill the adulteress, and he bends down and draws in the dirt until eventually they all drop their stones. There's that time the soldiers come to arrest Jesus, and Peter pulls out a sword and cuts off a guy's ear. (He'd be in big trouble around here.) Jesus rebukes him and then grabs the dude's ear and puts it back on. That must have been a little awkward for everyone, especially the soldiers. How do you arrest a guy who just put your buddy's ear back on? Jesus' theological stunts and prophetic imagination surprise and disarm. They make people laugh and catch folks off-guard, even folks who wish they could hate him. And of course,

---

10. Charles Marsh, *The Beloved Community* (New York: Basic, 2005).

there's the dazzle of the resurrection; that's got to be the best one ever. (Even David Copperfield couldn't pull that off.) Colossians says that in his death and resurrection, Jesus "disarmed the powers and authorities" and "made a public spectacle of them" (Col. 2:15).

One of the women in our community, Adrienne, is the mother of a three-year-old, Bianca, who has an inordinate amount of energy and bounces from place to place and from emotion to emotion. Adrienne is one of the more innovative and persistent women I know and has taught me a thing or two about creatively disciplining and disarming three-year-olds. One day she took Bianca to the toy store, and she became obsessed with a toy she could not have, so she began throwing a horrific temper tantrum. She flung herself to the ground and began screaming and rolling around. Without a second thought, Adrienne threw herself down beside her and began doing the same thing. Bianca jumped to her feet, saw everyone staring, and became timid, telling her mother how embarrassed she was. And Adrienne just said with a grin, "Good, now you know how I feel." And on they shopped. We give tons of other examples of the "third way"—neither fight nor flight—in *Jesus for President*. Hands down, one of my favorites involved a young woman from Brazil in the early days at the Simple Way. Lydia was petite, and like many of the women in our community, she was a fireball—sassy, bold, somehow able to be both gentle and direct. One day as she was traveling on the train, a fellow sat down next to her and pulled a knife. "Listen carefully," he said, "here's what's gonna happen. You are going to hand me your bag, get off at the next station, and not say a word." She looked at him unflinchinchingly. "My name is Lydia," she said winsomely, firmly, "and I am from Brazil." The man stared at her blankly, taken aback. She continued, "My bag is filled with photos and addresses of my family and those mean a lot to me, but will do you no good. I'd imagine what you want is money. There is no money in my bag. However, I have some money in my pocket. So here's what we'll do. I'll get out my money, give you twenty dollars, you get off at the next station, and we won't say a word." And it worked.

One of our cohorts here in Philly was jumped by some inner-city youth. They beat him up pretty badly, leaving him with a broken jaw. He came home pretty shaken up. With his mind racing, he began to pray about what to do in response. He decided to go back to the corner where the youth hung out and post a flyer with his picture on it. The flyer read something like this: "I was beaten up by some guys on this corner. If anyone knows who did this, please let them know I do not hold this against them but care about them, and if I have done anything against anyone, I ask for forgiveness. I want whoever did this to know that I am not angry with you. I care about you and invite you to get to know me. Maybe we could play some kickball or something." And it listed his contact info.

We get another glimpse of extreme love in the musical *Les Miserables*, in which a priest allows a vagrant, Jean Valjean, to stay in his home, only to get knocked unconscious and be robbed. The next day, the authorities catch Jean Valjean and drag him before the priest. They say Valjean claimed that the priest had given him the silver goods in his bag. And the priest instinctively, beautifully, says, "I am so thankful you have come back, as you forgot the candlesticks." As the guards release Jean Valjean, the priest whispers in his ear, "With this, I have ransomed your soul."

Sounds good (musicals can do that for you), but it's not that easy. When someone stole our power drill (and we all knew who), we didn't run after the person with the drill bits saying, "Hey, my friend, you forgot these." We'd rather teach the person a lesson of justice than a lesson of love.

That kind of love takes courage. One of the neighborhood kids who hangs out at our house all the time came up to me one day very upset because one of the bullies in his school was picking on him. I told him, "Rolando, that means you get to show him how friends treat each other. He must not know what love and friendship feel like, so you get to teach him." Rolando said, "Aww man, love is so hard."

This love is not sentimentality but the dreadful kind of love Dorothy Day spoke of, saying that it is such a harsh and dreadful thing to ask of us, but that it's the only answer. The only thing harder than hatred is love. The only thing harder than war is peace. The only thing that takes more work, tears, and sweat than division is reconciliation. But what more beautiful things could we devote our lives to? Until the courage that we have for peace surpasses the courage that we have for war, violence will continue to triumph, and imperial execution rather than divine resurrection will have the final word.

I saw one of those World's Best Video clips a while back. One of them captured a hockey game in which one of the key players went for a shot, and then everything went crazy and erupted into a brawl. This player was famous for his gentle spirit and love for the game. He hated it when players fought, so when the fight broke out, he pulled aside. And as it escalated, he decided to create a distraction, so he ripped his clothes off and started streaking around the hockey rink. As you can imagine, the fight didn't last long.

Whenever there is a fight on our block, my first instinct is to run inside and grab our torches and begin juggling them, to upstage the drama of violent conflicts in our neighborhood. Perhaps the kids will lose interest in the noise of a good fight and move toward the other end of the block to watch the circus. I truly believe we can overwhelm the darkness of this world by shining something brighter and more beautiful. It's sort of like the celebration we had on Wall Street. We didn't have to "lock down" the entrance and keep people out. We just celebrated an alternative that was so incredibly contagious they couldn't keep people in that place. In the same way, we continue to declare God's beautiful vision even in this world, and in the darkness, it shines brighter and brighter.[11]

Our world is desperately in need of imagination, for we have spent so much creativity devising ways of destroying our enemies that some folks don't even think it's possible (much less practical) to love them.[12] We have placed such idolatrous faith in our ability to protect ourselves that we call it more courageous to die killing than to die loving. The faith we have in the market and in the imagination we employ to acquire wealth has so far surpassed our ingenuity to share that we cannot help but wonder if the contemporary gospel remains good news to the poor whose bellies scream out to God.

---

11. Our friends in the New Jerusalem community here in Philly lead us in a workshop called the Alternatives to Violence Project. The project is designed to help us recognize our own violence and learn to creatively resolve conflict. It's a holistic program trying to root out violence from our world by beginning within each of us. Many of the teacher-learners have been perpetrators or victims of violence themselves. Check out *www .avpusa.org*.

12. Another good book on creative nonviolence is *Is There No Other Way?* by Michael Nagler, which argues that the problem is not that we have tried nonviolence and it has failed but that we have rarely had the courage and imagination to try it.

Perhaps it should not come as a surprise that when I returned from Iraq, it wasn't the Christian press but *SPIN* magazine, a leading mainstream pop-culture magazine, that came knocking at our door. Meeting some resistance from me as we discussed doing an interview for a feature story, the journalist said in frustration, "I want people to see another face of Christianity." He explained that most of his readers were not Christians and that many of them were in favor of the war or were simply ambivalent. He went on to confess that he had been raised Catholic and became quite disenchanted with it all. Now he just wanted people to catch another glimpse of what Christianity could look like. He and the photographer came down to Philly and hung out, and we talked for hours. They fell in love with our community and life, and we with them. The photographer gave us a beautiful camera we share with our neighbors. The writer gave us a van. And out of the whole experience came an article that spoke of my Christian faith and vision for God's peace (sandwiched between Radiohead and the Fugees, smothered by ads for beer, SUVs, and the Navy). While it was hard to find language that transcended culture (the article called me the "bulletproof monk" and a "Christian punk activist" and gave props to my fantastical band The Dumpster Divers, who have never had a show or cut a record), it made me recognize how thirsty the world is for another way of life. For the record, I did actually write one song, which you can hear my friends sing here: *https://www.youtube.com/watch?v=KKmBRP9noQw*. Our culture is starving for answers, as the old ones have gone bankrupt. In response to the *SPIN* article, I got many letters from non-Christians who were fascinated by the gospel I preached and the God I've grown to love, and I got many letters from religious folks and church elders who were upset that I would talk with such heathens. We must have done something right.

I was able to be the face of another kind of Christian extremist, another ordinary radical ready for a revolution that dances and laughs.

CHAPTER 11

MAKING REVOLUTION IRRESISTIBLE

Dumbfounded and outraged by the apathy of the church, I've at times gravitated toward circles of social dissenters, protesters, and activists. We've shouted at the system that was hurting so many of our friends, and we've yelled at the church to wake up. But I saw very little fruit from those days. My ripped jeans and punk rock hair made me feel pleasantly distant from the "filthy rotten system," but I also found myself estranged from sincere folks who were polarized by the way we preached the truth.

I went to the rallies and marched in the streets. I got arrested for "nonviolent direct action" and "civil disobedience" over and over, losing count after around a dozen times. But my hopes for a perfect revolution were dashed by human imperfection. Among my activist friends, I began to feel a self-righteousness mirroring that of conservative Christianity. I felt an aggressiveness and judgmentalism reminiscent of that which I had grown to despise in the church. I sat through meetings to plan rallies and marches where people argued and gossiped like the best church committee or trustee meeting, destroying one another in their fervor to build a better world. I handed out flyers to convert people to the movement and felt as coercive and detached as I did handing out Christian tracts at the mall.

FACING STATISTICS THAT HAVE FACES

But then I discovered a different kind of protest. Years ago, I attended a rally against sweatshops overseas. The organizers had not invited the typical rally speakers—lawyers, activists, academics. Instead, they brought the kids themselves from the sweatshops to speak. I listened as a child from Indonesia stood to share and pointed to the giant scar on his face. "I got this scar when my master lashed me for not working hard enough. When it began to bleed, he did not want me to stop working or to ruin the cloth in front of me, so he took a lighter and burned it shut. I got this making stuff for you." I was suddenly consumed by the overwhelming reality of the suffering body of Christ. Jesus now bore not just the marks from the nails and scars from the thorns but a gash down his face, for when we have done it to the "least of these," we have done it to Christ himself. How could I possibly follow Jesus and buy anything from that master? The statistics now had a face. Poverty had become personal. And that messes with you. When I was traveling in Europe, I stumbled across a reality show that was fascinating. The producers had rounded up some fairly wealthy adults—some were shopping, others eating. And they challenged them to track some of their favorite products to their source. Some of them went out on boats to gather shrimp, some headed to the tuna factory in the Philippines. Others visited sweatshops and factories. What they saw shocked and horrified them. Some of them ended up on their knees vomiting, nauseated by the smell of the factory and the smell of injustice. Others were moved to tears as they met the invisible faces behind their products. Over and over they said, "I will never be the same." Some of them said they will no longer buy products from that company, and others said they will be launching a campaign to change the injustices. Once again, I was reminded that one reason we do not care is that we do not know. I also learned that apparently the UK has much better reality TV than we do.

Not too long ago, I was speaking at Princeton, and some of the students asked me how they were to choose which issue of social justice is the most important. The question made me cringe. Issues? These issues have faces. We're talking not only about ideas but also about human emergencies. My response to the well-intentioned Princeton students was, "Don't choose issues; choose people. Come play in the fire hydrants in North Philly. Fall in love with a group of people who are marginalized and suffering, and then you won't have to worry about which cause you need to protest. Then the issues will choose you."

Don't get me wrong. There are times when injustice will take us to the streets and might land us in jail, but it is our love for God and our neighbor—not our rage or our arrogance—that counts. One of my favorite old protest songs goes like this: "We are a gentle, angry people . . . and we are fighting for our lives." Street protest signs and bumper stickers often flash the slogan, "If you're not angry, then you're not paying attention." I got angry and was often ready to flip some tables. I rocked out to Rage Against the Machine: "I got no patience now, so sick of complacence now . . . the time has come to rage." In college, we prided ourselves on stirring stuff up. Our group raged against complacency. In fact, originally we tried to call ourselves Youth Against Complacency, but YAC sounded like someone was about to hurl, so we went for Youth Against Complacency and Homelessness Today. The YACHT Club kind of had a ring to it (and we hoped to squeeze some money out of curious boaters). The YACHT Club continues to be a vibrant group on Eastern University's campus, with weekly trips to hang out with friends on the street. And they continue to fight complacency. When an issue of injustice arises, they are often the "first responders," sort of a special-ops team. What's also great is that they are careful not to separate prayer and action. They love Jesus and holy mischief.

While most activists could use a good dose of gentleness (after all, it is a fruit of the Spirit), I think most believers could use a good dose of holy anger. Years ago, I came across an old prayer of a Danish pastor named Kaj Munk, which I had torn out of a community newsletter printed by our friends. Munk was an outspoken priest and playwright who uttered these prophetic words before he was killed, with his Bible next to him, by the Gestapo in January 1944 (careful, it could get you killed):

> What is, therefore, our task today? Shall I answer: "Faith, hope, and love"? That sounds beautiful. But I would say—courage. No, even that is not challenging enough to be the whole truth. Our task today is recklessness. For what we Christians lack is not psychology or literature . . . we lack a holy rage—the recklessness which comes from the knowledge of God and humanity. The ability to rage when justice lies prostrate on the streets, and when the lie rages across the face of the earth . . . a holy anger about the things that are wrong in the world. To rage against the ravaging of God's earth, and the destruction of God's world. To rage when little children must die of hunger, when the tables of the rich are sagging with food. To rage at the senseless killing of so many, and against the madness of militaries. To rage at the lie that calls the threat of death and the strategy of destruction peace.

To rage against complacency. To restlessly seek that recklessness that will challenge and seek to change human history until it conforms to the norms of the Kingdom of God. And remember the signs of the Christian Church have been the Lion, the Lamb, the Dove, and the Fish . . . but never the chameleon.

There were plenty of violent revolutions during the time of Jesus, and Jesus had several Zealots in his inner circle. But he was teaching them another way of life. I am reminded of how Gandhi said that if he had to choose between a violent person and a coward, he would choose the violent person. For a violent person can be taught to love, but very little can be done with a coward. We are students of a gentle revolution, and that is what the world needs more of, whether you're conservative or liberal. It was Argentinian doctor and pop-revolution icon Che Guevara who said, as he was leaving Cuba for Africa, "Let me say, at the risk of seeming ridiculous, that the true revolutionary is guided by great feelings of love."[1]

Just as "believers" are a dime a dozen in the church, so are "activists" in social justice circles nowadays. But lovers are hard to come by. And I think that's what our world is desperately in need of—lovers, people who are building deep, genuine relationships with fellow strugglers along the way, and who actually know the faces of the people behind the issues they are concerned about. We are trying to raise up an army not simply of street activists but of lovers—a community of people who have fallen desperately in love with God and with suffering people, and who allow those relationships to disturb and transform them.

---

1. Che Guevara, *Reminiscences of the Cuban Revolutionary War* (New York: Penguin, 1969).

TOWARD A GENTLER REVOLUTION

While I was at Eastern University, the YACHT Club stirred up all kinds of dust. When the administration bought fancy trash cans, we found out how much they had cost (hundreds of dollars each) and then put huge three-foot price tags on each one to creatively critique the expenditure. We stirred up students on various campuses to research who makes their athletic teams' clothing and whether those companies use sweatshop labor. But the moments that were most transformative, that had the most lasting significance, were those done with gentleness and personalism. One of the most creative things we did was Arthur Jackson Appreciation Day. Arthur Jackson Inc. was the company that provided all of the housekeeping staff for the college. As students built relationships with the housekeeping staff, we wanted to show the folks who cleaned up after our messes and held our campus together that we cared about them and appreciated their continual work. YACHT Clubbers organized an annual holiday, when dozens of students cleaned up the entire campus so that the staff could have a paid day off and know that they were celebrated and loved. Arthur Jackson is no longer the company Eastern works with, and some of the issues around wages and immigration status continue to raise new questions of what justice looks like at Eastern and universities around the country. But just this year, I was able to participate in what I hope is becoming a tradition at Eastern: Housekeeper Appreciation Day. I wrote about it here: *http://www.redletterchristians.org/blessed-housekeepers/.*

For those of you thinking about college, consider this: don't just ask how strong the academics are or how good the football team is or even how you like the campus or the town. All of those are good questions, but make sure you also ask, "What do you pay your housekeeping staff?" One of the true tests of a good college is how they treat their workers, and certainly a decent indicator of that is how the lowest paid workers fare in contrast to the highest paid administrators. A good question of any college president is whether she or he would be comfortable exchanging salaries for a year with the janitor. After all, both are just as valuable in the eyes of God.

Years later, we began asking new questions. One of the janitors happened to end up living on our block in Kensington. We found out that he wasn't making enough money to support his family, earning just over six dollars an hour. The administration, students, and alumni had already begun to ask questions about the workers' wages at Eastern University. That same year, David Black, the president of Eastern University, came down to the Simple Way for our Christmas party. It just so happened that my neighbor, the janitor, also showed up. So we said, "Hey, let's all sit down and talk!" That's when things are transformed, when people become human, neighbors, family. Thanks to the hard work and courageous voices of faculty, students, and Dr. Black himself, Eastern University made a courageous step. They agreed to provide a living wage to workers, along with transportation assistance and benefits. Now when I speak to students, especially Christian students, I remind them that we must not ask only about the academic quality, social life, and aesthetic beauty of the universities we are considering attending; we must also ask how these institutions incarnate the values we believe in, especially Christian institutions that proclaim the gospel of God's justice.

Students have begun talking about how Eastern could be more faithful caretakers of God's creation, tread more lightly on God's earth, and use renewable energy. In a respectful dialogue, the administration again took a bold step to move toward wind energy, one of the first Christian colleges to do so. And they, in turn, are finding that they will also gain, as they attract the sorts of Christian disciples who care about things like workers' rights and the environment. The gentle revolution.

THE INVISIBLE PEOPLE

One of the groups many of us in Philly have grown to admire, because they exemplify the gentle revolution, is the Coalition of Immokalee Workers.[2] They are farm workers and day laborers who pick tomatoes for companies like Taco Bell. We've worn out some shoes together marching hundreds of miles in protest. One summer a few years back, the workers told us they were organizing a walk from their fields in Florida to the growers association in Orlando. As usual, we joined them. On the back of a truck, a fourteen-foot Statue of Liberty led the way, only instead of a tablet, she held a bucket, and in place of the torch, she lifted up a tomato. Along the way, hundreds of pedestrians came by to voice their support, along with actors, musicians, politicians, and clergy. They made headlines in nearly every town we passed through. As we neared Orlando, public attention had reached a pinnacle, and the police told the workers they could no longer have the statue on the back of the truck. We were disappointed. But one of the workers grabbed me. "They said we cannot have the statue on the truck," he said pensively, "so we will carry her." He was serious. So each of us grabbed a corner and hoisted her up on our shoulders, and we began walking, taking turns.

---

2. *www.ciw-online.org.*

One of the mighty women who helped carry the statue whispered, "If Jesus can carry that cross, we can carry this statue." The statue is now housed in the Smithsonian Museum in Washington, D.C., evidence of how monumental their movement has become. And we did. Dripping with sweat, singing, and chanting, we carried her to the front doors of the growers association.

It was a sacred moment. The executives tried to ignore them. They issued a statement that "the tractors don't come up to the farmer and tell him how to run the farm." With tears in their eyes, these workers with calloused hands and leathery skin from long days in the sun-scorched fields cried out, as if to God, "We are not tractors. Tractors do not bleed and cry. Tractors do not have families and children. We are not machines; we are human beings." It seemed to me the whisper of James was never as clear as it was on that day: "Look! The wages you failed to pay the workers who mowed your fields are crying out against you. The cries of the harvesters have reached the ears of the Lord Almighty. You have lived on earth in luxury and self-indulgence. You have fattened yourselves in the day of slaughter. You have condemned and murdered the innocent one, who was not opposing you" (James 5:4–6).

It is the warm joy and humility of these workers that has wooed people into their movement. I remember one of the more recent marches we went on, when we walked to the corporate headquarters of Yum! (the company that owns Taco Bell and many others). The workers simply hung out their dirty work clothes, hundreds and hundreds of shirts stained by hours of sweating beneath the sun in the fields. Another prophetic stunt to reach the ears of powerful people who had grown so detached from the sweat and tears of peasants and workers, and to make it personal.

And it was not like before. The Presbyterian Church joined the workers in the boycott of Taco Bell. One congregation had received a grant from the Yum! Corporation, but they said that, while the grant money would really come in handy for their poor congregation, they wanted to give it to the workers, to whom it belongs, and they signed the check over to them. Student boycotts closed down Taco Bells on college campuses until they would listen to the farm workers. Congregations and youth groups told me they were writing letters to the owners of Taco Bell—not angry letters, but kind letters that hoped for and believed in redemption. And a few months ago, after I had gone nearly five years without chalupas (I always said, "Why couldn't it have been Checkers or something . . . not Taco Bell?"), the owners of Taco Bell agreed not only to meet the workers' demands but to sit down and meet with them face to face. Taco Bell's executive even issued a statement encouraging other fast-food franchises to ask who the hidden faces are behind their food, and how they are being treated. So now you can eat your chalupas with pride—or at least the tomatoes on the chalupa. That's the irresistible revolution. (Though of course, it's not the end of their struggle.) The Coalition of Immokalee Workers has been making modern-day slavery history. They've won all sorts of awards, and even more significant, they've managed to get a dozen of the largest corporations in the world to commit to their campaign, which includes ending slavery. Among them are Whole Foods, McDonald's, Walmart, Trader Joe's, Chipotle, Subway, Burger King, and yes, Taco Bell. (Yum! Brands.) But the struggle's not over. Last I heard, Publix and a few others are still holding out. About a year ago, I joined the coalition on a march to the Publix headquarters. My favorite part was when we arrived. We blasted some Aretha Franklin from the flatbed: R-E-S-P-E-C-T (*http://ciw-online.org/blog/2013/03/ social-media-chatter-surges-around-the-march-for-rights- respect-and-fair-food/*).

The world of efficiency and anonymity dehumanizes us. We see people as machines, as tractors, or as issues to protest. We live in an age when machines act like people, and people act like machines. But machines cannot love. We have to ask who the invisible people are. Who makes our clothes? Who picks our vegetables? And how are they treated? Growing up, I was told not to wear a T-shirt that advertised a band unless I agreed with what they stood for, but I was never told to do the same with the companies I advertised inadvertently. What do they stand for? What gospel do they proclaim?

There is a brilliant scene in Michael Moore's documentary *The Big One* where Philip Knight, founder and former CEO of Nike, which has become notorious for its abuse of workers overseas,[3] invites Moore to talk with him. So Moore goes in to meet with Knight bearing a gift—two first-class tickets to Indonesia. And he invites Knight to fly to Indonesia and simply walk through his factories. Phil busts out laughing and shakes his head, "No, no, not a chance." Moore tells him that he just wants to walk through and check out the operation, and then asks, "Have you ever been to see your factories where your shoes are made? Have you ever been to Indonesia?" Knight says, "No,

---

3. Nike's shoes are produced in factories in Indonesia, China, and Vietnam. Human rights abuses occurring in these factories range from torture to rape and have made headline news in recent years, especially since the *New York Times* front-page article on November 8, 1997. The workers make about $1.50 to make Nike's shoes, half of what it costs to live, and folks in the US buy them for $100 or more. And folks like Michael Jordan and Tiger Woods earn more money wearing the shoes for ads than all the workers combined earn for making the shoes.

and I am not going to go." These are the layers of separation that allow injustice to happen. It's not that people are malicious. I do not think we are naturally able to hurt each other. Even Philip Knight seems like too nice of a guy for that. But we keep ourselves at a safe distance.

I am also reminded of the gatherings each year down in Fort Benning, Georgia, outside the US Army's School of the Americas,[4] a military camp that trains soldiers from Latin America and has a notorious and humiliating past. Graduates of the school have committed atrocities in Latin America, including the 1980 assasination of Archbishop Oscar Romero, along with the massacres of the indigenous poor and religious leaders who have joined their struggle. Each year over ten thousand folks gather for a silent procession onto the property, simply holding white crosses with the names of the thousands who have lost their lives. In 2015, Romero was officially declared a martyr by Pope Francis, paving the way to sainthood. He was shot in the heart as he served communion during worship. As the vigil

---

4. Graduates have been linked to some of the worst human rights abuses in Latin America. In 1996, the Pentagon was forced to release training manuals used at the school that advocated torture, extortion, and execution. Among the SOA's nearly sixty thousand graduates are notorious dictators Manuel Noriega and Omar Torrijos of Panama, Leopoldo Galtieri and Roberto Viola of Argentina, Juan Velasco Alvarado of Peru, Guillermo Rodriguez of Ecuador, and Hugo Banzer Suarez of Bolivia. According to human rights watch groups, lower-level SOA graduates have participated in human rights abuses that include the assassination of Archbishop Oscar Romero and the El Mozote Massacre of nine hundred civilians. In an attempt to deflect public criticism and disassociate the school from its dubious reputation, the SOA was renamed the Western Hemisphere Institute for Security Cooperation (WHINSEC) in 2001, a cosmetic change that would ensure that the SOA could continue its operations during a time when opponents were poised to win a congressional vote that would have dismantled the school. Somehow it is still open. See *www.soaw.org and www.soawne.org.*

proceeds, each name is read aloud and everyone responds, "Presente" (present). This is the spirit of gentleness that moves us to imagine new alternatives, driven by the sacredness of each life, which is no longer hidden in the shadows.

BECOMING HUMAN

Over and over, people have told me that the power of my trip to Iraq is that it humanized the war, even for folks who otherwise might not have given a second thought to the morality of what we were doing there. The war took on a face other than just Saddam or Osama, or even a family member in the US military. A few days before I left for Iraq, I settled into my seat on an airplane next to two strangers. They began talking to each other, discovering that they had much in common, particularly their political affiliation. They cracked some jokes about liberals and boasted about the military presence in Iraq. I tried to read, tried to sleep, tried to resist the temptation to start an intense debate, which would have made for a long plane ride. Finally, I got out some homemade cookies and offered them to my neighbors. They continued talking about how much they traveled, all the places they've been, and then they turned to me. "Where's your next trip to?" one of them asked. I got a lump in my throat and paused, since the honest answer was "Baghdad." And I proceeded cautiously. "Actually, next week I plan to go to Iraq." Their jaws dropped. Puzzled, one man asked, "With the military?" I giggled. (I don't exactly fit the military prototype, with my dreadlocks and all.) "No," I replied, "I will be going as a Christian Peacemaker to be with the families there and voice opposition to the war."

I was amazed that they did not start arguing with me. They were intrigued that I believed in something so much that I would risk my life for it. We actually had a nice talk. And I will never forget what they said as we parted. These two people, whom I had just met, told me with great drama how they would be glued to the TV as they worried about me, wondering if I would make it back safely. I stood in awe, knowing that this is the great tragedy: we have not put a face on the war. Degrees of separation allow us to destroy human beings we do not know except as the enemy. So in one hour, the walls came down a little. I thought of how powerful it was to have a face in Iraq, albeit a face these two had met for only a couple of hours on a plane. But now they hesitate as they hear the drums of war. And in the moment of hesitation, the world is pregnant with possibilities. Granted, I would like for my two new friends to oppose the war because of the families in Iraq, but if they oppose the war because of some goofball they met for an hour on a plane, that'll work for now.

There is power in a name. One of the things happening in our country around racial justice right now is that people are "naming" injustice. No longer are we just talking about statistics, numbers, and data. We are lifting up the names of the victims of a failed justice system. Injustice becomes a name or a hashtag and goes viral. And there is something in a name that humanizes, personalizes, and wakes us up. Trayvon Martin. Mike Brown. Eric Garner. Tamir Rice. Anthony Hill. Tony Robinson.

The statistics have faces now. The numbers have names. They remind us of the collateral damage of a failed system, and the urgency of this moment. We can't make injustice history until we make injustice personal. For many people of color, the victims of injustice have had names for a long time. Names like Emmett Till help us know how far we have come, and names like Eric Garner remind us how far we still have to go.

I've written more about the power of a name here: *http://www.redletterchristians.org/naming-injustice*.

THE TEARS OF RIZPAH

Before and during my time in Iraq, I studied the powerful biblical story of a heroic woman named Rizpah (2 Sam. 21:1–14). It took on completely new meaning for me as I lived among the women of Iraq who had seen their loved ones killed in war and faced the reality of more suffering. Rizpah lived in a time like ours. Kings were making treaties and breaking them (v. 2). The land was stained with the blood of war. To heal the famine that cursed Israel, David makes a deal in order to make amends with the Gibeonites. The currency he uses is human lives, as with our present war. He hands human beings over to be massacred; of course, they are not his own children. He takes the sons of Rizpah (Saul's concubine) and Merab (Saul's daughter), and the children are "killed and their bodies exposed before the Lord." Not only were they killed, but they were left on the hill without proper burial, left to be devoured by wild animals. And yet, despite David's effort, God does not heal the land . . . yet.

With the reckless love that only a grieving mother has, Rizpah takes sackcloth and spreads it out on a rock beside the bodies. She sets up camp. The text says she stays from the "beginning of the harvest till the rains poured down," implying she was there for the season. Day after day, week after week, she protects the bodies from the birds and animals. And word of her encampment spreads across the land, making it all the way to the ears of King David. When he hears of her courage, he remembers Saul and his friend Jonathan. An incredible thing happens: he is moved to gather up the bones of all the dead. Human suffering has the power to move even kings to feel again.

Rizpah pricks the humanity of a king who had become so dehumanized that he could exchange children like currency and see them die without remorse. Then there can be a true liberation, where even kings can be set free. True revolution is when, as antiapartheid leader and Nobel Peace Prize–winner Bishop Desmond Tutu says (with a huge smile), "the oppressed are freed from being oppressed and the oppressors are freed from being oppressors." And this is when God heals the land (v. 14).

When I was in Iraq, I prayed that as lives were lost in that ancient land again, mothers would set up camp beside the bodies of their dead and wail so loudly that word of the travesty would spread throughout the earth. Maybe people from around the world would hear and come out and sit with them on the rock beside the bodies. And we would groan together so loudly that even the kings would hear.[5] One also thinks of Emmett Till's mother, who insisted on having an open-casket funeral after the brutal racially motivated murder of her son, so that everybody could see what they did to her baby. Her words: "There was just no way I could describe what was in that box. No way. And I just wanted the world to see." His casket is now in the Smithsonian, a continual reminder of what we did. Perhaps the kings would be moved to be human again, and then God would heal our land. Maybe that's the most transformative thing we could have done after September 11th.

And when the Scriptures in Isaiah (2:4) and Micah (4:3) say that "the people" will beat their swords into

---

5. I wrote this section long before Cindy Sheehan's son Casey was killed in Iraq in April 2005, but consider the power with which her presence captured the attention of the nation as she set up camp outside the president's Texas ranch. Even for those who don't dig her style or politics, her mourning and loss are hard to ignore.

plowshares and their spears into pruning hooks, the verses end with the words, "Nation will not take up sword against nation, nor will they train for war anymore." The transformation begins with the people—with ordinary radicals, courageous mothers and grandmothers like Rizpah. When we begin enacting the new world, the nations will follow. Nations will not lead us to peace; it is people who will lead the nations to peace as they begin to humanize the nations. There's something holy about beating a gun into oblivion. The most powerful guns-to-plows events we've held have involved victims of violence doing the beating on the gun. We've had moms who lost their kids, police chiefs, and veterans participate. And there is something so visceral, holy, and captivating about seeing an instrument of death become a tool that cultivates life.

Our first weapon conversion was on the tenth anniversary of the September 11th attacks after hearing that some of the metal from the World Trade Center was used to build a warship, the antithesis of the prophetic call to bring life out of death. We took an AK47 and turned it into a rake and a shovel. Then we started getting messages from around the world of other weapons conversions—handguns turned into guitars, machine guns made into saxophones, war metal transformed into art.

I'll never forget one of the moms who had lost her son, as she beat on the handgun we got off the streets of Philly. With every *thup* of the hammer, she said, "This . . . Is . . . for . . . my . . . son." It is this prophetic, imaginative, stubborn witness that says we refuse to wait any longer. We have prayed for peace, and we will continue to pray for peace. But we also have realized that sometimes we think we are waiting on God when actually God is waiting on us. We cannot wait on politicians or governments. The new world the prophets of old told us about begins with us. It begins with you. We are the ones that we have been waiting on.

You can see more here: *https://www.youtube.com/watch?v=dWH4R0_-4hg*. And here: *www.rawtools.org*.

PROTESTERS AND PROPHETS

One of the moments when I felt myself move toward a gentler revolution was during the Republican National Convention when it came to Philadelphia in 1998. It was election year, and once again poor people were running— for their lives. Somehow my community partner Jamie and I got into the convention. Call it divine providence or savvy politics, we got special passes onto the main arena floor. We were dropped off at the front door by our own private golf cart. The friendly, enthusiastic GOP volunteers escorted us in. (We need not fear their surveillance too much!) So there I was in my young Republican suit-and-tie disguise (complete with a little gold elephant pin). But underneath, I was ready. I had painted my shirt to read, "Woe to those who deprive the poor of their rights (Isaiah 10)," and on the back were the words of Jesus, "Woe to you who are rich . . . but blessed are the poor (Luke 6)." We were able to get very close, about twenty yards from the stage. After the introduction of George W. Bush, as soon as the thundering applause faded into eager silence, I rose and tore off my outer layer to reveal my shirt. And at the top of my lungs I began quoting the Scriptures. In their distress, the conventioneers tried to drown me out by interrupting George's first words with applause. The ovation died down. And the words of Jesus blared forth: "Blessed are the poor . . . but woe to you who are rich." Again they clapped. Then Romans 8: "Creation is groaning for liberation!" Security people frantically ran around. I was soon pounced on by the Secret Service and removed. They locked me in a closet "so we could talk." Through the locked door, I could hear them conferring with each other. I heard them say, "Maybe we can charge him with protesting. If so, we can hold him for several days." So they came back in and asked, "Are you a protester?" I thought for a second (a very brief second). "No sir," I said plainly, "I am not a protester . . . uh . . . I am a prophet." I was held in custody a bit longer and then released with no charges but a few strange grins. (They even gave me a golf-cart ride back to the car.)

I said it half in jest with a little smile, knowing that if I agreed that I was a protester, I would go to jail. To be honest, I wouldn't normally claim such a pretentious title as Prophet, nor do I see many of the biblical prophets running around throwing the title around. Besides, protesters might go to jail, but prophets usually get killed. (As old Bob Marley sings in "Redemption Song": "How long shall they kill our prophets while we stand aside and look?") But it did warrant more thought, and as I watched the riots in the streets of Philly over the next few days, my heart sank at all the violence and hatred. It didn't feel like we were moving closer to a better world.

Protesters are everywhere, but I think the world is desperately in need of prophets, those little voices that can point us toward another future. *Prophet* means "mouthpiece of God." Prophets are truth-tellers, whistleblowers of the best kind. They are God's MCs, trying to listen to God, feel with God, and speak the things on the heart of God. And they amplify the voices on the margins. They have a profound sensitivity to good and evil. Rabbi Abraham Heschel wrote a classic titled (creatively) *The Prophets*, and he throws it down like this: "To us a single act of injustice— cheating in business, exploitation of the poor—is slight; to the prophets, a disaster. To us injustice is injurious to the welfare of the people; to the prophets it is a deathblow to existence: to us, an episode; to them, a catastrophe, a threat to the world." Some of us have spent so much time fighting what we are against that we can barely remember what we are for. Whether in the church or in circles of social dissent, there are plenty of people who define themselves by what they are not, whose identity revolves around what they are against rather than what they are for. It's sort of in the DNA of *Protest*ants. Church history shows how good Protestants are at dissent, but once they are in charge, no one knows what to do. Most people are aware that something is wrong. The real question is, What are the alternatives?

Protesters are still on the fringes like satellites, revolving around the system. But prophets and poets lead us into a new world, beyond simply yelling at the old one. As I read this again ten years later, it felt like one could hear me saying that we shouldn't be in the streets protesting. Don't hear me say that. As the adage goes, "If you're not upset, you're not paying attention." There is some serious injustice that needs to be protested. So we need to protest. But we need to do more than that. That's why I call myself an activist. The best protest is the proclamation and practice of something better. The prophetic witness has everything to do with that. It's not just about saying what is wrong but also about how it can be made right again. Let's be known not just by what we are against but also by what we are for. In many ways, protesters fit into the dominant system, legitimizing the current order with carefully compartmentalized dissent. A one-dimensional society[6] can absorb dissent in a way that

---

6. A phrase coined by social philosopher Herbert Marcuse in his classic book *One-Dimensional Man* (Boston: Beacon, 1964).

even further empowers its domination. People watch it on TV and know that they are not "one of those," and teach their kids the comfort of slavery rather than the slavery of comfort. And sympathetic liberals applaud the valiant courage of the resisters from their comfortable couches as if someone made a touchdown.

A REVOLUTION THAT LAUGHS

During the war, people became so polarized that hatred and anger seemed to dominate, no matter which side you were on. Friends at the Camdenhouse, a sister community to the Simple Way, did something beautiful. They each dressed in sackcloth branded with one of the fruit of the Spirit— love, joy, peace, patience, kindness, goodness, faithfulness, gentleness, and self-control—fruit that most revolutions are starving for. And then they walked into the middle of the protests, a witness of the Spirit to both the warmongers and the Bush bashers. That's the sort of thing that makes us laugh and nudges us all a little closer to God.[7]

One night, a couple of my housemates sneaked into my room carrying a life-size poster of President Bush hugging a little girl. They climbed up on my bunk and hung it from the ceiling just a few feet above my bed. I came in late that night, and my roommate was already asleep, so I crawled into bed in the dark, oblivious to it all. The next morning, the first thing I saw when I awoke was George W. Bush staring me dead in the eye and nearly lying on top of me. Now that's funny. I left it there so that I see him every night when I go to bed and each morning when I get up. That

---

7. The women in several of the communities in Philly organized a similar witness at a March for Women's Rights, which featured a polarizing counterdemonstration by pro-life activists. They went as bridge builders to bridge the gaps between them and talk with people on both sides.

would give some folks nightmares. For others, it would help them to rest secure. For me, it reminds me that President Bush is human, neither the Antichrist nor the Savior, and that allows me to sleep well. Humor. That's something most liberals and conservatives have in common—they've forgotten how to laugh. And the world is starving for joy. This poster remained above my bed until it went up in flames when our house burned down in 2007. If you have an extra life-size poster of George W. lying around, mail it to me. Thanks.

I'll never forget one of the times I became convinced that God is committed to making us laugh at ourselves, especially those of us who take ourselves so seriously. First, you need to know that I have been to a fair amount of protests against the death penalty.[8] It's a big deal here in Pennsylvania. Philadelphia, like many cities and states, has passed a moratorium bill to halt executions because of significant proof of a class and ethnic bias.[9] In 2015, Pennsylvania Governor Tom Wolf declared a new moratorium on the death penalty. Hallelujah! I wrote a response here: *http://www.post-gazette.com/opinion/2015/02/19/ Shane-Claiborne-Dealing-out-death-in-Pennsylvania/stories/201502190024*. (Recently several people have been exonerated after serving years in prison and nearly being

---

8. The death penalty has always messed with my theology, as I really believe that Jesus died both for, and from, my sins. In a sense, my sins put Jesus on the cross. So if murderers should be killed, I'm at the top of the list. And there's that pretty clear instance where Jesus is asked for his support of the death penalty and he answers, "Let any one of you who is without sin be the first to throw a stone at her."

9. A great group of folks we work with locally, many of whom share a deep Christian faith and have done tremendous research and collaboration, is Pennsylvania Abolitionists United Against the Death Penalty (*www.pa-abolitionists.org*).

executed.) There is also the high profile case of Mumia Abu-Jamal, who in a very dubious trial was convicted of killing a Philadelphia police officer and has spent over twenty years in prison. And of course, we have friends on death row, some of whom are innocent. (One man wrote us a letter that just said, "Please help.") So I have done a fair amount of organizing and educating on the death penalty, and the issue has human faces for me. I have spent many days outside the office of the district attorney, Lynne Abraham. For seeking the death penalty on so many cases and building up Philadelphia County's death row to the country's third largest, the *New York Times* dubbed her America's Deadliest DA. Now here's the beautiful event. A few years back, I was invited to speak to a gathering of thousands of Christians. I was led onto the stage, where I was seated in a line of people who would be speaking. I guess I expected to see the cast of usual suspects—you know, preachers and teachers. As I sat down, I looked to my left only to see Lynne Abraham! I recognized her from seeing her face plastered on posters.

I had no idea what to do. I thought of interrupting her speech. I thought of spending my talk time reacting to her. Instead, I just listened and prayed. I felt a strange peace and must admit I was quite prepared to feel some prophetic fire. But I just sat there as the words of the prophets demanding God's justice for the poor danced in my mind. I wrote a few of them down on a piece of paper, and when she sat back down next to me, I quietly passed it to her, along with a note that said I would be praying for her to be filled with God's love and grace and begging her to pray the same for me. She smiled at me and said thank you as she left (before listening to my speech, I might add). Her name has joined the host of those engraved in our chapel, for whom

I regularly cry out to God. And she left her cup at that gathering, so I picked it up and it's in my closet. Hopefully someday I will have the chance to give it back to her and chat with her over coffee.

I take great courage from the fact that many of us are taking steps toward a gentler revolution. We need more prophets who laugh and dance. In our living room, we have an Emma Goldman quote: "If I can't dance, then it is not my revolution." Whenever people talk about injustice, usually there is a cloud of guilt looming over them. Joy and celebration don't usually mark progressive social justice circles, or conservative Christian circles, for that matter. But the Jesus movement is a revolution that dances. Celebration is at the very core of our kingdom, and hopefully that celebration will make its way into the darkest corners of our world—the ghettos and refugee camps, and the palaces and prisons. May the whispers of hope reach the ears of hope-hungry people in the shadows of our world.

CHAPTER 12

GROWING SMALLER AND SMALLER...
UNTIL WE TAKE OVER THE WORLD

You may recall the old comic in which two pastors are talking, and one of them asks the other, "How's your church?" The other pastor boasts, "Quite well, I should say. When I got there, we had only thirty members, and I have been there only a year. Now we are seeing over four hundred people on Sunday morning. And how's your church?" The first pastor says, "Well, I don't know. When I got there, we were seeing about a hundred. I've been preaching the gospel, and I've preached that ole church down to ten."

I'm not sure the Christian gospel always draws a crowd. People may not stand in line for a Roman cross; after all, it's hard enough to wait in line at the shopping mall. In a culture so in fear of death that we stockpile water for Y2K or duct-tape our windows to be safe from terrorists, people may not flock to an invitation to lose their lives. This is a dated reference to something that happened after September 11th. It's almost forgotten now, but across the nation, fear of chemical and biological weapons created a frenzied rush to buy duct tape to tape up windows and "air-proof" homes. It made national news as stores began to sell out of duct tape. It shows how wildly we can react to our fear. I remember my mom calling and asking if we had duct-taped our windows.

(She had seen a news story that insisted this was a good idea.) I burst out laughing and said, "No, Mom, I'm pretty sure that is all part of an unreasonable panic." She said, "I knew it! Exactly what I was thinking." There is still some suspicion that the duct-tape companies started the idea. Wink. The invitation to come and suffer may prove to be quite inconvenient and not as sexy as the cool culture we are taught to emulate. There may be plenty of spectators, skeptics, or antagonists (just as was the case two thousand years ago), but followers may be hard to come by. Sometimes I wonder, amid our crowds, if we are really preaching the gospel.

I've learned that a lot of good things start small and grow smaller. It seems to be the story of the early church. Certainly, thousands were added to their number in the early church— the poor, outcasts, people fed up with the world. They were the scum of the earth. The Scriptures describe the early Jesus movement like this: "We go hungry and thirsty, we are in rags, we are brutally treated, we are homeless. . . . We have become the scum of the earth, the garbage of the world" (1 Cor. 4:11–13). Our context is quite different. We live among the wealthiest people of the world (top 2 percent), a tough mission field. We are preaching a gospel that declares that it's easier to fit a camel through the eye of a needle than for the rich to enter the kingdom. But look on the bright side. After we preach the crowds down, we will not need such expensive buildings. And of course, in a Christian culture shopping for the cheapest grace, the temptation is always to tone things down a little bit. People will be more comfortable around a domesticated Jesus than the Lion of Judah.

And yet whether it's the *Prayer of Jabez*[1] or the war in Iraq,

---

1. The Prayer of Jabez is based on a thirty-word prayer by an obscure Old Testament person named Jabez, who is never again mentioned in the Bible (1 Chron. 4:10). His prayer used the phrase "enlarge my territory," which is

many Christians seem to be hoping that the kingdom of God will come in triumphal greatness, expanding God's territory and taking over the world with glory and power—shock-and-awing the masses, if you will. But that's the very temptation Jesus faced in the desert, the temptation to do spectacular things like fling himself from the temple or turn stones into bread, to shock the masses with his miracles or awe them with his power. And yet he resists. The church has always faced the same temptation, from the time of Constantine's sword to now. We are tempted to do great things like rappel from the rafters in the newest church gym or throw the best pizza party so that kids might bow before the altar.

But amid all the church-growth tacticians and mega-church models, I want to suggest something a little different: God's kingdom grows smaller and smaller as it takes over the world.

GOD OF LITTLE THINGS

Mother Teresa offers us that brilliant glimpse of hope that lies in little things: "We can do not great things, only small things with great love. It is not how much you do but how

---

quite popular in Christian jargon nowadays. But the book doesn't talk about the bloodshed that happens after the territory enlarges (1 Chron. 4:41–43). Nor does it mention why, if the prayer is so important, Jesus never told us about ole Jabez. There are plenty of prayers in the Bible that are best not emulated, like Psalm 109, where David curses his enemy and prays that his enemy's children would become beggars forced to wander the streets. Ouch. To be fair, the author, Bruce Wilkinson, probably never envisioned the ripples the book would make or that there would be a children's version on the market. If you are trying to figure out how to pray, I'd suggest the Prayer of Jesus, which has some significant differences from that of Jabez; namely, the constant echo of "me" and "my" of Jabez does not appear once in the Prayer of Jesus (only "us" and "our") and the "keep me from harm" is trumped by "thy will be done." You can find it in Matthew 6:9–13, and if you really want to read a book on it, *Praying Like Jesus* by James Mulholland (San Francisco: HarperSanFrancisco, 2001) is a decent one.

much love you put into doing it." Above our front door, we have hung a sign that says, "Today . . . small things with great love (or don't open the door)."

It is easy to fall in love with the great things, whether we are revolutionaries or church-growth tacticians. But we must never simply fall in love with our vision or our five-year plan. We must never fall in love with "the revolution" or "the movement." We can easily become so driven by our vision for church growth, community, or social justice that we forget the little things, like caring for those around us. An older charismatic woman told me, "If the devil can't steal your soul, he'll just keep you busy doing meaningless church work."

There is a brilliant truth I have come to see, largely because of Dietrich Bonhoeffer, spiritual writer and fellow resister, whose words are now inscribed on my wall: "The person who loves their dream of community will destroy community [even if their intentions are ever so earnest], but the person who loves those around them will create community." This has proved to be one of the most helpful quotes over the years. I visited another community that had their own version of it: "Everybody wants a revolution, but nobody wants to do the dishes." A reminder that we've gotta have more than a vision and more than passion. We have to be willing to serve and love each other in real ways. I heard a friend who is a prominent worship leader say something similar about worship. Worship is singing love songs to God, but if all we have are songs, we're in trouble. I can sing my wife a song, but she really knows I love her when I do the dishes. Those we live in community with really know we love them when we show them love in action. Maybe that's what Jesus was up to when he washed his disciples' feet. Perhaps today he'd be cleaning the hair out of the shower drain or other work no one seems to want to do. Many congregations are in love with their mission and vision and rip one another apart in committee meetings trying to attain it. And many social activists I know tear each other up and burn themselves out fighting for a better world while forgetting that the seeds of that world are right next to them.

It's not easy to wrap your hands around a God who is evident in all of creation, who when asked for a name says, "I AM." It's not easy to grasp a vision for the world that is a kingdom or an empire[2] bigger than Rome but as small as a mustard seed. This is the God who creates the universe but chooses to be born in a manger. This God continues to pop up in little things like burning bushes, stubborn donkeys, and little kids. And we like it when God feels a little closer to us. We like the possibility that God might even be, as singer Joan Osborne puts it, "one of us . . . just a stranger on the bus." But we also want a God who is at a safe distance "out there." It's a good thing God is bigger than our minds. Floundering in our attempts to wrap our hands around that mysterious God (dare we even utter the name), we are tempted to enshrine that transcendent God in golden calves, golden eagles, or golden crosses (or golden WWJD bracelets) that we can touch and hold and market all over the world. And we like to have a temple where we know we can find God.

We have a God who enters the world through smallness—a baby refugee, a homeless rabbi, the lilies and the sparrows. We have a God who values the little offering of a couple of coins from a widow over the megacharity of millionaires. We have a God who speaks through little people—a stuttering spokesman named Moses; the stubborn donkey of Balaam; a lying brothel owner named Rahab; an

---

2. The word Jesus uses for the kingdom of God is the same word that was used for the Roman Empire (*basilea*).

adulterous king named David; a ragtag bunch of disciples who betrayed, doubted, and denied; and a converted terrorist named Paul.

SUPERSIZED CHURCH

Bigger is better, so we hear. We live in a world that wants things larger and larger. We want to supersize our fries, sodas, SUVs, and church buildings. Cities build bigger stadiums and conventions want to draw the biggest crowds. Amid all the supersizing, I want to make a modest suggestion: our goal should be not to get larger and larger but to get smaller and smaller. I think of the kingdom of God as bubbling up from the bottom rather than trickling down from the top. The pendulum has swung in the other direction, from megachurch to microchurch. It's ironic to see how much of the curriculum coming out of megachurches is on how to get people into small groups. Small groups in megachurches. The philosophy of many denominations is simply to keep hiving off a new congregation any time we get beyond a couple of hundred so that we keep growing in a way that reproduces like mustard rather than redwood trees. Others suggest that just like the "slow food" movement pushes back on the cheap, quick, zero-nutrition fast-food movement, we need a "slow church" movement that does the hard, steady, patient work of discipleship and formation so that we see real life-change and world-change, not just quick conversions. My friend Chris Smith wrote a book titled *Slow Church*—highly recommend it. Contrary to the pattern of the world, it is like a mustard seed. To enter it, we must become like a little child. God is indeed taking over the world, but it is happening through little acts of love.

There was a majestic megachurch in the time of Jesus. People flocked to it, hoping to meet God there. They bought all kinds of stuff in the temple market, hoping it would bring them closer to God. And yet it is in the middle of that religious market that Jesus flips the tables and drives out the money-changers. He rebukes the religious elite who take the last pennies of homeless widows to build their palaces for God (Mark 12:38–44). When the disciples stand in front of that temple marveling at its gargantuan beauty and saying, "What massive stones! What magnificent buildings!" he quickly admonishes them, saying, "Do you see all these great buildings? . . . Not one stone here will be left on another" (Mark 13:1–2). (And we wonder why people hated him so much.)

It is this monopoly on the sacred that Jesus dismantles as he redefines the temple as his body, as our bodies, the mystical body of Christ. There is something precious about corporate worship, but corporate is whenever two or three of us gather with God. We must resist the ancient temptation to centralize worship, especially at the expense of justice for the poor.[3] The human-made temples will be split open, and no stone will be left on another, as Jesus says. (And of course, the powers, looking for an excuse to execute him, accused him of threatening to destroy the temple.) Acts 17:24 reminds us that God "does not live in temples built by human hands." The Scriptures remind us that we are God's temples, that the Spirit lives in us. And in a very special way, as Jesus says in Matthew 25:40, in the least of these, we find Jesus in disguise. Perhaps we are just as likely to encounter God over the dinner table or in the slums or in the streets as in a giant auditorium. Of course, suggesting that God doesn't need these million-dollar

---

3. The words of the prophets, like in Amos 5:21–24, even declare that God hates our worship and singing if they are devoid of justice, and God demands that they cease until we practice justice for the poor and oppressed.

megacathedrals is the sort of thing that gets you in big trouble.

GOD OF THE REFUGEES

In an age of million-dollar mansions for God, it's hard to imagine that our God prefers tents. But God has always had a thing for camping. In the Hebrew Scriptures, such as in Exodus, God "tabernacles" with the Israelites, a word that essentially means "sets up camp." God was with Rizpah as she set up camp on the rock next to her children's massacred bodies, collateral damage of kings and their wars (2 Sam. 21:1–14). In the baby refugee Jesus, God becomes Emmanuel[4] ("God with us"), crashing in the manger. And it is in the life of Jesus that God puts skin on to show us what love looks like. John's Gospel calls this incarnational act "pitching God's tent among us." And then God wanders the Galilean countryside with "no place to lay his head," a stranger looking for a house of hospitality to welcome him.

Despite the fact that God's Word insists that "God does not dwell in temples built by human hands," we insist that God should. In 2 Samuel 7, King David finds himself in a supersized mansion, living in a "palace of cedar," and starts to think that maybe God needs a fancier place to dwell. But God rebukes David: "Are you the one to build me a house to dwell in? I have not dwelt in a house from the day I brought the Israelites out of Egypt to this day. I have been moving from place to place with a tent as my dwelling" (vv. 5–6).

God just digs camping. No wonder when I think of my most powerful encounters with God they seem to involve

---

4. Interestingly, Emmanuel was also a name used by emperors like Antiochus IV Epiphanes, who claimed to manifest the incarnation of the gods.

camping of some kind—crashing on the marble floor of abandoned St. Edward's cathedral, camping out in tents in Baghdad outside the Al Monzer children's hospital, sleeping in church parking lots as we marched with migrant workers, standing around barrel fires in shantytowns and tent cities, and camping in the wilderness of God's creation. That is where I have met God. God still dwells there. No doubt there is power in corporate worship, and there are times when I feel God among the masses (and during Masses), but it has had nothing to do with the color of the carpet or the comfort of the chairs.

One of the communities I love is a group of folks who gather below an interstate bridge in Waco, Texas, each week for worship. They creatively call themselves Church under the Bridge.[5] Over a decade ago, homeless folks and their friends began meeting for Bible study and grub, and now there are hundreds of folks from all walks of life trying to figure out what it means to live God's little revolution together. They just pull up a flatbed truck, and God shows up. No fancy carpet or pews. Whenever I speak or worship there, I always tell them it's the most beautiful sanctuary I've ever seen. (Apologies to folks reading this from the Crystal Cathedral[6] out there in California.) I still go to Church under the Bridge every chance I get. They still don't have a building—probably never will. And it is one of my favorite sanctuaries of all time. On a recent visit there,

---

5. *http://churchunderthebridge.org.*

6. The Crystal Cathedral in California has a building with 10,000 windows, a 52 bell carillon, gigantic 90 foot tall doors that electronically open behind the pulpit, a 17 foot 18 karat gold cross, and an outdoor movie screen for "drive-in" worshipers. Don't take my word for it, visit *www.crystalcathedral.org.* The Crystal Cathedral went bankrupt in 2010. The Catholic Church bought the building.

they told me the story of why they have a fellow who plays air guitar in the worship band. This fellow, a committed, regular member of their community, had an adventuresome imagination and sometimes got a little overly ambitious during worship. He tended to jump on stage and join the band. And he played air guitar like a rock star. Sometimes he would grab the mic or knock over a stand and occasionally detracted from the overall worship experience just a little. Instead of kicking him out, like some congregations might, they made him part of the worship band. And to keep him from taking over the stage, they created a little duct-tape square that marks his special spot. Last I heard he now has his own guitar. They just don't plug it in. And everyone likes it that way, including him. I am convinced his worship is a "sweet incense to the Lord."

In fact, Jesus and the disciples would probably get in a lot of trouble in most fancy churches. They'd probably be turning water fountains into wine fountains, inviting kids to swim in baptistries, ripping holes in the roofs when the crippled can't get in the doors, flipping over the cash registers in the bookstores—at which point a trustee would scold Jesus and ask, "Jesus!?!? What, were you born in a barn?" And Jesus would nod.

TEARING DOWN THE WALLS

A few years back, Willow Creek Community Church announced its vision for "Chapter 2," which included a building expansion costing tens of millions of dollars. My heart sank. Many of us in the evangelical church, both within and outside of the Willow Creek community, voiced tremendous concern about the new venture. I chose not to speak publicly about it, but anytime I was asked in private, all I could do was weep. It broke my heart. I began writing back and forth with folks in leadership at Willow, including the pastor, Bill Hybels, whom I deeply respect.

I did a ton of research on tithes and offerings in Scripture, and discovered they are unmistakably intended to be used for redistributing resources to the poor and not to go toward buildings and staff for the church. I quoted the church fathers and mothers, who had much to say about the shameful use of church offerings for anything other than Jubilee redistribution. Tertullian, Justin Martyr, Augustine, Irenaeus, Basil the Great, and Gregory of Nazianzus, Jerome, John Chrysostom, Aristides—all attest that the church offerings are to be given to the poor as their right. Ambrose, on becoming bishop of Milan, melted all of the objects of gold in the temple, saying, "The church has gold not to store up but to lay out and spend on those in need, for would not the Lord himself say: why didst thou suffer so many to die of hunger?"

I expressed to the leadership of Willow Creek in solemn earnestness that I feared our church is guilty of theft and embezzling from the poor. And I told them a story about our Catholic Worker friends. When the Catholic archdiocese decided to build a multimillion dollar cathedral, our Catholic friends decided to kneel in prayer in front of the bulldozers. They were eventually arrested, which led to a transformative conversation that included not simply church leaders but also the poor and marginalized. I mentioned in good humor to the folks at Willow that I had no plans to "lock down" on the bulldozers (though the thought did pass through my mind), but urgency demanded that we fast and consider the cost of the building, and not just the price tag but the cost in terms of our global neighbors. So we did. I went on to remind them of the early days of Christianity, that when there was not enough food for everyone to eat, the whole community would fast until all could come to the table together. We considered doing a prolonged communal fast on the site of the new building, to remind ourselves of the cost. Bill and I wrote back and forth, wrestling with the weightiness of this decision. The greatest thing was that no defensive walls went up. All of this was done with deep respect and gentleness. In fact, it was an attempt to tear down the walls that keep people isolated from each other and trapped in the ghettoes of wealth and poverty.[7] It has been fascinating to watch Willow Creek evolve over the years. They take their mission of forming "fully devoted followers of Jesus" very seriously. They distinguish between what it means to be a believer and what it means to be a follower, and their goal is not simply to see people come to believe in Jesus but to see people actually follow Jesus. Some years ago they wanted to see how they were doing at that goal, so they surveyed the community. What they found was less than encouraging. To their credit, they released it publically. What it revealed was a problem not just at Willow but throughout much of evangelicalism. Our fervor for evangelism has often come at the cost of discipleship. In the words of one prominent pastor, "Our Christianity is a mile long and an inch deep." Thankfully there is a renewed focus on discipleship and formation, and

---

7. They went forward with the building project. And the weird thing is, it didn't make me angry, just sad. I felt sad that we had settled for another building when God might have had so much else in mind. I must also add that Willow Creek has continually made remarkable strides toward justice and reconciliation, the fruits of which are the substantial financial gifts Willow has given to relieve the suffering of our global neighbors, such as those afflicted with AIDS in Africa. Willow continues to be a place that is hungry for fully devoted discipleship. After all, it is Willow Creek who taught many of us that 90 percent discipleship is 10 percent short of full devotion.

this is also true at Willow. In the years since that study, they have made massive shifts to deepen their commitment and be true to their goal. I did a little snooping around to see what that looks like. And I did have to snoop, because they don't brag about it. But I "know people," if you know what I'm sayin'. An inside source whose identity I won't reveal gave me this credible info.

Here's a glimpse at a few of the things Willow Creek has done in the period of a year: They have distributed 2.8 million pounds of food to neighbors in need; opened eleven clinics in Latin America, sharing over 3.1 million dollars; installed twenty-eight solar-powered water systems and dug 106 wells in Africa, providing water for 200,000 people; hosted one of the largest fair-trade expos in the United States; mobilized 16,000 folks to sort seeds for half a million seed packs sent to Zimbabwe; had 16,000 people pack 3.6 million meals for kids in Africa; filled eighteen forty-foot shipping containers to be sent to some of the toughest corners on earth; packed 13,000 hope packs, including mosquito nets to save lives in Zambia; provided free legal counsel for 893 folks from a volunteer team of lawyers; visited 5,000 inmates at eight local prisons; and gave away 10,728 coats to folks who are cold. More than 35,000 volunteer opportunities were filled in 2010 at Willow. No doubt these are some stunning examples of compassion. And they challenge not just megachurches and evangelicals but all congregations and all Christians to put their faith into action.

Oh—and I did write Bill Hybels another letter, after all the other ones. This one was a happy letter, celebrating the things I just listed, and all the folks who have come to know Jesus through the ministry of Willow Creek. After all, it's important to speak truth not just as criticism but also as affirmation. And Bill wrote me the nicest letter back.

THE MYTH OF MULTIPLICATION

The pervasive myth is that as we grow larger, we can do more good. But there is little evidence that this is ever realized. My own research and experience would suggest that as congregations grow in terms of staff and property, their giving to causes outside of operating expenses decreases dramatically, especially money given directly to the poor. I just read a recent study that showed that rich people are significantly less generous (proportionately) than poor people, and that large congregations give proportionately far less to people in poverty than do small ones. (In fact, they rarely even have poor people among them.) We cannot magically arrive at a community that allows us to give everything if we do not currently nurture a culture of sacrificial giving. As Gandhi taught, the means must express the end that we desire; the journey is as important as the destination. If our community, in its current state, does not reflect the brilliant cultural and economic diversity that marked the early Jesus revolution, how can it reflect that in its later state?

Usually when things grow fast and large, they also grow homogeneously. Whether it's the crowds in the streets during the Republican National Convention or the folks flocking into the megachurches, we like to be around people who look and think like us. Our big visions for multiculturalism and reconciliation will make their way into the church only when they are first lived out in real relationships, out of our homes and around our dinner tables and in our living rooms. Perhaps this is why Jesus begins it all by sitting around a table with a Roman tax collector, a Zealot revolutionary, a fisherman, a Pharisee, and a prostitute.

As we build our buildings, human temples are being destroyed by hunger and homelessness. The early prophets would say that a church that spends millions of dollars on buildings while her children are starving is guilty of murder. Imagine the scene in a biological family: a father building a mansion while his children are going hungry. He'd be institutionalized or jailed. How much more preposterous should this be in our family of rebirth, in which we have been given new eyes to see others as brothers and sisters?

The more personal property is retained as private space, the more corporate property becomes a necessity. And the cycle continues, for as we enlarge the territory of corporate property, private property remains comfortably sacred. So as congregations build larger buildings, gyms, and food courts, we find ourselves less likely to meet in homes and kitchens and around dinner tables. We end up centralizing worship on corporate space or "on campus." Hospitality becomes less of a necessity and more of an optional matter, a convenient privilege. On the other hand, as members open their homes and yards and share vehicles and recreation spaces, less and less corporate property is necessary.

One of the underlying assumptions is that money from the offering or tithe belongs to the church. But the Scriptures consistently teach that the offering is God's instrument of redistribution and that it belongs to the poor. Giving to the poor should not make its way into the budget; it *is* the budget. One could argue that small portions of the Israelite offering (no more than 10 percent) were given to the Levitical priesthood (Neh. 12:47), and that in the early church an even smaller contribution could be given to the church's itinerant evangelists, who, incidentally, were themselves poor (1 Cor. 4:11). But it is not a coincidence that the first major organizational structure in the early church was created to assure order in the redistribution of resources to widows and orphans (Acts 6:1–6).

So historically, church offerings were part of God's economy of redistribution, and over 90 percent was to be given to the poor. We live in an age when we have nearly reversed what God set in place. An average of 85 percent of the church offering is used internally, primarily for staff and buildings and stuff to meet our own needs. And this borders on embezzlement, as theologian Ray Mayhew points out in his essay "Embezzlement of the Church: The Corporate Sin of Contemporary Christianity."[8] No wonder most churchgoing Christians give only less than 3 percent of their income to the church and find other ways of giving money to the poor.

OUR GLOBAL FAMILY

In the vein of loving our global neighbors as ourselves, I have been able to propose to Willow Creek and to other congregations an alternative vision called a Jubilee Campaign which would match dollar for dollar the money spent on building projects. The idea came after hearing of a congregation that consistently gives 51 percent of its offerings outside the walls of the church, ensuring that they are committed to loving their neighbor as themselves. Since pitching this idea several times and at some conferences for pastors, I've actually had a bunch of folks send me letters saying they did it! It's always exciting when people take an idea and run with it, especially when originally it sort of came off the cuff. It doesn't even seem that farfetched to say that some denominations could make it more of a protocol and

---

8. Ray has become a dear elder and friend whose scholarship has given birth to many experiments in reimagining the tithe as God's instrument of redistribution. His essay can be found on the website of Relational Tithe: *http://relationaltithe.com*.

we could see a movement of congregations that create a Jubilee fund alongside their capital campaigns.

Imagine the ripples something like this could cause. For instance, we have close friends in El Salvador. Some of them are indigenous folks trying to build wells; an estimated fifteen thousand people died in El Salvador last year simply because they didn't have clean drinking water. My good friend Atom, the scientist who lives on my block, and the water team he and his wife, Tara, have organized found that it costs $2,000 to build a well for an entire village. What if evangelical megachurches became known around the world for things like providing water access for entire countries or fighting to end the AIDS pandemic? Imagine what integrity that would give to the good news we preach, especially the gospel that Jesus declares is good news to the poor.

RELATIONAL TITHE

If nothing else, the dialogue with folks at Willow Creek became a catalyst for many of us to pluck the plank from our own eyes rather than trying to get the speck out of our neighbors' eyes. Church father Ignatius said that if our church is not marked by caring for the poor, the oppressed, and the hungry, then we are guilty of heresy. A new reformation is long overdue. We began to dream of what it would look like to reimagine the offerings, since God intended them to be instruments of a redistributive economy. We considered how the early church brought their offerings and laid them at the apostles' feet to be redistributed to folks as they had need. And we came up with something beautiful and small—the relational tithe.[9]

---

9. *http://relationaltithe.com.*

A relational tithe is a network of reborn friends around the world organized in little cells, like in a body, taking care of each other. Like the early church, all offerings and needs are brought to the community. Unlike the early church, we have a blog and can wire money across the globe. We pool 10 percent of our income into a common fund. Regularly, the needs of our neighborhoods and villages are also brought before the community, and we meet them as we are able. Meanwhile, we are building relationships that radically tear through the economic walls that divide us, from economists to homeless folks, all the time trusting that we can do more together than we could do alone. Together, we've helped friends get cars, keep their utilities on, create new jobs, send kids to summer camp, throw birthday parties, and send people on their first vacation. And it all happens through relationships. No one is giving or receiving who is not grounded in sincere friendships. When the tsunami hit in 2004, two folks from the RT went over to Thailand, and as they brought before the community the needs of people they met, we helped repair fences and boats and playgrounds (and even got a write-up in the *Bangkok Post*, one of Thailand's most prominent papers). After the 2005 hurricane hit the Gulf, folks from the Relational Tithe and other friends sent supplies and people down to Louisiana on a bus running off veggie oil (which was particularly delightful at a time when gas prices were nearing four dollars a gallon!).[10] Folks in the RT also organized a network of families and communities who opened up their homes to folks displaced by the hurricane. Whew! That all sounds like God's vision for

---

10. The bus belongs to and was converted to veggie oil by our dearest comrades, a dazzling crew of ordinary radicals in the band mewithoutyou (*mewithoutyou.com*).

a human family with a parent with a big, divine wallet and a lot of love. The Relational Tithe is still going as strong as ever—actually it seems to get stronger every year. We now have a global movement, with little clusters scattered all over the world under a larger umbrella now called Common Change. (Relational Tithe is still what we call the charter community, the thirty-five or so of us who started it ten years ago.) We've seen entire congregations and communities start their own chapters. (I think we have more than fifty affiliated groups now.) At the core is the fundamental belief that there is enough for everyone's need, and that we are all better off together than on our own. But to love those in need, we have to first know those in need, so we still give only to people we know, folks we are friends with (no gifts to organizations or people we read about in newsletters). With knowing comes true community—and wisdom, as we discern how to most responsibly share the resources and the needs among us. Recently we've sent folks to college, repaid money lost in a robbery, repaired vandalism done to a car, paid a dowry, and bought someone dentures. Since its inception in 2005, we have shared more than $850,000 with thousands of families around the world. And true to the vision of "growing small," these little clusters continue to multiply, as do our resources. But it is still friends sharing with friends. Check it out: *https://www.commonchange.com*. Heck, think about starting your own common-change experiment right where you are.

THE MUSTARD SEED REVOLUTION

Jesus uses some unlikely metaphors for God's kingdom—like yeast, for instance. Jews were not big fans of yeast. After all, it was the same metaphor he had used to describe the infectious arrogance of the Pharisees that everyone was to beware of. So then, for the folks not digging the yeast imagery, he says God's kingdom is like mustard. And I'm not sure they would have liked that any better. Was Jesus just running out of metaphors? I don't think so. I've heard plenty of cute sermons about the mustard seed parable, talking about how God takes little seeds and makes big trees out of them, but I think there's much more than that going on here.

Matthew strategically places the mustard seed parable in the middle of a story about gardening in which Jesus commands people not to tear up the weeds from the garden but to let the wheat and weeds grow together (Matt. 13:24–30, 36–43). Then he tells his listeners that the kingdom of God is like mustard, which grows like a wild bush (Matt. 13:31–35). I once heard a farmer say it is like kudzu,[11] and a city preacher compared it to the wild weeds that grow out of the abandoned houses and crack the sidewalks. The mustard seed's growth would have been familiar to first-century Jews and its symbolic meaning unmistakably clear. It may have even been growing in the wild around them as Jesus spoke.

Jews valued order and had very strict rules about how to keep a tidy garden, and one of the secrets was to keep out mustard. It was notorious for invading the well-trimmed veggies and other plants and for quickly taking over the entire garden. (Kind of like yeast works its way through dough . . . hmm.) Then they'd be left with only mustard! Jewish law even forbade planting mustard in the garden (*m. Kil'ayim* 3:2; *t. Kil'ayim* 2:8). When those first-century peasants heard Jesus' images, they would have giggled, or maybe they would have told him to hush before he got killed. Here he is using this infamous plant to describe God's kingdom subtly taking over the world.

---

11. Kudzu is a wild vine that vigorously takes over an area. (I grew up playing in it.) Rather unassumingly, it can blanket entire mountainsides, smother trees, and crack cement buildings.

Plenty of people had lofty expectations of the kingdom coming in spectacular triumph and were familiar with the well-known "cedars of Lebanon" imagery from the prophets, who described the kingdom as the greatest of all trees, not unlike a giant redwood tree. The cedars of Lebanon imagery would have brought some enthusiastic amens from the crowd, maybe even gotten some people dancing. But Jesus ridiculed this triumphal expectation. After all, even mature mustard plants stand only a few feet high, modest little bushes.

The Jesus revolution is not a frontal attack on the empires of this world. It is a subtle contagion, spreading one little life, one little hospitality house, at a time. Isn't it interesting that Saul of Tarsus went door to door (Acts 8:3) trying to tear up the contagion like it was a cancer? But the harder people tried to eradicate it, the faster it spread. And in the end, even Paul caught the contagion. The mustard weed grabbed him.

Another convert I have fallen in love with is a dude named Minucius Felix. Felix, a persecutor of the early Christians, cursed the early followers of the Way as a "profane conspiracy" and an "impious confederacy" that was multiplying all over the world "just like a rank growth of weeds." He went on to say that it should at all costs be exterminated and ripped up from the roots. Years later, Minucius caught the infectious fires of God's love and joined that little mustard seed conspiracy.[12]

---

12. The story of Minucius is a beautiful glimpse of irresistible revolution. As a lawyer who was persecuting Christians, Minucius understood the empire and the religious establishment well. But he soon caught the contagion of love. Here's what he had to say about Christians before his conversion in AD 200: "They despise temples as if they were tombs. They despise titles of honor and the purple robe of high government office though hardly able themselves to cover their nakedness. . . . They love one another before being acquainted. They practice a cult of lust, calling one another brother and sister indiscriminately."

Mustard has always been known for its fiery pungency. In the days of the Roman Empire, it was a sign of power. Darius, king of the Persians, invaded Europe and was met by Alexander the Great. Darius sent Alexander a bag of sesame seeds as a taunt, indicating the multitude of soldiers he had. Alexander sent back a bag of mustard seed with the message, "You may be many, but we are powerful. We can handle you." And they did.

So there goes Jesus turning power on its head again. His power was not in crushing but in being crushed, triumphing over the empire's sword with his cross. Mustard must be crushed, ground, broken in order for its power to be released. In John's Gospel, Jesus compares his death and resurrection to a seed that is broken: "Unless a kernel of wheat falls to the ground and dies, it remains only a single seed. But if it dies, it produces many seeds" (John 12:24). This is the crazy mystery that we celebrate, a Christ whose body is torn apart and whose blood is spilled like the grains and grapes of the Eucharist that give us life. Mustard was

---

And here's what he said after his conversion: "Why do they have no altars, no temples, no images? . . . What temple shall I build him [God] when the whole world, the work of his hands, cannot contain him? Should we not rather make a sanctuary for him in our souls? The whole heaven and the whole earth and all things beyond the confines of the world are filled with God. . . . I would almost say: we live with him. What a beautiful sight it is for God when a Christian mocks the clatter of the tools of death and the horror of the executioner; when he defends and upholds his liberty in the face of kings and princes, obeying God alone to whom he belongs. Among us, boys and frail women laugh to scorn torture and the gallows cross and all the other horrors of execution" (Eberhard Arnold, ed., *The Early Christians: In Their Own Words* [Farmington, PA: Plough, 1998]). By the way, this spectacular book, *The Early Christians in Their Own Words*, is exactly what its title says—the edited words of dozens of the earliest Christians and their stories. Not only is it one of my favorite collections, it is also free. (Thanks, Plough and Bruderhof!) Here you go: *http://www.plough.com/en/ebooks/e/early-christians*.

also known for healing; it was rubbed on the chest to help with breathing, sort of like Vicks vapor rub. Mustard— the official sponsor of the Jesus revolution; a healing balm, a sign of upside-down power, and a good dip for a kosher meal.

As if that weren't enough (and we wonder why people were so angry!), Jesus adds one more thing: "the birds come and perch in its branches" (v. 32). Another aspect of the popular Hebrew imagery of the cedars of Lebanon is that the nations can build nests in the branches of the cedars. But Jesus puts an interesting spin on it when he says the "fowls" can come and rest in the branches of the mustard bush. The word *fowls* is not a reference to the mighty eagles that dwelt in the cedars but the detestable birds, the ones that ate animal carcasses (Gen. 15:11; Deut. 28:26). Farmers did not want fowls in their gardens. That's why they put up scarecrows. Bless his heart, Jesus is saying the kingdom of God is "for the birds." The undesirables find a home in this little bush.

WHEN GRASS PIERCES CONCRETE

Many today would point to the mega model of growth as the way the kingdom comes. And yet we forget what happens when we build our towers and sanctuaries, hoping to reach God (figuratively or physically). We find ourselves growing farther and farther from the God who was with us in the garden, who camped out with us in the wilderness, who pitched his tent with us in Jesus, who comes like a little seed. To be clear, we want to grow. Just as thousands were added to the early church in Acts, we want to see thousands of folks fall in love with Jesus and join his revolution. But the growth is not up but out. It's about a movement, not a monument. Think about Alcoholics Anonymous. While I don't think the church needs to replicate AA, I do think we can learn some things from them. Most of us have heard the Twelve Steps, but not we're not as familiar with the Twelve Traditions, which are phenomenal: *http://www.aa.org/assets/ en_US/smf-122_en.pdf*. The leadership of AA has been called a nonhierarchal "inverted pyramid," very different from much of the church. AA is also self-supporting—no outside donations. (They give the donor too much power.) Anonymity and the inverted pyramid model means no spokesperson. (It has been called a "benign anarchy.") They neither have nor need any buildings or professional staff. The public relations policy is one of attraction rather than promotion. And it is one of the most pervasive movements in the world—hundreds of thousands have found healing and community.

One of the earliest moves recorded in Scripture is from the beauty of the little garden to the beast of the big city (Gen. 11:1–9). The people decided to build a sky-scraping tower, Babel, and the land around became known as Babylon. Scripture says the people wanted to "make a name" for themselves. They hoped to attain the beauty of the heavens, only to find themselves growing farther and farther from the God who dwelt with them in the garden. God quickly ended their building project, scattering the people throughout the land to form different tribes with different languages. And God is ultimately in the process of bringing down what the Bible calls the Great Prostitute Babylon. My friend Tony Campolo pointed out to me that when Babylon falls in Revelation 19, there are two responses to her fall. The kings of the earth and all the merchants and business folks weep and wail; they are devastated. But the angels rejoice and celebrate that Babylon is no more. It raises a question: when Babylon falls, will we be weeping with the merchants and the kings, or rejoicing with the angels? Israel is rebuked over and over for her lack of loyalty to God, as she runs to empires like a harlot, eager for the power, wealth, and chariots of the imperial cities.

It all begins in the garden, but it ends in the city. It is a beautiful thing that, as the city of God, the New Jerusalem, is unveiled (Revelation 21), there are no fancy church buildings, not even a temple (v. 22), for God lives among us again, as in the garden, as in the wilderness. We are to bring the garden to the city. I was talking with one of my neighbors, who explained well the theology behind what we are doing with urban gardens: "We are bringing the garden of Eden to North Philadelphia." Amen. The river of life and the tree of life have taken over the world. It's a campout with God, in the middle of the city! Rather than our towers and temples reaching up to heaven, the God of heaven reaches down to earth and lives among us (v. 3).

This is good news to us when we notice the fragility of our towers, when we feel the emptiness of the market, when we see a failed attempt at imperial peace. This bringing of the garden to the city is not only what we are expecting but also what we are beginning to enact— tossing seeds on toxic waste sites, making mosaics from toy weapons, reclaiming trash-strewn lots for urban gardens, and taking over the concrete world, where old tires and hollowed out TVs and computer monitors become pots for flowers on our roof. And the contagion of God's love is spreading across the land like a little mustard plant, growing smaller and smaller until it takes over the world.

CHAPTER 13

CRAZY BUT NOT ALONE

We live in a world of oxymorons and contradictions. You know the old joke: "Why do we park on driveways and drive on parkways?" Then there are the everyday oxymorons we bump into, like "good mornings," "school food," "plastic silverware," and "reality TV." And of course, there are the ones we see occasionally, like "working vacations," "bad luck," "old news," "bankrupt millionaires," "United Methodists," and "diet Oreos." And finally, there are those contradictions that deeply disturb our logic and ethics, like "military intelligence," "peacekeeping missiles," "just wars," "smart bombs," and "friendly fire." Hmm. It's a wonder anyone knows left from right or right from wrong.

I used to think that those of us who hope for things we cannot see and who believe that the world can be different than it is were the crazy ones. We are usually called that by people who spend their lives trying to convince everyone that the crazy things they do actually make sense. Now more and more people are starting to imagine that maybe another world is possible and necessary and actually quite imaginable. I'm starting to wonder if, actually, we have gone sane in a mad world. In a world of smart bombs and military intelligence, we need more fools, holy fools who insist that the folly of the cross is wiser than any human power. And the world may call us crazy.

The good-humored teacher and street-corner prophet Peter Maurin, cofounder of the Catholic Worker movement, put it this way: "If we are crazy, then it is because we refuse to be crazy in the same way that the world has gone crazy." What's crazy is a matter of perspective. After all, what is crazier: one person owning the same amount of money as the combined economies of twenty-three countries, or suggesting that if we shared, there would be enough for everyone? Abba Anthony, one of the famous desert fathers, said something similar 1,600 years ago: "The time is coming when people will be insane, and when they see someone who is not insane, they will attack that person saying: 'You are insane because you are not like us.'" What is crazier: spending billions of dollars on a defense shield, or suggesting that we share our billions of dollars so we don't need a defense shield? What is crazier: maintaining arms contracts with 154 countries while asking the world to disarm its weapons of mass destruction, or suggesting that we lead the world in disarmament by refusing to deal weapons with over half of the world and by emptying the world's largest stockpile here at home? What's crazy is that the US, less than 6 percent of the world's population, consumes nearly half of the world's resources, and that the average American consumes as much as 520 Ethiopians do, while obesity is declared a "national health crisis." Someday war and poverty will be crazy, and we will wonder how the world allowed such things to exist. There was a great moment when Martin Luther King Jr. was accused of being maladjusted. He responded with his characteristic brilliance by saying how proud he was to be maladjusted in this world. We need to be maladjusted people in a world that has become way too adjusted to segregation, racism, inequity, violence, and discrimination. We need to be maladjusted people in a world that has become way too adjusted to injustice. Some of us have just caught a glimpse of the beauty of the promised land, and it is so dazzling that our eyes are forever fixed on it, never to look back at the ways of that old empire again.

RISING FROM THE DEAD

Late-nineteenth-century German philosopher Friedrich Nietzsche knew the deadness of the church all too well. (He came from a rich heritage of Lutheran ministers.) He told the famous (or infamous) story of the madman who runs into the market early one morning screaming, "I seek God! I seek God! Where is God?" The townspeople make fun of him. Their laughter convinces him that God is dead, and he says to the crowd, "Whither is God . . . I will tell you—we have killed him, you and I." He goes on to wonder how we have sucked up the sea and the sky and now are plunging into emptiness with no up or down or left or right. The madman asks the people if they can feel the world getting colder and the night taking over the day. He asks them what will wash the blood off them and what games could allow them to forget. He asks them if they can smell the death of God around them and why the churches all look like tombs. And the madman falls silent, as the town stares in astonishment.[1]

I know it's a bit morbid, but look around. We live in a world of zombies, amid a deadness that has infected even the church. The prophet Ezekiel saw a similar deadness and wondered if the dead bones would ever rise. Deadness is in the air. You can see it on the subways, in the airplanes and

1. Friedrich Nietzsche, *The Gay Science*, ed. Walter Kaufmann (New York: Vintage, 1974), 181–82.

skyscrapers, empty and lonely people wondering if there is more to this life than the meaningless toil they fill their days with. (I used to want to buy a hearse to drive around with the words "Rise from the dead" painted on it, but my friends convinced me this wasn't the best idea. Hearses don't get good gas mileage.) Still looking for a hearse, if you have one handy . . . but it needs to be diesel so I can run it off veggie oil. I remember one of the first sermons I ever gave, a clever little talk about how the world is filled with the walking dead, people who breathe air but are not truly alive. I compared the deadness to vampires and said that vampires can't stand light. They cannot stand the cross. (And they apparently don't like garlic, but I left that one out.) Okay, it was a really bad sermon and an embarrassing analogy, but as I think back on my youthful dreams, I just wanted to rise above the suffocating deadness, to rise above people who no longer feel or dream but just exist.

CRAZY BUT NOT ALONE

We are not alone, but the eerie silence can make us think we are. For a long time, I have said, "We have to remind each other that we are not crazy, or that if we are crazy, at least we are not alone." Jesus and most of the apostles were accused of being crazy. Lots of the saints were nearly institutionalized, and some actually were. (And perhaps some televangelists really should be, but that's for another book.)

During even the darkest eras of imperial infection, when the identity of Christianity seemed all but lost, tremendous renewals and prophetic voices have declared that another future is possible. Many of us have grown to look to the monastic movements within the church as preserving the way of the cross, especially during times of distorted Christianity and counterfeit revolutions. We look to them for hope and courage, even as we see the Spirit giving birth to a powerful movement in the North American church.

I believe we are amid a great awakening in the slumbering body of Christ. I once heard someone call us the Lazarus[2] generation, for we are a generation rising from the apathetic deadness of this world, a church that is awakening from her slumber. There's a beautiful verse in which Jesus scolds his listeners for having grown numb and cold, for having forgotten how to laugh and cry and feel. He says, "To what can I compare this generation? They are like children sitting in the marketplaces and calling out to others: 'We played the pipe for you, and you did not dance; we sang a dirge, and you did not mourn'" (Matt. 11:16–17). A new day is dawning. We are playing the flute and folks from Wall Street to the ghetto are beginning to dance.

Little communities are being born all over—Zealots, tax collectors, prostitutes, cowards, all being reborn together. There is a new tribal confederacy of faith communities, a community of communities, emerging and dreaming ancient visions. We are not a neo-denomination, because we are not trying to spread a doctrine or theology. We are not even trying to spread a model of community. We are just trying to discover a new (ancient) kind of Christianity. We are about spreading a way of life that exists organically and relationally and is marked by such a brilliant love and grace that no one could resist it. Now we just get to connect the dots. I always liked those stinking connect-the-dots things, seeing a bunch of dots become a beautiful piece of art. Everywhere I travel, I find groups of people dreaming new and ancient dreams

_____

2. Referring to the incident when Jesus raised his friend Lazarus from the dead. Lazarus still had his grave clothes on and the stench of death on him, but he was alive.

of what it means to be the church and to love our global neighbors. Nearly everywhere we speak, young people come up with tears in their eyes, no longer alone in their dreams for another world. Over and over, we hear, "I knew there was more to Christianity." We are waking up. What seemed impossible is becoming normal.

Because it is small like the old mustard seed, it is possible to miss the little revolution spreading across our land, cross-pollinated by an ongoing web of relationships and a common vision—of alternatives to existing worldly structures, of bartering economies, of money collectives for emergencies (instead of insurance), of prophetic interruptions to war and theft, of sustainable urban gardening and eco-energy alternatives, of using the trash and wreckage of the consumptive world to create things that bring life and beauty. I had a whole series on Facebook of cool stuff made out of trash. And man, was there some cool stuff. Folks who made jewelry out of bullet casings, and doormats from plastic bags. My wife has a purse made by women who used juice boxes from a dump in Thailand. We have planters in our garden made from tires, and beautiful sunflowers made from painted hubcaps on poles. I was with a clothing company that started Trash Fashion, a clothing line made from recycled and discarded materials. And there is a whole orchestra with instruments made out of trash from a landfill in Paraguay: *http://www.npr.org/blogs/deceptivecadence/2012/12/19/167539764/the-landfill-harmonic-an-orchestra-built-from-trash*. That's what we mean by creating a new society in the shell of the old one. We have been deeply polluted by the world, as James would say, so it takes incredible creativity and all of us learning together to be faithful to the Way. Meanwhile, these little acts of love are taking over the world like mustard spreads through the garden. And Jesus promises that the world will hate us, for we are not of the world. If the world does not hate us, we must wonder whether we are really imagining an alternative.

ASLEEP IN THE LIGHT

When the darkness of our world, and all of the fears we hold in that darkness, are pierced by the light of God's love and by the possibility that God has other ideas in mind for how we are to live, something liberating happens. But there is also the danger of our becoming mesmerized by the dazzle of the light. It can become quite comfortable, like a campfire. We can crawl up into the hands of God and fall asleep in the sweet aroma and cozy warmth, asleep by the fire. And so much of the world lies in the cold, clammy darkness of human suffering, oppression, inequality. My friend John Francis Maher sings a beautiful song that whispers to the groaning masses, "Don't let your eyes adjust to the dark." Perhaps we could also add for those by the fire, "Don't fall asleep in the light." We must neither get used to the darkness of human suffering or fall asleep in the comfort of the light.

I once heard our brother Steve Chalke, a church leader and minister in the UK, describe a little kid stumbling across a raging house fire. As he looks around, he notices a water hose, which he quickly grabs, but then, as he frantically goes to put out the fire, he notices something else, something peculiar. All around him are fire engines with firefighters on them, but all of the firefighters are sound asleep. Now the little boy is left with a decision. He can attempt the hopeless task of trying to put out the fire by himself, or he can take that water hose and begin spraying down all of the firefighters, waking them up so everyone can put the fire out together.

The choice seems pretty clear when we see how large the inferno is in our world and how small each of our hands are. It is a world of big beasts and little prophets, but also of ordinary radicals rising from the deadness. The darkness of our world will try to smother the light, so we have to surround ourselves with people who make us shine brighter.

WILDFIRE

My grandfather used to bale hay, and he was notorious for buying new tractors and equipment without my grandmother's consent. So this one summer, he had just gotten a brand-new truck and trailer and wanted to "break 'em in." So he and my uncle began loading up the hay bales scattered across the field, stacking them higher and higher, pushing it to the limit. Finally, they hit the road with the hay, my uncle driving and my grandfather riding along proudly. What they didn't notice was that one of the hay bales was rubbing against a tire. Which is pure trouble, thanks to a little thing called friction.

Before long, the hay bale caught on fire, then another and another. (It's hay.) Eventually, the truck looked like a comet headed down the highway. And they didn't notice. They were probably just talking about how nice the truck ran or jamming to the Chuckwagon Gang. People began to wave hysterically, and my uncle nodded back. (That's how we roll in East Tennessee.) But eventually, he looked in the mirror and saw the flames behind them, and they quickly pulled over and got out of the truck. This created new problems, since now the flames that had been behind them raged upward and began to melt the back of the truck. My uncle noticed my grandfather had the glove compartment opened, and he asked what he was doing. My grandfather pointed to the pile of stuff he'd pulled out and said, "Well, I don't want this stuff to burn too." But my uncle was not so quick to give in. He snapped back, "No, get back in the truck." So they did. My uncle hit the pedal and they were on the highway again, this time with the goal of getting rid of the fire. He began to swerve so the hay bales fell off behind them. But then the fields began to catch on fire. Pretty soon fire trucks from all the neighboring counties were following along behind them, trying to limit the damage, and they finally managed to extinguish the inferno. Some folks have questioned whether this story "really happened like that," since some preachers tend to "remember big." In my defense and for the sake of my credibility, I want to say that my uncle—the driver in this story—confirmed it. He came to hear me speak once when I told this story. Afterward, he told me, "That's exactly how it happened. I couldn't have told it better," he said. Although he said I did leave out one part—where they considered driving the entire thing into the lake.

My grandfather told me, after he got out of jail (just kidding), "Shane, we caught half of East Tennessee on fire." We laughed and laughed. And I thought to myself, That is what the kingdom of God looks like. Christians blaze through this dark world and set it on fire with their love. It is contagious and spreads like wildfire. We are people who shine, who burn up the darkness of this old world with the light that dwells within us. And perhaps the world will ask what in the world passed through here.

We are not just called to be candles. Candles make for nice Christmas services and for a nice peace vigil (or a pretty Elton John song). They can remind us that God's light dwells within us and that we are to shine that light in this dark world. But we are not just called to be candles. We are called to be fire.[3] Candles can be snuffed out by the

3. And when I say fire, I mean the kind of fire that purifies and cleanses, not the kind of fire that destroys. This is the gentle fire that the Scriptures speak of, the fire that melts away the impurities of precious metals. The fire that burns away the chaff and dead branches so that we may be more

slightest wind or by the smallest child on their birthday. But it's harder to put out a fire. We are to be fire, to weave our lives together so that the Spirit's inferno of love spreads across the earth. We are a bride, not a harem.

MOMMA CHURCH (BLESS HER HEART)

It's weird that while many of the traditional mainline denominations and old-school Anabaptists are trying to figure out how to fill empty pews or how to get rid of pews and bring in drums and drama to attract the young 'uns, there are so many communities and visionaries starting things up that I can hardly keep up with them. We are bursting at the seams at times. Nearly every week, people call wanting help starting a community or a house of hospitality. People have even ended up on our front steps ready to follow Jesus but with no idea where to begin.[4] Meanwhile, I just saw a sad, sad billboard. The Catholic Church was advertising for priests, trying to recruit a few good men. So many of the circles we are in are packed with young visionaries who could use some good eldership. So to the young 'uns: we have to remind ourselves to stay anchored in the church, for we need roots and wisdom. This is one of the reasons I hang out with older folks, and why I have written books with several folks over sixty. The old need the young, and the young need the old. Plus, when people tell you radical Christianity is just a phase, you can say you know folks who have been in the phase for more than fifty years.

---

fully alive, as people and as a planet. The fire that consumes bushes and sinners without destroying them.

4. Tony Campolo called a few years ago and said he had just spoken to a bunch of young people about selling everything and giving it to the poor, and they actually did. He said one of them was on a Greyhound bus coming to our house. I told Tony we'd give the kid his address (ha!).

It seems to me that God could surround us with elders as we bring new energy into an aging body, but it will take tremendous courage from old folks to dream new dreams and allow a new generation to make their own mistakes. And it will take great humility from the new generation of the church to listen to the wisdom of our elders and know that we can learn from others' mistakes.

There are so many signs of hope, dear friends, and not just within the Christian underground. The crazy thing is that we are beginning to make sense; ordinary radicals are all around us. So we mustn't allow ourselves to detach from the church in a self-righteous cynicism. That's too easy and too empty. To those communities that have severed themselves from the established church, please build a bridge, for the church needs your prophetic voice. We can do more together than we can do alone. One of the most important projects I've been a part of is a book called *Common Prayer: A Liturgy for Ordinary Radicals*. It took nearly five years to create, and we did it with dozens of folks from different traditions—Protestant, Catholic, Orthodox, Pentecostal, and everything in between. Our goal was to move toward the unity Jesus prayed for, that we be "one as God is one." And as we did it, we discovered there are more than 35,000 denominations. Our hope is that this project, which consists of songs, prayers, biographies of saints, and spiritual practices, builds up the church. There's a book, website, and even an app for your phone: www.commonprayer.net.

If you have the gift of frustration and the deep sense that the world is a mess, thank God for that; not everyone has that gift of vision. It also means that you have a responsibility to lead us in new ways. Recognizing that something is wrong is the first step toward changing the world. So for those of us who have nearly given up on the church, may we take comfort in the words of St. Augustine: "The Church is a whore, but she's my mother." She is a mess and has many illegitimate children. But she is also our momma and managed to give birth to us and to give us enough of the truth that we have been able to ask the questions that we have in this book.

I once heard a pastor say, "The church is like Noah's ark. It stinks, but if you get out of it, you'll drown." I visited a congregation in Tennessee my family goes to, and the greeters at the door welcoming people in wore shirts that read, "No Perfect People Allowed." We are the church. If she were perfect, we'd mess her up as soon as we joined. So may we have some grace, even with those Christians and pastors who make us nauseated and put us to sleep. After all, they have given us enough of the story that we have been able to stumble into God and community. A friend just told us that perhaps we should relate to the church as a dysfunctional parent. We honor, submit to, and love her. But we do not allow her to destroy those we love with her dysfunction. We recognize that our beauty and our broken-ness are inseparable from hers. The Creator and the church are our parents, and having one without the other leaves us very empty. Though our mother has many illegitimate children, we still love her.

Maybe we are a little crazy. After all, we believe in things we don't see. The Scriptures say that faith is "being sure of what we hope for and certain of what we do not see" (Heb. 11:1). We believe poverty can end even though it is all around us. We believe in peace even though we hear only rumors of wars. And since we are people of expectation, we are so convinced that another world is coming that we start living as if it were already here. As prominent evangelical activist Jim Wallis says, "We believe despite the evidence . . .

and watch the evidence change." So may we begin living as if poverty were over, and we will see it come to pass. May we begin beating our swords into plowshares now, and the kingdom will begin to be not simply something we hope for when we die but something we see on earth as it is in heaven, the kingdom that is among us and within us.

I pray that we will have the integrity of the early church, which, in the same breath that it denounced their empire in Rome, was able to invite people into the Way—little communities scattered throughout the empire. We have a tremendous responsibility to provide an alternative to the children who see military service as their only hope for college, to young people who see the market economy as their only hope for providence. May we spend our lives making the Jesus way of life accessible to people. The world is thirsty. All creation is groaning. Christianity as it is has not satisfied the souls of those who hunger for another way of life.

One friend was asked by a skeptic, "You all are just a little group of radical idealists. What makes you actually think you can change the world?" And she said, "Sir, if you will take a closer look at history you will see . . . that's the only way it has ever been done." Welcome to the irresistible revolution, a new and ancient way of life that is so attractive, who would settle for anything else? Welcome to the revolution of little people, guerrilla peacemakers, and dancing prophets, the revolution that loves and laughs. The revolution begins inside each of us, and through little acts of love, it will take over the world. Let us begin to be Christians again. Jesus, give us the courage.

THE BEGINNING

So it's the end of the book, and I feel like I should give an altar call. But let me remind us that altar calls originated during the fiery revivals of nineteenth-century evangelists like Charles Finney. The reason they gave them was to register new converts for the antislavery movement. They were not simply calling people forward to become believers; they were calling people forward to join a movement of ordinary radicals. On the altar, belief and action kissed, and extremists for love were born. So once again, it is time for an altar call, but this one is a little different. It is an altar call to the world, an invitation to see a new kind of Christianity and to hear the confession of a church on its knees asking your forgiveness for the mess we have helped create. And it is an "alter"[5] call to the church, to alter our vision from the patterns of this world and create new ways of living. So it's a little different from the tear fests of my youth, where we flooded to the altar *en masse* to get born again every year. The tears we shed are not just for ourselves but for our world. The sins we confess are not just drinking too much beer but also getting drunk on the cocktails of culture. We are not just laying our lives at the altar with nothing to pick up but we are also picking up an irresistible revolution that the world is waiting for.

So with every head bowed and every eye closed, let's get started.

---

5. I don't even like puns, much less stealing them. But I stole this one from some friends. In the fall of 2005, some dynamic folks gave birth to a magazine called *Geez*, which is a promising effort to harmonize the voices of ordinary radicals. They have a delightful pun on the altar call, calling themselves an "alter" call on the fringes of the faith, cleverly inviting restless and overchurched souls to create alternative ways of living. Check out *http://geezmagazine.org*.

CHAPTER 14

SCRAP NOTES FROM THE REVOLUTION

Frequently Asked Questions from the Past Decade

One of the things we decided I should do for the anniversary edition is add a new chapter. It made sense.

But it felt a little clunky—in part, because I like the way the original book ends. So we kept thinking of what we could do to add some new content but keep the old intact. We came up with this idea. (Actually my wife came up with this idea . . .) Let's do a new chapter of frequently asked questions, since I've had tons of great conversations over the past decade and there are several themes that keep coming up. Here you go. Imagine we're just drinking sweet tea in rocking chairs on the front porch.

How do you sustain yourself and not burn out? (Seems like a good question to start with, since this is the ten-year edition.)

I remember hearing a mentor of mine getting asked the same question. This was the answer of my wise, old Catholic friend: "Every morning, I crawl into a little ball and listen to Jesus tell me how much he loves me. And that gives me energy for another day." I get that. Jesus energizes me.

Seeing what he survived gives me courage every day. So keep falling in love with Jesus—fresh every day.

Community is also clutch. I heard a friend say, "Even Jesus didn't carry his cross on his own," referring to the fact that Simon helped him, but also to the fact that our burdens, our little crosses, our hard days, get a little more bearable when others are walking alongside us.

Practically, we also rest. God had this idea that we should take a day off—a Sabbath. Crazy, huh? So we do take time to rest—and play and rejuvenate. On the Sabbath, we often don't answer the phone or door or check emails. We rest and do things that energize our souls.

I also live an integrated life, and by that I mean that I try to do things that complement each other well. If I am going to spend a lot of time writing, then I like to spend some time in the garden first. My best writing comes when I type with dirt under my fingernails. I love to travel and speak, but I make sure my travel is integrated into the rest of life and that I am home more than I am away. That way I make sure I am not just talking about what we do but also doing what we do. If I am only out speaking and haven't hung out on the street or helped a kid with homework in a while, I start to get tired.

Likewise, if all I did was give out food without addressing why people are hungry, I think I'd start to grow weary. The macro and micro, or the global and the local, belong together like the yin and yang or Oreos and milk. I believe in changing systems and structures, but I also believe in hanging out with real people. When we work only on policies without hanging out with real people, we get tired. And if we are only bandaging people's wounds without doing something about the systems running them over, we start to burn out. That's why we give people fish, and also teach people to fish, and then also do something about who owns the pond.

These all have to go together like a tripod or a three-legged stool. Without one leg, the stool get a little wobbly and out of balance. Charity workers need to also have a vision for justice. And justice workers need to keep their feet on the streets of injustice.

Another good piece of advice I got from a friend is this: If you know you are going to encounter a lot of ugly things, be sure to surround yourself with beauty. That's part of why we paint murals and plant gardens and hang out with kids. And you need to hang out with people who make you smile. If you can't laugh, the devil has already won. (That's another good reason to ride a unicycle, by the way.)

You talk a lot about community. What exactly is it and how do I find it?

My buddy says community is like a potluck on steroids.

When we think of community, I don't think we should limit ourselves to "intentional communities" where folks share a house, though these can be beautiful things.

Here's why. I know lots of folks who live together with a dozen other folks crammed into a house, but they do not have a healthy community. And there are other folks who don't all live in the same house, but they have deep, rich, authentic community.

Most of the vital communities I've seen have some model of cohousing or sense of a parish or village where folks have decided to live near each other and do life together. What we have at the Simple Way started as an intentional community house and now feels more like an intentional village. We've created rhythms for our days, weeks, and years so that we move together, mourn together, and celebrate together.

The good news is that we are not alone in the world. There is a longing in all of us to love and be loved. We are made in the image of a God who reflects community—Father,

Son, Spirit. God said it's not good to be alone; we are better together. And Jesus lived in community, sent the disciples out in pairs, and said whenever two or three gather in his name, he is with them.

Community is about realizing that others can make us better, that we can do more together than we can on our own. When we are teenagers, we hear about peer pressure as a negative thing, and it can be. But we can also surround ourselves with a critical mass of people who create a gravity that moves us toward God, and toward the kind of people we want to be. In one sense, community is about surrounding ourselves with people who resemble the kind of person we want to be, and we rub off on each other. It is about positive peer pressure.

So if you want to be more courageous, hang out with courageous people. If you want to be more generous, hang out with generous people. Surround yourself with people who remind you of Jesus, and they will move you closer to him.

As a society, our "communal muscles" have atrophied, so we have to start by exercising them slowly. You don't dive into the deep water until you learn to swim a little. I see a lot of folks dive into the deep end without ever wading in the water. It's important to visit and learn from folks who have been at it for a while. We've tried to create some good resources for that on our websites and with some "come and see" weekends for folks to visit.

I see a lot of new communities set the bar so high that they set themselves up for disappointment. They want to share every dollar together, eat every meal together, pray every morning together, and they end up like the seed that Jesus spoke of that springs up into a plant that initially blooms beautifully but dies quickly because it has no roots. I suggest starting small—with one meal a month—and do it well. Then you desire more community instead of less, and you can grow into it naturally. It's kind of like growing a baby tree—community needs a lot of tender love and care as it establishes its roots.

Community can be a nebulous and elusive thing, so it needs definition; it needs some DNA. We may share money and meals and prayer and gardens and cars, but those are more the fruits of community. The foundation must be built out of some shared values, beliefs, and practices that we hold each other accountable to.

Community also needs structure to be healthy. The structure is like a trellis in a garden. Without some structure for your tomato plants to grow on, your tomatoes will rot, but if you have too much structure, you'll stifle life instead of supporting it. Community is kind of like that, and we have to learn what kind of structure best creates an environment where it is easier to be good and where the Spirit flows freely among us.

We've found it helpful to think of community sort of like an onion, with different layers. We invite folks to move deeper in (and sometimes joke that the outer layers are a little flaky). This can also be helpful for other faith communities like traditional congregations—not to think of membership as being in or out, but to think of it as a process of going deeper together. Sometimes we cheapen membership by making it something you just decide to do and then sign a doctrinal statement. In the early church, joining the community of Christ was a process that took years to become fully committed.

I also heard a good metaphor from a rancher. He was talking cows, but I think it works with people too. He explained that there are two ways to keep your cows together. One is by building fences and gates. The other is by creating a really good food source. When you create a really good food source in the center, you don't have to worry as much about all the gates and fences and who's in and who's out.

Do you all have a worship service?

We have chosen not to start a church but rather to join the church in our neighborhood. We saw that what most inner cities need is not more churches but a unified, revitalized church. Rather than do our own worship services, we join congregations in our area. That may mean going to the storefront Pentecostal service or heading to Mass with the Catholics down the street. I saw a T-shirt that said, "Don't go to church . . . be the church." We do both—we go to worship, and we do our best to be the church, knowing that what happens around dinner tables and living rooms is also church.

It is impossible to be a Christian without the church. We need to be a part of a worshiping community. The sacred rituals of the church—communion, baptism, confession— these things have deep roots thousands of years old. I am very suspicious of the "spiritual but not religious" trend. I get the reasons for it. But I also think we can be both spiritual and religious.

Should I give money to homeless folks or beggars?

Jesus said to give to everyone who asks. That's a tough command. Sometimes we wonder what Jesus would do in the Calcutta slums or in our heroin-haunted streets, where folks ask for change on every corner.

What we can say with confidence is that Jesus would not ignore them. "Give to everyone who asks" means "do not ignore people." We can always give dignity, attention, time, a listening ear. Sometimes we give money, sometimes not. But we can always give love.

Ironically, giving money can be a cheap way to love someone. Many folks give money because they don't want to have an interaction; they just want to get someone off their back. There are times when giving money can even be a way to avoid the responsibility that a real relationship might demand. So I want to suggest, sure, give money, but give more than money . . . give yourself.

When Jesus speaks in Matthew 25 about caring for "the least of these," the actions he speaks of are not distant acts of charity but personal actions of compassion—visiting the prisoners, caring for the sick, welcoming the strangers, sharing food with the hungry. Better than sharing money is sharing life, a meal, a home.

Sure, wisdom has its place, but so does risk-taking. Many of us don't have enough stories of being taken advantage of or of having something stolen because we don't take enough risks. Any time we love someone, we risk being hurt. But it's worth the risk.

Sometimes folks ask this question about giving to beggars and panhandlers with suspicion, speculating that homeless folks will just use their money for drugs or alcohol, which happens sometimes. But we don't always ask what CEOs are doing with our money when we give it to their companies, and they may also be buying drugs or pornography (or yachts) with our money!

In the end, if we cannot take someone to dinner or give them a ride when they ask for money, we might as well give some money. It's better to err on the side of grace than on the side of suspicion. Maybe that woman asking us for diapers really does need them. And we doubt that Jesus is going to reprimand us for giving too much money to addicts. More likely, we will discover we could have been a bit more generous than we were. So if you make a mistake, err on the side of generosity.

Do you use Twitter and Facebook, or are you antitechnology?

There are some things I think we need to turn off so we can make space for community and other lifegiving things. Like television. We don't have a TV, and one of the reasons kids come to our house is because we don't have a TV. People love hanging out at the house because we play games, paint on walls, hang out in the yard, and cook food together. If they want to stare at a box, they can do that anywhere. Now we occasionally watch a movie or something. (We have an awesome ten-foot TV painted on one of the walls and can project a movie onto it.) If you do have a TV, I suggest keeping it in the closet and bringing it out on special occasions, or at least not having it in a prominent place.

Other things like computers and smart phones I think of as tools. I like having a drill, but I don't want my drill telling me when it is time to work. I like keeping my phone on airplane mode most of the time and checking it on occasion, but on my terms, not its terms.[1] Technology can be used for good or for bad, to build or to destroy—whether it's a hammer or Skype. We've had some incredible calls on Skype with people around the world. I can speak in Finland without having to go to Finland. (No offense, Finland.) We see what happened in Egypt with the Arab Spring and how instrumental Twitter has been in the movement for racial justice. But I also see how the technology is changing the way we interact. We need to beware of virtual friends and still have real ones. Everywhere you look, there will be virtual revolutions, virtual networks, virtual friends, but *virtual* also means "almost

---

1. Okay, in my notes for this chapter, my wife wrote, "Be honest." I guess I should add that it's not easy to keep our tools in their proper place. One of my biggest struggles is freeing myself from feeling like I have to respond to every current issue on Twitter and Facebook. It is liberating to remember that Jesus did pretty well without Twitter, and the world really doesn't fall apart if we go a month without using a computer, but that doesn't mean it's easy.

real." Virtual relationships come without any responsibility or accountability, which is what makes them dangerous. There is a word we have for intimacy that comes without obligations or responsibilities: infidelity. So don't replace real community with virtual community. The person with many virtual friends is likely to be very lonely. You have probably found that as we connect virtually to the world, we often lose connection with the people right next to us; we gain the whole world and lose our soul. If we eat only virtual food, we will starve to death.

Having said that, please follow me on Twitter and Facebook @ShaneClaiborne.

Do you think everyone needs to live like you?

There are certain things we can say are clear gospel mandates, like caring for the poor and sharing the salvific love of Jesus with others. But Jesus doesn't tell everyone the same thing when he invites them to follow. To one person (Nicodemus) he says, "Be born again." To another (the rich ruler) he says to sell all he has and give it to the poor. There is an unmistakable call in Scripture to "not conform to the patterns of the world," but just because we are called to be radical nonconformists doesn't mean that we all end up doing the same thing.

Nonconformity doesn't mean uniformity.

We are all called to carry a cross, but that doesn't mean all the crosses look alike. Consider the two tax collectors who follow Jesus: Matthew and Zacchaeus. Even though they are both tax collectors, their responses to Jesus are not identical. Matthew leaves everything and follows Jesus, walking barefoot on the streets. Zacchaeus doesn't. He sells half of everything he owns and gives the money to the poor, and then he begins paying people back four times what he owes them. He is a different kind of tax collector, doing Jubilee economics and spinning debt on its head. Neither of them are conforming any longer to the patterns of their world and the oppressive systems of taxation they find themselves in. But they respond in different ways. As we "seek first the kingdom of God," some of us may lose our jobs. Some of us may redefine them. Others may turn the systems on their head as they pursue the upside-down kingdom of Jesus.

Paul said, "Follow me as I follow Christ."

What's more important than your following me is that you are following Jesus. I'm interested not in your being me but in your being you. And in all of us becoming more like Jesus.

What does it mean to be a "red letter" Christian?

A friend of mine was being interviewed on the radio by a DJ who commented about how he liked some of the Bible and found other parts troubling. Then, referring to how the words of Jesus are often set apart in red font, the DJ said to my friend, "But I sure like the stuff in red. You seem to like the stuff in red too. You should call yourselves 'red-letter Christians.'" And so we did.

Some will say, "Aren't the black letters important too?" Of course. And yet Jesus over and over declared that some of the things that Moses taught about divorce, adultery, killing, getting even with those who hurt you, and the use of money needed to be transcended by an even higher morality. So Jesus is not contradicting them as much as he is fulfilling them. Now we do not just have words on paper, but the Word has become flesh. We can see what God is like in the flesh, with skin on. Jesus becomes the lens through which we understand Scripture and the world around us.

I don't think you can really understand what the black letters in the Bible are telling you until you first come to know the Jesus revealed in the red letters. This in no way diminishes the importance of those black letters; we believe that the Holy Spirit directed the writers of Scripture so that all of Scripture was inspired by God.

Many of us have become uncomfortable with labels like "evangelical" which have come to be closely associated with some of the very things Jesus spoke so clearly against. We want a Christianity that looks like Jesus again, that takes the Sermon on the Mount and the Beatitudes seriously. We are simply asking, What if Jesus meant the stuff he said? And what would the world look like if Christians lived by those red letters of Scripture?[2]

What's more important: saving souls or feeding bellies?

So often we separate things that were never meant to be separated. Faith and works. Saving souls and feeding bellies. Jesus and justice. The Great Commandment and the Great Commission.

I think that is why Jesus said the most important thing in the world is this: Love God and love your neighbor. It's one thing. They cannot be separated. Like two sides of a coin. Or two blades of the scissors—they only work together. Scripture says that if we have material possessions and pass by our neighbor who is in need without having compassion, how can we say the love of God is in us (1 John 3:17)? Jesus says if we come to the altar holding a grudge, we should get up and go reconcile (Matt. 5:24). True religion, says James, is

---

2. Now we have a Red Letter Movement on our hands. Tony Campolo and I wrote a book together unpacking this even more, titled *Red Letter Revolution*. My public ministry of speaking and writing is a part of Red Letter Christians. We've got the blog: *www.redletterchristians.org*. And we have an entire network of speakers and writers who are communicating the message of Jesus and justice. I am still very much a part of the Simple Way, and I think of that as our local revolution. If you want to support or keep track of our local work, go here: *www.thesimpleway.org*. And if you want to connect with and support the movement work around the world, check out *www.redletterchristians.org*.

caring for the widow and orphan and keeping ourselves from being corrupted by the world.

So what's more important: to love God or our neighbor, feeding bellies or saving souls? Neither. It is impossible to separate them. "No one has ever seen God; but if we love one another, God lives in us and his love is made complete in us" (1 John 4:12).

Some will say, "Are you saying that works can earn our salvation?" We can do nothing to earn our salvation. Our salvation is a gift from God. But I am saying that our works demonstrate our salvation. If our love for God does not translate into acts of love and compassion for the most vulnerable people on the planet, how can we say that we love God? If we truly experience mercy, it should make us merciful.

One of the problems, as I look at history, is that not only have we pitted things against each other that were never meant to be at odds, but we also end up overcorrecting when we've gone astray. When folks talk about the "social" gospel and the "evangelical" gospel, you see this. We end up emphasizing one thing at the expense of another. That is what most heresies were—focusing on one truth at the cost of neglecting other truths. It's sort of like someone driving a car and running off the right side of the road, and then yanking the wheel so hard they run off the left side of the road. So let's not be reactionary. Let's refuse to create false dichotomies, and instead let's say yes to the whole gospel. And the whole gospel is about loving God and loving people. It is about heaven and about earth. It is about saving souls and feeding bellies.

One of the big obstacles to Christ has been Christians who have so much to say with their mouths, but so little to show of God's love with their lives. And many of the folks who love so loudly don't always share about Jesus with their words. Let's be people who share Jesus with our words and with our lives.

How important is prayer, and what does your prayer life look like?

I grew up thinking of prayer mainly as bringing our requests before God. It could feel a little like the old story of the kid going up to bed who said, "I'm going to pray now. Does anybody want anything?" As if God were Santa Claus. That may be part of prayer—I think God wants to hear the desires of our hearts, our anxieties and hopes—but I've also come to see that prayer is not just about trying to get God to do what we want God to do. It is just as much about getting ourselves to do what God wants us to do, and training ourselves to be the kind of people God wants us to be.

I noticed in India many of the prayers we prayed were about inviting Jesus to live in us and to love people through us. We prayed that the fruit of the Spirit—love, joy, peace, patience, kindness, goodness, gentleness, faithfulness, self-control—would grow in us, that where there is hatred, we would bring love, that where there is darkness, we would bring light. I pray these same prayers all the time. I carry some beads in my pocket to pray with, not as a good luck charm but just as a tool to help me focus. As I hold each bead, I pray a line of the Lord's Prayer or I think about one of the fruit of the Spirit.

As a community—with Catholics and Protestants, Pentecostals and Quakers, and everything in between—we had a hard time learning to pray together. That's part of what gave birth to the *Common Prayer* book.[3] We collected songs, prayers, biographies of saints, quotes from different traditions, and made a marvelous collage. It is like a treasure chest. In *Common Prayer*, there are prayers for each morning, midday, and evening, and prayers for special occasions like a

---

3. There is a big book, a pocket edition, even a phone app, and you can find a lot of it online: *www.commonprayer.net*.

housewarming or a baby dedication. It felt like a holy project from the beginning. In the years since its release, we have gotten stories from folks around the world who are using it to pray together—people in prison, even in mental health hospitals. I had one couple say that using *Common Prayer* to pray together helped save their marriage. Thanks be to God.

I also think it's critical that prayer and action go together. Lots of people pray and don't do much else. Other folks are very active and forget that there is a God at work—the weight of the world is not on our shoulders alone, thanks be to God.

How do you respond to your critics?

My critics are my best teachers, but only when they will talk with me, not at me.

Unfortunately, a lot of critics, even Christians, are not willing to talk with me (contrary to what Jesus commands in Matthew 19). I had one speaking event where a small group of very vocal critics wanted to uninvite me. I, along with the organizers, offered to use my honorarium to fly them in to have a robust, public conversation about issues they were concerned about. Unfortunately, they would not come. In the end, the controversy caused such a stir that the audience ended up being twice the size it would have been. And we ended with communion and a prayer for those who vilify us. It was a sacred event. Still, I wish I could have had a conversation with the people who were so upset. And had communion together.

Even if 90 percent of what our critics say is false, that means 10 percent is true, so I try to look for the truth. Critics sharpen you in ways your friends do not.

I've found that one of the ways we bear witness to Christ is in the way that we disagree. We need to be able to disagree well—as Christians, as a church.

Just as important as being right is being nice.

Look at both the liberals and the conservatives, and you can see that having good ideologies and arguments is not enough. You can have great ideas and still be mean and arrogant, and no one really likes listening to mean people. It makes for good TV but doesn't look much like our Lord Jesus. Remember that anyone can be set free, both oppressed and oppressor, and do not forget that our Lord's table has room for both Zealot and tax collector.

I was traveling in Texas when I was approached by this tough, Southern cowboy of a man. He said to me with a strong Southern draw, "I gotta confess. I am a redneck. A textbook redneck—gun totin', pickup-truck drivin' redneck— but I've been reading your stuff, and it has messed me up. I just wanna say thanks and ask you to pray for me. I am a recovering redneck now."

We have a God who welcomes recovering rednecks. Heck, I'm one of them.

And just because we don't agree with someone doesn't mean we can't work together. When we build subversive friendships and create unlikely alliances, we broaden our influence and amplify our message. One of our best partners in the fight against gun violence has been Hunters against Gun Violence.

We should never think that Christians have a monopoly on goodness. In Scripture, God uses pagan kings, lying brothel owners, reborn terrorists, and even a donkey, so never set limits on where God is at work. Just because the church is God's primary instrument for the kingdom doesn't mean God is not at work in others.

There's a story in the Gospels where the disciples come to Jesus and say, "There's a guy down the street doing miracles and prophesying, but he's not one of us. Should we tell him to stop?" Jesus says absolutely not. "If he is not against us, he is for us." Sadly, we Christians have often said, "If we don't have the same religion or political beliefs, we can't work together." That's a shame. We should be the best collaborators in the world.

Are you ever scared?

There are certainly times I am scared, but they aren't always when I expect to be scared. One of the scariest moments in our community was when the police raided our house (on "accident") and the SWAT team threw everyone on the floor and ripped one of the women's shirts. Those are moments when you think, "Who do we call now?!"

We've certainly had scary things happen. My mom is a wise woman. She said to me, "I used to pray that you would be safe, but now I pray that you would be careful, and those are not the same." That's a beautiful distinction. Just because we are not called to be safe does not mean that we should not be wise. We have created many important guidelines for life here in the neighborhood. Some have come from mistakes. Others have come from Jesus, like always going out in pairs. That's wise no matter where you are.

At the end of the day, the best security is knowing your neighbors. And we are proud to be a part of a tight-knit neighborhood where dozens of families are always looking out for each other. The gospel does not promise us safety— only that God will be with us in the danger. That doesn't mean that nothing bad will happen. (Look what happened to the disciples . . . and Jesus . . . and Christians throughout history!) When Jesus speaks of fear, he talks about how we fear those things that can destroy our bodies (like guns and knives), but he says we should fear all the more those things that can endanger our souls, and those are the more subtle dangers, including suburban demons like insulating ourselves from suffering or cluttering our lives with possessions while others live in poverty. These are the things that can destroy our souls. So don't just pray on the street corners of the inner city. Make sure you also go to the shopping malls and cast out the demons of Mammon and materialism!

Fear is a dangerous thing. And we live in a culture that is held hostage to fear. We do a lot of damage when we live in fear. Some of the worst violence in the world has come when we let fear overcome our love—after all, perfect love drives out fear. When love is absent, fear holds us hostage.

But love casts out fear.

How do I know what God's will is for my life?

I grew up asking this question and feeling a great deal of pressure when it came to decisions like whether I should get married, which college to go to, what career to choose. Now, rather than asking what God's will is for *my life*, I find it helpful instead to ask what God's will is and how my life might fit into that. Maybe that's what it means to seek first the kingdom of God—the world does not revolve around us, but rather we are revolving around God. That relieves the pressure a bit because we know that God's will is for the hungry to have food, the homeless to have housing, the oppressed to be set free, and we get to be a part of that. The question then becomes how we can contribute to the redemptive work God is doing. Instead of asking God to bless what we're doing, we can align ourselves with what God has already promised to bless—the poor, the merciful, the peacemakers—and know with confidence that God is blessing us, or more important, that we are blessing God.

It's also helpful to remember that God promises to be a lamp unto our feet and a light unto our path, which means we may not be able to see the whole path ahead of us, but we can see the next few steps, and as we take them, we see that the light continues to guide us one step at a time.

There's also something to be said for the role that community can play in discerning God's will in important decisions. Sometimes we act as though we have to hear God speak directly to us in an audible voice. That may happen. But for me, more often what happens is that I hear the Spirit speaking through friends I know and trust. The Quakers have a whole process for discernment; they are good at listening—to each other and to the Spirit.[4] When it comes to important decisions in my life, I gather some friends and elders and invite them to listen with me and to reflect back to me what they sense God might be saying. The decision to write this book and the decision to get married were both made this way. Many ears help us hear better.

Do you think Christians should be involved in politics?

Jesus spent a lot of time talking about the real stuff of his world—day laborers and unjust judges, widows and orphans, strangers and immigrants, abused women and exploited workers, redistribution of wealth and reconciliation with enemies. The real question is not, Do we engage? but rather, How do we engage? If we are to love our neighbors as ourselves, then we care about legislation and laws and policies, because they affect people we are trying to love. But the danger is to limit our politics to a party or a candidate, rather than focusing on Jesus. We have already cast our ultimate vote, and now we are trying to align with anyone and anything that moves the world toward the kingdom of God.

In a world where pledging allegiance to Rome meant declaring, "Caesar is Lord," substituting Jesus for Caesar offered the early Christians a new political orientation. Every time Christians proclaimed, "Jesus is Lord," they were also

---

4. There are lots of helpful resources from the Quakers here: *http://www.fgc quaker.org/resources/clearness-committees-what-they-are-and-what-they-do*.

saying, "Caesar is not." It was deeply and subversively political. It was as strange to say, "Jesus is my Lord," two thousand years ago as it would be to declare him commander-in-chief today. It was an invitation to a new political imagination centered around the person, teaching, and peculiar politics of Christ. This political orientation invites every political leader and worldly power to conform to the norms of the upside-down kingdom of God, where the poor are blessed, the last come first, the hungry are filled, and the mighty are cast down from their thrones. It means aligning ourselves with the prophets, who spoke of beating our weapons into farm tools, rather than conforming to the patterns of violence and the business of war.

We need imagination.

When Jesus spoke of the kingdom of God, he used the word *empire*, and the empire he spoke about was not just one we hope to see after we die. We are to bring it "on earth as it is in heaven." It's about bringing God's reign to earth. It's about making Jesus king—or president—now. Joining the politics of Jesus is about joining God's redemptive plan to save the world. It is about allegiance, hope, and a new kingdom.

And our hope is not in a party or a candidate but in Christ. *Vote* shares the same root as *devotion* and has to do with where we put our hope. Our hope is not in a donkey or an elephant but in the Lamb. As the old hymn goes, "My hope is built on nothing less than Jesus' blood and righteousness . . . all other ground is sinking sand." And there is a lot of sinking sand these days.

So we may vote on the Tuesday after the first Monday in November, but we also vote today and tomorrow and the next day.[5] We are convinced that change is not confined to

---

5. Another way to think of political engagement, or voting, is that we are doing damage control. We are limiting the collateral damage of the principalities and powers.

one day every four years. Change happens every day. We vote with our lives.

You have been a big advocate of singleness. Why did you get married?

The truth is I still feel just as passionate about the gift of singleness and how badly the church has dropped the ball on this subject. I'm able to advocate for it now from a new angle, but I'm an advocate nonetheless. To be a good spouse, one needs to be thoroughly content to be alone. And to be a good single person, one needs to be comfortable around others. Folks who can't be alone are dangerous married, and folks who can't imagine living with someone else will not be very healthy alone either. I learned so many things from my thirty-five years of unmarried life (sometimes I say I was single as long as Jesus was single!), things marriage doesn't teach you. And now I am learning new lessons, new dynamics to love and sacrifice. Both singleness and marriage can be lonely, and both can be invigorating. Both can be selfish, just as both can be holy. The real question is, Which one helps me love better? Do I love God and my neighbors better alone, or together? Do I seek first the kingdom of God better single or married? And I still see our faith as less of a theory and more of a romance. Mother Teresa was once asked by a reporter if she was married (a strange question for a nun, but maybe he was new to the whole nun thing). She responded, "Yes, I am deeply in love. And sometimes my Spouse can be so demanding." The wedding rings Katie and I chose are rosary rings identical to those Mother Teresa and the Sisters of Charity wore as a reminder of their vow to Jesus. A friend made them for us by melting down the band of my deceased father. Every time I look at it, I am reminded of my amazing wife, and I am also reminded of my amazing Savior—both are the loves of my life.

There is profound truth in these words: We can live with-out sex, but we cannot live without love. Plenty of people have lots of sex but aren't loved, and other folks go their entire lives without ever having sex, but experience immense love. The deepest longing in our souls is not for sex but for love, for community, for friendship. Our communities and congregations must be places where everyone can feel loved and experience authentic community. Too often we focus on sex—sexual identity, sexual behavior, sexual attraction—and we forget to talk about love. The starting point must be that the church is a place where everyone can feel loved by God and by people, and then the other stuff gets a little easier, or at least a little safer.

What would you do if someone attacked your wife?

Usually this question is asked as a bit of a trap—if you don't fight, you are a coward; if you do fight, you have con-tradicted your nonviolent theology.

So let me have a little fun and answer a hypothetical question with a hypothetical answer. Use your imagination.

Katie was asleep, and I was downstairs writing. I heard the window break and then Katie's scream. I ran for the kitchen to grab a knife.

(Heck, this is a fantasy . . . I can do better than that.)

I remembered that Katie had a pistol her grandfather had left her. She kept it loaded and hidden under a loose floor board, so I grabbed it and headed upstairs to the rescue. I opened the door—

No, I kicked in the door, shattering it to pieces like the Incredible Hulk, and then I saw him.

A large seven-foot hairy beast of a man was staring at me. I thought he might jump out the window, but I couldn't wait.

I shot.

Six times. Three hit him (I'm not a great shot), and he fell. One ricocheted and hit our beloved dog, Bella, in the leg. But I couldn't think about that. All I could do was stare at the bloodied body on our floor and hug my wife, tears streaming. We were safe.

Two weeks later Katie and I were on a trip, and the brother of the man came to retaliate. While away, Katie's sister Gwen watched our house and took care of Bella, our (now three-legged) dog. But the brother didn't know that. He broke in while we were away and brutally killed Gwen, leaving the dog whimpering over her body.

Katie and I were so devastated. We burned with rage. We couldn't think clearly or rationally. We decided to burn down the brother's house. But as we set it ablaze, unbeknownst to us, he was working the night shift and his two teenage girls were home. The fire consumed them.

We were charged and convicted of murder. I got the death penalty, and Katie got life in prison as an accomplice to the crime. The state is going to kill me by lethal injection. And that hairy beast of a man is still free. But thank goodness Katie is alive. That was always my goal—to protect my wife. And that I did.[6]

And now our three-legged dog lives with my mom in Tennessee.

All I know is that if someone ever attacks my wife, I hope I will react in a way that honors Jesus, the same Jesus who forgave his killers. I'm not sure I have the kind of mercy he had, but I can at least hope I will.

That doesn't mean I'd simply stand by and watch someone kill my wife. I would do everything I could to put my body on

---

6. I later found out the hairy beast of a man was actually a roofer working on my neighbor's house when his ladder broke and threw him through our window. Oh well.

the line. There is no greater love than this—to give our lives for another person. But I would not dishonor Christ, and my wife, by trying to destroy the life of another person, especially a person who evidently is very much in need of grace. My wife would not want me to kill for her. Nor would I want her to kill for me.

My wife always gets frustrated that people don't ask her what *she* would do if someone attacked *me*. And apparently—according to my sources—she would kick them in the nuts—or ovaries—and we'd run like crazy. And she is fast.

Why did you cut your hair?

Lice.

Just kidding. Actually, I did get lice, but that was after the trim.

The truth is you probably need a haircut every decade. After more than ten years without one, I took the plunge. The final push for me came when I went to Afghanistan and my friends suggested it. (In Iraq, I wore a head covering.) I asked them if it was because I would stand out as an American. They said, "No, you might be mistaken for Al Qaeda." I said, "Well, what are you waiting on—grab the scissors." That's why I cut it. Now, about why I have kept it short. My wife sort of liked it and offered to give me a forty-five-minute massage each week I keep it short. She gives a good massage.

What is the most pressing issue?

It is impossible to rank one issue more important than another, especially when we're talking about lost lives. Sex trafficking, mass incarceration, drone warfare, the death penalty, economic inequities, gun violence, immigration, abortion, slavery, domestic violence, police brutality—all of these are issues of life and death. It is time for a movement of Christians to consistently get in the way of death and interrupt patterns of violence with the love we see on the cross. Some might say we need a new pro-life movement— not your granny's pro-life movement.

The culture wars of our parents left us polarized by party platforms and paralyzed between imperfect options. There is no Life Party, but maybe one is emerging.

Convinced that every human life is breathed upon by God and stamped with God's image, we are ready for a movement of Christians who insist on protecting life in all of its dazzling forms. This consistent ethic of life permeates and impacts every social issue—from abortion to militarism, from poverty to immigration, from capital punishment to gun control. I hope that we can decrease and eliminate abortion, embrace the immigrant and orphan, end the death penalty, and see poor people cared for and militaries turn their weapons into farm tools to cultivate life.

We live in a nation where gun violence kills more than ten thousand people a year, and we are one of the only industrialized countries that still executes its own citizens. The US has 5 percent of the world's population, and 25 percent of the world's prison population. That makes us the world's largest jailor. Military spending is about $20,000 a second, and we have the capacity of 100,000 Hiroshima atomic bombs in our arsenal. So it is time for a revolution.

Pro-life doesn't just mean anti-abortion. Let's be pro-life from the womb to the tomb, from the cradle to the grave. To be for life means standing against death in all of its ugly forms, and against everything that dehumanizes and suffocates the good in us.

By articulating a strong and consistent ethic of life as our framework, I think we can take on many of the issues. And issues must become faces, names, friends, not just campaign platforms. To really be an advocate for life, we have to know the names and the stories of those whose lives are at stake. Otherwise, all we have is ideology. And ideology cannot fuel the movement. Love must fuel the movement.

Do you believe in miracles?

Yes. Not only do I believe in miracles, I have seen them with my own eyes.

I also know that miracles happen when we take risks, and many of us don't see many miracles because we don't take many risks. I want to live in a way that makes miracles possible—and necessary.

One of my favorite miracle stories is the classic "fish and loaves" story. It begins with the disciples noticing the hunger around them. (And it's great that they noticed!) They see thousands of hungry people and realize that something has got to be done. So they come to Jesus and say, "You need to do something. The people are hungry."

Jesus' response is brilliant. He looks back at them and says, "You do something. Feed them." Their minds begin to spin as they wonder how they will ever come up with enough money and where the nearest supermarket is. But Jesus challenges them to think deeper. "What do you have?" he asks. And according to one account, there is a little child who has a few fish and loaves and is willing to give them up for the common good. The disciples offer them to Jesus, and he takes the fish and loaves and adds a little God-stuff. Everyone eats, and there are basketsful left over. My favorite part is that the little kid got to be a part of the miracle.

One of the great mysteries of our faith is that the God of the universe does not want to change the world without us. Sometimes when we ask Jesus to do something about the needs of our world, Jesus throws our prayers back to us and invites us to be part of the answer to our prayers. When we ask God to move a mountain, God may hand us a shovel.

When we see the needs of our world, all the poverty and violence and pain, it's easy to throw our hands up at God and say, "Why don't you do something?" And if we listen closely, we may hear God say back to us, "I *did* do something. I made you."

The End . . . Again

In the past few decades, our passion for evangelism has come at the cost of discipleship. Our megachurches have left us with a Christianity that is a mile long and an inch deep. We have created a church of believers, not disciples. But let us remember that the Great Commission sends us into the world not just to make believers but to form disciples. So let's rediscover the practice of disciple-making. That's what Christians are meant to be—people who remind the world of Jesus.

There is a whole new generation that wants a Christianity that looks like Jesus again. I have a pile of letters here beside me[7]—hundreds of them—and many of them say, "Thank you . . . I knew there was more to Christianity." When it comes to Christians in public, the loudest voices haven't always been the most beautiful voices, but that is changing.

When I first wrote this book, I was told, "Social justice books don't really do that well, especially in the Christian book world." But you have proved them wrong. Not just because you bought this book, along with hundreds of thousands of other people, but because you care. You care about Jesus and about the world around us.

Let's continue to show the world that our faith is not just

---

7. By the way, I like letters. Letter writing has been an important pasttime for the church. I can't promise I'll write you back, but I will read your letter, and I'll do my best to reply. Right now, I'm running about six months behind on writing. And I prefer old-school snail mail: Shane Claiborne, PO Box 12798, Philadelphia, PA 19134.

a ticket into heaven and a license to ignore the world around us. We care. We care about injustice and racism and inequity. We care because Jesus cared, and love causes us to care about life before death just as much as life after death.

Amen.

So this is the end . . . for now. I guess we might have another edition ten years from now, the twentieth-anniversary edition. Until then, I hope you enjoyed the book again—or for the first time.

Now, enough words. Let's live the revolution.

LOCAL REVOLUTIONS AND ORDINARY RADICALS

Here are a few of the local revolutions and ordinary radicals who have inspired this book and with whom the money from the sales of this book is being shared. Over the past ten years, we've shared at least half a million dollars with more than 150 groups. We add new ones each year. You can also feel good when you buy a book—it is fueling the revolution.

5 Small Loaves, Fort Defiance, AZ: *http://5smallloaves.org/*

ALARM Rwanda: *http://alarm-inc.org/where_we_serve/rwanda*

Alterna Community, LaGrange, GA: *http://www.alterna community.com/*

The Alternative Seminary, Philadelphia, PA: *http://www .alternativeseminary.net/*

Area 15, Charlotte, NC: *http://areafifteen.com/*

Atonement Lutheran Church, Philadelphia, PA: *http://atone mentlutheranchurch.beliefnet.com*

Bartimaeus Cooperative Ministries, Oak View, CA: *http:// www.bcm-net.org/*

Beloved Community Center, Greensboro, NC: *http://www .belovedcommunitycenter.org/*

Bethel Temple Community Bible Church, Philadelphia, PA

Beyond Borders: *http://beyondborders.net/*

Black Lives Matter: *http://blacklivesmatter.com/*

Black Women's Blueprint, Brooklyn, NY: *http://www.black womensblueprint.org/*

Blessed Earth, KY: *http://www.blessedearth.org/*

Blood Water Mission, Nashville, TN: *http://www.bloodwater .org/*

Brandywine Peace Community, Swarthmore, PA: *http:// www.brandywinepeace.com/*

Bread for the World, Washington, DC: *http://www.bread.org/*

Broad Street Ministry, Philadelphia, PA: *http://broadstreet ministry.org/*

Bruderhof: *http://www.bruderhof.com/*

Casa Shalom, Albuquerque, NM

Cedar Ridge Community Church, Spencerville, MD: *http:// www.crcc.org/*

Center for Action and Contemplation, Albuquerque, NM: *https://cac.org/*

Center for Death Penalty Litigation, Durham, NC: *http://www .cdpl.org/*

Center for New Ideas, St. Louis, MO: *http://www.ideabounce .com/ssf/2628.html*

Centurion's Guild, Durham, NC: *http://centurionsguild.org/*

Chosen 300 Ministries, Philadelphia, PA: *http://www.chosen 300.org/*

Christian Community Development Association, Chicago, IL: *https://www.ccda.org/*

Christian Healthcare Ministries: *www.chministries.org*

Christian Peacemaker Teams, Chicago, IL: *http://www.cpt .org/*

Christ the King United Church of Christ, Florissant, MO: *http://www.christthekingucc.org/*

Church of the Savior Servant Leadership School, Washington, DC: *http://www.slschool.org/*

Church of the Sojourners, San Francisco, CA: *https://church ofthesojourners.wordpress.com/*

Church under the Bridge, Waco, TX: *http://www.church underthebridge.org/*

Cielo Azul: *http://cieloazulfund.blogspot.com/*

Circle of Hope, Philadelphia, PA: *http://www.circleofhope.net/*

Coalition of Immokalee Workers, Immokalee, FL: *http://www.ciw-online.org/*

Common Change: *www.commonchange.com*

Common Ground Community, Shreveport, LA: *http://commongroundshreveport.blogspot.com/*

Communality, Lexington, KY

Communities United for Police Reform, New York, NY: *http://changethenypd.org/*

Cred Jewelry, London, England: *http://www.cred.tv/*

Death Penalty Information Center, Washington, DC: *http://www.deathpenaltyinfo.org/*

Do Caminho, Salvador, Brazil: *http://www.mansaodocaminho.com.br/*

Dorothy Day Catholic Worker, Washington, DC: *http://www.catholicworker.org/*

Dream Defenders: *http://www.dreamdefenders.org/*

EAPE, St. Davids, PA

Eastern University, St. Davids, PA: *http://www.eastern.edu/*

Ecclesia Houston, TX: *www.ecclesiahouston.org/*

Ekklesia Project, Indianapolis, IN: *http://www.ekklesiaproject.org/*

Equal Justice Initiative, Montgomery, AL: *http://www.eji.org/*

Equal Justice USA: *http://ejusa.org/*

Esperanza College, Philadelphia, PA: *http://esperanza.eastern.edu/*

Esperanza Health Center, Philadelphia, PA: *http://www
.esperanzahealthcenter.org/*

Evangelicals for Social Action, Wynnewood, PA: *http://
www.esa-online.org/*

Exodus Transitional Community, New York, NY: *http://www
.etcny.org/#home*

Faith in New York, New York, NY: *http://www.faithinnewyork
.org/*

Families for Peaceful Tomorrows, New York, NY: *http://
www.peacefultomorrows.org/*

Flatlanders Inn, Winninpeg, Manitoba, Canada:
http://flatlandersinn.org/

The Forgiveness Project, London, England: *http://www
.theforgivenessproject.com*

Gandhiji Prem Nivas Leprosy Centre, Calcutta, India

Geez magazine, Winnipeg, Manitoba, Canada: *http://www
.geezmagazine.org/*

Global Exchange, San Francisco, CA: *http://www.global
exchange.org/*

Hands Up United, Florissant, MO: *http://www.handsupunited
.org/*

Harambee Community, Pasadena, CA: *http://www.harambee
ministries.org/*

Heeding God's Call, Philadelphia, PA: *http://heedinggodscall
.org/*

Hip Hop Caucus, Washington, DC: *http://www.hiphopcaucus
.org/*

Hope International, Lancaster, PA: *http://www.hopeinter
national.org/*

House of Grace Catholic Worker, Philadelphia, PA

Hunting Park Christian Academy, Philadelphia, PA: *http://
www.hpcaphilly.org/*

Hyaets Community, Charlotte, NC: *http://allianceofbaptists .org/AllianceStories/detail/hyaets-community*

Iglesia del Barrio, Philadelphia, PA: *https://www.facebook .com/pages/Iglesia-Del-Barrio/*

Imago Dei, Portland, OR: *http://www.imagodeicommunity.com/*

InnerCHANGE, Anaheim, CA: *http://www.innerchange.org/*

Innocence Project, New York, NY: *http://www.innocence project.org/*

Interfaith Center of NY, New York, NY: *http://interfaithcenter .org/*

International Justice Mission, Washington, DC: *http://www .ijm.org/*

Jesus People USA, Chicago, IL: *http://www.jpusa.org/*

Jesus Radicals: *http://www.jesusradicals.com/*

Jonah House, Baltimore, MD: *http://www.jonahhouse.org/*

Journey of Hope: *https://www.journeyofhope.org/*

Jubilee Partners, Comer, GA: *http://www.jubileepartners.org/*

Kensington Welfare Rights Union, Philadelphia, PA: *http:// www.kwru.org/*

Kid Brothers of St. Frank: *http://www.richmullins.com/*

Koinonia Farm, Americus, GA: *http://www.koinoniafarm.org/*

Lawndale Community Church, Chicago, IL: *http://www .lawndalechurch.org/*

Little Flower Catholic Worker, Trevilians, VA: *https://www .facebook.com/HouseOfTheLittleFlower*

The Marin Foundation, Chicago, IL: *http://www.themarin foundation.org/*

Mars Hill Bible Church, Grand Rapids, MI: *http://www .mhbcmi.org/*

Mennonite Central Committee: *http://www.mcc.org/*

The Message Trust, Manchester, England: *https://www .message.org.uk/*

mewithoutyou: *http://www.mewithoutyou.com/*

Micah Institute, New York, NY: *http://www.nyts.edu/ the-micah-institute/*

Millennial Activists United: *http://millennialau.tumblr.com/*

Missio Dei, Minneapolis, MN: *http://www.mennoniteworker .com/*

Missionaries of Charity, Calcutta, India

MissionYear, Atlanta, GA: *http://www.missionyear.org/*

Missourians Organizing for Reform and Empowerment, St. Louis, MO: *http://www.organizemo.org/*

Murder Victim Families for Human Rights, Boston, MA: *http:// www.mvfhr.org/*

Murder Victim Families for Reconciliation, Raleigh, NC: *http:// www.mvfr.org/*

Mustard Seed Associates, Seattle, WA: *http://www.msainfo.org/*

My Brother's Keeper, Hop Bottom, PA: *http://www.uglyquilts .org/*

My People International, St. Paul, MN: *http://www.mypeople international.com/*

NAACP, Baltimore, MD: *https://www.naacp.org/*

National Coalition to Abolish the Death Penalty, Washington, DC: *http://www.ncadp.org/*

Nebraskans for Alternatives to the Death Penalty, Lincoln, NE: *http://nadp.net/*

Nehemiah House, Springfield, MA: *https://www.facebook .com/NehemiahMinistriesInc/*

New Jerusalem, Philadelphia, PA: *http://www.libertynet.org/ njl/*

New Providence Community Church, Nassau, Bahamas: *http://www.npcconline.org/*

New Sanctuary Movement, Philadelphia, PA: *http://www .sanctuaryphiladelphia.org/*

Nueva Esperanza, Philadelphia, PA: *http://www.neacademy .net/*

Oasis, London, England: *http://www.oasistrust.org/*
ONE Campaign, Washington, DC: *http://www.one.org/*
One Day's Wages, Seattle, WA: *http://www.onedayswages .org/*
Open Door Community, Atlanta, GA: *http://www.opendoor community.org/*
Organization for Black Struggle, St. Louis, MO: *http://obs-stl .org/*
Our Community Place, Harrisonburg, VA: *http://ourcommunity place.org/*
PA Abolitionists, Philadelphia, PA: *http://www.paabolition.org/*
PICO, Washington, DC: *http://www.piconetwork.org/*
The Pink House, Fresno, CA: *http://fiful.publishpath.com/*
Place of Refuge, Philadelphia, PA: *http://placeofrefuge.net/*
Plant with Purpose, San Diego, CA: *https://www.plantwith purpose.org/*
Poor People's Economic Human Rights Campaign: *www .economichumanrights.org/*
Preemptive Love Coalition: *http://www.preemptivelove.org/*
Project HOME, Philadelphia, PA: *https://projecthome.org/*
Project TURN, Durham, NC: *http://www.schoolforconversion .org/programs/project-turn/*
Psalters, Philadelphia, PA: *http://www.psalters.com/*
Radical Living Community, Brooklyn, NY: *http://www.radical livingnyc.com/*
RAW Tools, Colorado Springs, CO: *http://rawtools.org/*
The Ray of Hope Project, Philadelphia, PA: *http://www .therayofhopeproject.org/*
Reba Place Fellowship and Church, Chicago, IL: *http://www .rebaplacefellowship.org/*
Re-Imagine, San Francisco, CA: *http://www.relmagine.org/*
Relational Tithe: *http://www.relationaltithe.com/*

Revolution Church, Brooklyn, NY: *http://www.revolution
church.com/*

Revelation Church, United Kingdom: *http://www.revelation
.org.uk/*

Riverbend Commons, Corona, CA: *http://riverbendcommons
.org/*

Rivercity Church, Chicago, IL: *http://www.rivercity.cc/*

Runaway Circus

Rutba House, Durham, NC: *http://emerging-communities.com/
tag/rutba-house/*

Sacred Heart Catholic Church, Camden, NJ: *http://www
.sacredheartcamden.org/*

School for Conversion, Durham, NC: *http://www.schoolfor
conversion.org/*

Shalom Mission Communities: *http://www.shalomconnections
.org/*

Shekina Baptist Church/Shalome Baptist Church, Santa
Ana, El Salvador

Simple Cycle, Philadelphia, PA: *http://www.simplecycle.org/*

Simple Homes Fuller Center, Philadelphia, PA: *http://www
.fullercenter.org/philadelphiapennsylvania*

The Simple Way, Philadelphia, PA: *http://www.thesimpleway
.org/*

SOA Watch, Washington, DC: *http://www.soaw.org/*

Sojourners, Washington, DC: *https://sojo.net/*

Solomon's Porch, Minneapolis, MN: *http://www.solomons
porch.com/*

Spirit and Truth Fellowship, Philadelphia, PA: *https://www
.facebook.com/pages/Spirit-and-Truth-Fellowship-Church/*

St. Louis Emerging Leaders Institute, St. Louis, MO

Tearfund International: *http://www.tearfund.org/*

Tierra Nueva, Burlington, WA: *http://www.tierra-nueva.org/*

Timoteo Flag Football, Philadelphia, PA: *www.timoteo football.com*

Transform Network: *http://transformnetwork.org/*

Twin City Peace Campaign, Minneapolis, MN

University of the Poor: *http://www.universityofthepoor.org/*

Urban Mentors Network, Oakland, CA: *http://www.urban mentors.com/*

Urban Promise, Camden, NJ: *http://www.urbanpromiseusa .org/*

Vocal New York, New York, NY: *http://www.vocal-ny.org/*

Voices for Creative Nonviolence: *www.vcnv.org*

Voices in the Wilderness

Walnut Hills Fellowship, Cincinnati, OH

The Water Team: *http://www.circleofhope.net/venture/water.htm*

Wiconi International, Vancouver, WA: *http://www.wiconi.com/*

Willow Creek Community Church, South Barrington, IL: *http://www.willowcreek.org/*

Witness to Innocence, Philadelphia, PA: *http://www.witness toinnocence.org/*

Word and World: *http://www.wordandworld.org/*

Word Made Flesh, Omaha, NE: *http://www.wordmadeflesh.com/*

YACHT Club, St. Davids, PA: *http://www.eastern.edu/ student-life/student-programs-student-activities/ clubs-and-organizations*

Yes! And . . ., Philadelphia, PA: *http://www.yesandcamp.org/*

And the list goes on and on, so add your name . . .

APPENDIX 2

MARKS OF A NEW MONASTICISM

Moved by God's Spirit in this time and in this place called America to assemble at St. John's Baptist Church in Durham, North Carolina, we wish to acknowledge a movement of radical rebirth grounded in God's love and drawing on the rich tradition of Christian practices that have long formed disciples in the simple way of Christ. This contemporary school for conversion, which we have called a "new monasticism," is producing a grassroots ecumenism and a prophetic witness within the North American church that is diverse in form but characterized by the following marks:

1. Relocation to the abandoned places of empire.
2. Sharing economic resources with fellow community members and the needy among us.
3. Hospitality to the stranger.
4. Lament for racial divisions within the church and our communities, combined with the active pursuit of a just reconciliation.
5. Humble submission to Christ's body, the church.
6. Intentional formation in the way of Christ and the rule of the community, along the lines of the old novitiate.

7. Nurturing common life among members of an intentional community.

8. Support for celibate singles alongside monogamous married couples and their children.

9. Geographical proximity to community members who share a common rule of life.

10. Care for the plot of God's earth given to us, along with support of our local economies.

11. Peacemaking in the midst of violence, and conflict resolution within communities along the lines of Matthew 18:15–20.

12. Commitment to a disciplined contemplative life.

May God give us grace by the power of the Holy Spirit to discern rules for living that will help us embody these marks in our local contexts as signs of Christ's kingdom for the sake of God's world.

APPENDIX 3

TO IRAQ

I am going to Iraq because I believe in a God of scandalous grace. If I believed terrorists were beyond redemption, I would need to rip out half of my New Testament Scriptures, for they were written by a converted terrorist. I have pledged allegiance to a King who loved evildoers so much he died for them (and of course, the people of Iraq are no more evil or more holy than the people of the US), teaching us that there is something worth dying for but nothing worth killing for. While terrorists were nailing him to the cross, my Jesus pleaded that they be shown mercy, for they knew not what they were doing. We are all wretched, and we are all beautiful. No one is beyond redemption. May we see in the hands of the oppressors our own hands, and in the faces of the oppressed our own faces. We are made of the same dust, and we cry the same salty tears.

I am going to Iraq in the footsteps of an executed and risen God. I follow a Jesus who rode into Jerusalem on the back of a donkey at Passover, knowing full well what he was walking into. This Jesus of the margins suffered an imperial execution by an oppressive regime of wealthy and pious elites. And now he dares me and woos me to come and follow, to take up my cross, to lose my life to find it, with the promises that life is more powerful than death and that it is more courageous to love our enemies than to kill them.

I am going to Iraq to stop terrorism. There are Muslim and Christian extremists who kill in the name of their gods. Their leaders are millionaires who live in comfort while their citizens die neglected in the streets. I believe in another kingdom that belongs to the poor and to the peace-makers. I believe in a safe world, and I know this world will never be safe as long as the masses live in poverty so that a handful of people can live as they wish. Nor will the world be safe as long as we try to use violence to drive out violence. Violence only begets the very thing it seeks to destroy. My King warned his followers, "If we pick up the sword, we will die by the sword." How true this has proved to be throughout history. We armed Saddam in the conflict against Iran, and we armed Bin Laden in the struggle against the Soviet Union. Timothy McVeigh, the most terrifying domestic terrorist in US history, was trained in the Gulf War, where he said he turned into an animal.

I am going to Iraq to stand in the way of war. Thousands of soldiers have gone to Iraq, willing to kill people they do not know because of a political allegiance. I go willing to die for people I do not know because of a spiritual allegiance. The soldiers have incredible courage, courage enough to die for something they believe in. I pray that Christians would have that same courage. The command of the soldiers is handed down, through rank after rank, from a human commander-in-chief clinging to the myth of redemptive violence. My mandate is straight from the mouth of my heavenly King, through the lips of the Prince of Peace—to love my enemies—and yet I still falter. May we cling to the truth that every human is created in the image of God. Do we believe the children of Iraq are just as precious as the children of New York? A love for our own people is not a bad thing, but why should love stop at the border? We, the people of rebirth, have an allegiance that runs much deeper than nationalism.

I am going to Iraq as a missionary. In an age of omnipresent war, it is my hope that Christian peacemaking becomes the new face of global missions. May we stand by those who face the impending wrath of empire and whisper, "God loves you, I love you, and if my country bombs your country, I will be right here with you." Otherwise, our gospel has little integrity. As one of the saints said, "If they come for the innocent and do not pass over our bodies, then cursed be our religion." May our lives interrupt terrorism and war, in small ways, in large ways, in moments of crisis, and in everyday rhythms. These are extreme times. And I go to Iraq as an extremist for love.

"And now, compelled by the Spirit, I am going to Jerusalem, not knowing what will happen to me there. I only know that in every city the Holy Spirit warns me that prison and hardships are facing me. However, I consider my life worth nothing to me; my only aim is to finish the race and complete the task the Lord Jesus has given me— the task of testifying to the good news of God's grace" (Acts 20:22–24).[1]

---

1. You can read my Iraq journal in full at *www.thesimpleway.org/macro/shane_iraq.html*.

APPENDIX 4

HOLY MISCHIEF

Civil disobedience has had an important place in the black church in the US and in struggles for freedom throughout the world. Many Christians in the 1960s participated in sit-ins at lunch counters and wade-ins at swimming pools, and refused to honor laws that forbade them to enter certain restaurants or to sit in the front seats of public buses. First-century Christians were branded as lawbreakers for refusing to bow to the Roman emperor or his image. Martin Luther broke ecclesiastical laws of the Catholic church over freedom of religion. American abolitionists broke laws in order to bring about racial equality. Martin Luther King Jr. broke laws intended to enforce racial division. The American revolutionaries broke laws imposed by King George that oppressed the colonies. During the tyranny of Nazi Germany, Corrie ten Boom's family disobeyed German law by hiding and protecting Jews. And Dietrich Bonhoeffer and Martin Niemoller stood against German laws instituted by Hitler's Nazi regime. The Anabaptist, Quaker, Mennonite, and Brethren communities refused to adhere to laws pertaining to engaging in war. Christians smuggled Bibles into the Soviet Union and other Soviet bloc nations. The list of Christian civil disobedience is endless, and keeps getting new additions as time passes.

I prefer to think of civil disobedience as "divine obedience"—that we are obeying God even when the "laws of man" stand in the way. It becomes helpful to remember that whatever we call it—civil disobedience, divine obedience, holy troublemaking—disobeying bad laws not only has held an important place in the history of social change but also has been an ever-present part of the Christian story.

All the way back in the Old Testament, we have the Exodus story of the Hebrew slaves escaping Pharoah's plantation—an iconic act of liberation and of holy rebellion.

Shadrach, Meshach, and Abednego were thrown into a fiery furnace for refusing to obey a royal order that violated their commitment to God. Daniel ignored the king's law prohibiting prayer, and Darius flung him into the den of lions. And on and on.

Moses' very birth was an act of civil disobedience when his mother floated him down a river to escape Pharaoh's slaughter of the innocents, and the Hebrew midwives rescued him in defiance of royal orders.

Then there's Jesus. From birth, his life is marked with a subversive twist. The magi defy Herod's orders and protect Jesus. He challenges Caesar's power and is accused of insurrection. Eventually he is executed on a Roman cross, next to two other rebels . . . and crosses were reserved for the worst agitators in the empire.

Just as Jesus went to jail, so did many of his followers. John the Baptist, Jeremiah, and lots of the prophets were arrested, even executed for what were considered capital crimes at the time.

The book of Acts and the accounts of the early church are riddled with jail time, beatings, and even state-sanctioned executions of folks such as John the Baptist. Paul and Silas have a great story of the Spirit busting them out of that old jail. Paul's letter to Philemon was written to urge a former slave owner to illegally welcome back a fugitive slave (Onesimus) and to welcome him not as a slave but as a brother, a crime punishable by death.

Of course, the martyrs were known for their faithfulness to God over Caesar. One of the early Christians said that every time a Christian proclaimed, "Jesus is Lord," they were saying, "Caesar is not." The early Christians were known to be rebels and revolutionaries, albeit in a very different kind of revolution, a revolution that was as much for the freedom of the oppressors as for the freedom of the oppressed, a nonviolent revolution marked by enemy-love, gentleness, and audacious grace. But it was a revolution nonetheless. "These men who have caused trouble all over the world have now come here. . . . They are all defying Caesar's decrees, saying that there is another king, one called Jesus" (Acts 17:6–7). We see this holy mischief all the way through the Bible, even to the book of Revelation, where John, the writer of Revelation, gets exiled.

Here are a few quotes from the earliest days of Christianity:

> We are charged with being irreligious people and, what is more, irreligious in respect to the emperors since we refuse to pay religious homage to their imperial majesties. . . . High treason is a crime of offense against the Roman religion. It is a crime of open irreligion, a raising of the hand to injure the deity. . . . Christians are considered to be enemies of the State . . . we do not celebrate the festivals of the Caesars. Guards and informers bring up accusations against the Christians . . . blasphemers and traitors . . . we are charged with sacrilege and high treason . . . we give testimony to the truth.
> —TERTULLIAN

> The Christians form among themselves secret societies that exist outside the system of laws . . . an obscure and mysterious community founded on revolt and the advantage that accrues from it.
> —LETTER TO ORIGEN

They form a rabble of profane conspiracy. . . . They despise titles of honor and the purple robe of high government office though hardly able themselves to cover their own nakedness. Just like a rank growth of weeds, the abominable haunts where this impious confederacy meet are multiplying all over the world. Root and branch, it should at all costs be exterminated and accursed.

—MINUCIUS FELIX

Indeed, as we look at church history, it is hard to miss the collision between the kingdom of God and the kingdom of this world. Jesus promises the disciples that the world will hate them, that they will be dragged before courts and magistrates. It is a promise that if they live real good, they will get beat up real bad. But what is important is that they are to return love for evil. They are to stare into the faces of those who persecute them and say, "Father, forgive them, for they do not know what they are doing" (Luke 23:34).

You get the point. There is a subversive element all through the history of Christianity. Augustine himself, one of the most prominent ethicists in Christendom, said, "An unjust law is no law at all."

Actually there are only a couple of verses that can be used to argue that Christians should obey every leader and every law and never go to jail, even if the leader and the laws are in contradiction to God's law and God's love.

The most prominent verse used to debunk civil disobedience is Romans 13. It's noteworthy that the entire chapter before (Romans 12) is about not conforming to "the patterns of the world" and such. And then Paul writes Romans 13 about how we should submit to the authorities because they are established by God. The same Paul who wrote this in Romans 13 also wrote Ephesians, where he says that we wrestle not against flesh and blood (people) but against the powers and authorities (he uses the same word he used in Romans)—and he writes from jail. The same Paul who wrote that we are to submit to authority goes to jail for subverting authority. I suggest that there are two ways to respectfully submit to authority: (1) obeying the good laws and (2) disobeying the bad laws openly and being willing to suffer the consequences, thereby exposing injustice and making a spectacle of it. As Dr. King explains, when we go to jail, "we expose injustice and make it so uncomfortable that people can't help but respond." That's how movements change laws.

But one of the most important elements of Christian resistance is humility. We are willing to suffer the consequences of disobeying the laws or authorities. We are willing to suffer with those who suffer in order to end the suffering. This is exactly what Jesus did and calls his followers to do. John Howard Yoder calls this "revolutionary subordination." We can see how this has operated throughout history.

When I went to Iraq during the bombing in 2003, I went with a courageous group of folks that included a number of Christian pastors and doctors. We took medication to the hospitals, hung out with families, and worshiped with Iraqi Christians. This was all technically illegal, because US sanctions prohibited us from taking medication and other supplies to the people of Iraq. When we returned, the US State Department declared a lawsuit against the group, targeting the doctors who took medications in, with a penalty of up to twelve years in prison if convicted. What we argued, and continue to believe, is that the sanctions and bombing violated God's law to love our neighbors (or enemies, for that matter) as ourselves. And we were willing to go to jail for that.

In the end, no one went to jail. However, the court did issue a fine of $20,000 dollars. In an act of revolutionary subordination, our group paid it—in Iraqi dinar. It turned out that what was worth $20,000 in Iraqi currency a few years before had dwindled in value until it was worth less than eight dollars. It was an act that continued to expose the devastating consequences of the war—the destruction of life and livelihood.

I am convinced that our trip to Iraq was a holy endeavor, even though it was illegal. I am convinced that when we have gone to jail for feeding the homeless or sleeping in public, we were being faithful to God. As Gandhi and King said, "Noncooperation with evil is as much a duty as cooperation with good."

So yes, we have gone to jail. But we also have won in court, over and over. We have exposed bad laws. We have seen laws changed. We have had police officers who arrested us come to court and argue that we were right and the laws were wrong. Our goal is never to go to jail. But we are willing. And when we go to jail, we find, just as Dr. King did, that historically we are in pretty good company behind bars.

Jesus for President

Politics for Ordinary Radicals

Shane Claiborne and Chris Haw

Jesus for President is a radical manifesto to awaken the Christian political imagination, reminding us that our ultimate hope lies not in partisan political options but in Jesus and the incarnation of the peculiar politic of the church as a people "set apart" from this world.

In what can be termed lyrical theology, *Jesus for President* poetically weaves together words and images to sing (rather than dictate) its message. It is a collaboration of Shane Claiborne's writing and stories, Chris Haw's reflections and research, and Chico Fajardo-Heflin's art and design. Drawing upon the work of biblical theologians, the lessons of church history, and the examples of modern-day saints and ordinary radicals, *Jesus for President* stirs the imagination of what the church could look like if it placed its faith in Jesus instead of Caesar.

A fresh look at Christianity and empire, *Jesus for President* transcends questions of "Should I vote or not?" and "Which candidate?" by thinking creatively about the fundamental issues of faith and allegiance. It's written for those who seek to follow Jesus, rediscover the spirit of the early church, and incarnate the kingdom of God.

Jesus for President Tour DVD also available.

Available in stores and online!

Jesus, Bombs, and Ice Cream Study Guide

Building a More Peaceful World

Shane Claiborne, Ben Cohen, and Friends

Author and activist Shane Claiborne believes all people share a vision of a world where love triumphs over hatred, where life conquers death.

A couple of years ago, Ben Cohen, cofounder of Ben and Jerry's Ice Cream, and Claiborne crossed paths. Ben said to Shane, "I have read your books, and I like what I see." Shane said to Ben, "I have eaten your ice cream, and I like what I taste." They started dreaming and scheming, and *Jesus, Bombs, and Ice Cream* was born.

A host of talented friends have joined Shane and Ben for this multimedia presentation. The participant's guide is packed full of stories of reconciliation and grace, quotes, reflections, and questions for groups and individuals to discuss and discern how they can help make a more peaceful world a reality. The accompanying DVD (sold separately) contains more than two hours of testimonials, together with visual art and music, to provoke participants to imagine humanity with fewer bombs and more ice cream.

Available in stores and online!

Common Prayer

A Liturgy for Ordinary Radicals

*Shane Claiborne,
Wilson-Hartgrove, and
Enuma Okoro*

Common Prayer helps today's diverse
church pray together across traditions and
denominations. With an ear to the particulars of how various liturgical traditions pray, and using an advisory team of liturgical experts, the authors have created a tapestry of prayer that celebrates the best of each tradition. The book also includes a unique songbook composed of music and lyrics to more than fifty songs from various traditions, including African spirituals, traditional hymns, Mennonite gathering songs, and Taize chants. Tools for prayer are scattered throughout to aid those who are unfamiliar with liturgy and to deepen the prayer life of those who are familiar with liturgical prayer. Ultimately, *Common Prayer* makes liturgy dance, taking the best of the old and bringing new life to it for the contemporary renewal of the church. Churches and individuals who desire a deeper prayer life and those familiar with Shane Claiborne and New Monasticism will enjoy the tools offered in this book as a fresh take on liturgy.

Pocket edition also available.

Available in stores and online!

What would happen to our world if we took the words of Jesus seriously?

REDLETTER CHRISTIANS

www.redletterchristians.org

Blog. Radio Show. Books. Devotionals. Discussions. Podcasts. Speakers. Inspiration.